BEGINNING DirectX®11 GAME PROGRAMMING

ALLEN SHERROD AND WENDY JONES

Course Technology PTR

A part of Cengage Learning

COURSE TECHNOLOGY
CENGAGE Learning™

Australia • Brazil • Japan • Korea • Mexico • Singapore • Spain • United Kingdom • United States

COURSE TECHNOLOGY
CENGAGE Learning™

Beginning DirectX® 11 Game Programming
Allen Sherrod and Wendy Jones

Publisher and General Manager,
Course Technology PTR: Stacy L. Hiquet

Associate Director of Marketing:
Sarah Panella

Manager of Editorial Services:
Heather Talbot

Marketing Manager: Jordan Castellani

Senior Acquisitions Editor: Emi Smith

Project Editor: Dan Foster, Scribe Tribe

Technical Reviewer: Wendy Jones

Interior Layout Tech: MPS Limited,
  a Macmillan Company

Cover Designer: Mike Tanamachi

Indexer: Valerie Haynes Perry

Proofreader: Gene Redding

For product information and technology assistance, contact us at
Cengage Learning Customer & Sales Support, 1-800-354-9706

For permission to use material from this text or product,
submit all requests online at **www.cengage.com/permissions**
Further permissions questions can be emailed to
permissionrequest@cengage.com

DirectX is a registered trademark of Microsoft Corporation in the United States and/or other countries.

All other trademarks are the property of their respective owners.

All images © Cengage Learning unless otherwise noted.

Library of Congress Control Number: 2011920246

ISBN-13: 978-1-4354-5895-6

ISBN-10: 1-4354-5895-8

Course Technology, a part of Cengage Learning
20 Channel Center Street
Boston, MA 02210
USA

Cengage Learning is a leading provider of customized learning solutions with office locations around the globe, including Singapore, the United Kingdom, Australia, Mexico, Brazil, and Japan. Locate your local office at: **international.cengage.com/region**

Cengage Learning products are represented in Canada by Nelson Education, Ltd.

For your lifelong learning solutions, visit **courseptr.com**

Visit our corporate website at **cengage.com**

Printed in the United States of America
2 3 4 5 6 7 13 12

Acknowledgments

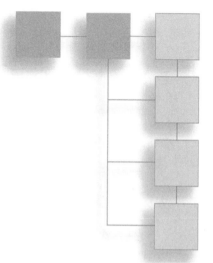

I would like to thank the men and women at Cengage Learning who helped make this book possible. I would also like to thank Wendy Jones for all her hard work on the previous editions of the book. And I would like to give a special thanks to Emi Smith, who has been very patient and helpful with this whole process.

—Allen Sherrod

Thanks to Allen Sherrod for taking over the writing duties for the DirectX 11 version of this book. I truly appreciate all the hard work and research he's put into it. I'd also like to thank Emi Smith for giving me the opportunity to work with Cengage Learning on multiple books.

—Wendy Jones

About the Authors

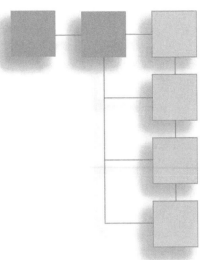

Allen Sherrod is an experienced author in the field of video game development. Allen's past works include two editions of *Ultimate Game Programming with DirectX*, *Ultimate 3D Game Engine Design and Architecture*, *Game Graphics Programming*, and *Data Structures and Algorithms for Game Developers*. Allen has also contributed to *Game Developer* magazine, the *Game Programming Gems 6* book, and the Gamasutra.com website. Allen is the creator of www. UltimateGameProgramming.com.

Wendy Jones is co-founder and CTO of Kitty Code LLC, a games studio working on mobile and console platforms such as iPhone, Windows Phone 7, and the Xbox 360. Wendy's past experience includes working on PC, console, and mobile game titles while working with Atari and Electronic Arts. Wendy also teaches DirectX at Full Sail University and is department chair of the interactive development department. Wendy can be reached through her website at www. fasterkittycodecode.com.

Contents

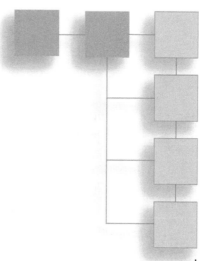

INTRODUCTION

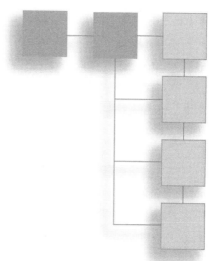

Many of us wish to create our own video games. For some, gaming is a hobby, and for others it is something fun to participate in casually. But for the rest of us, gaming and the dream of making our own games is more like a passion. Chances are, if you've purchased this book, you are looking to turn your desire and passion into something you can play and share with others.

About This Book

This book is the follow-up edition to Wendy Jones's *Beginning DirectX 10 Game Programming* book. In this book, we teach you the basics of getting started with game graphics using the latest iteration of Direct3D: Direct3D 11.

The goal of this book is to teach you the various aspects of DirectX 11. The target audience for this text is beginning/intermediate C++ programmers with little to no experience with DirectX. Although past DirectX or OpenGL experience can be useful, it is not required.

When you reach the end of this book, you will have had enough experience with DirectX 11 that you should be able to explore making simple video games and demos. Ideally, you will work your way up to make complex games and demos until you find yourself able to complete and release (even if for free at first) your own PC games.

Recommended Knowledge

This book assumes you have knowledge and familiarity of the C++ programming language. You are also assumed to have a comfortable working knowledge of Visual Studio 2010 and have completed at least a high-school level of mathematics. Since this book is centered on learning DirectX for the first time, knowing DirectX is, of course, not required for working through this book.

Throughout this book we use Visual Studio C++ 2010 Express, which can be downloaded from Microsoft's website at www.microsoft.com/express/Downloads. We are also using the June 2010 DirectX SDK, which can be downloaded from http://msdn.microsoft.com/en-us/directx.

Although not required for this book, it is recommended to try Adobe Photoshop for the creation of textures (www.adobe.com/products/photoshop/photoshopextended/) and XSI Mod Tool 7.5 for the creation of 3D models and meshes (http://usa.autodesk.com).

Companion Website: Code and Bonus Content

Almost every chapter has code samples and demos that give you hands-on exercises of the topics discussed. To follow along, view, execute, or manipulate these code samples, you will need the book's accompanying code, which can be downloaded from:

www.ultimategameprogramming.com/BeginningDirectX11/

or

www.courseptr.com/downloads

At either of these locations, you'll also find Web-only bonus content, including a ninth chapter, "Conclusions," Appendix A, "Chapter Answers" (which provides answers to all the end-of-chapter review questions), and Appendix B, "Audio in DirectX" (which introduces you to the various DirectX APIs, including XAudio2 and XACT3).

Errata

Sometimes there are errors that are not caught before the book is released or that can even arise due to outside circumstances that we could not anticipate. If you find any errors or issues with the book, please be sure to submit them to the companion website at www.ultimategameprogramming.com/BeginningDX11. Also be sure to check the companion website to see if there are existing issues that other readers have found that you might find useful to know.

Companion Website Downloads

You may download the companion Web site files from www.courseptr.com/downloads. Please note that you will be redirected to our Cengage Learning site.

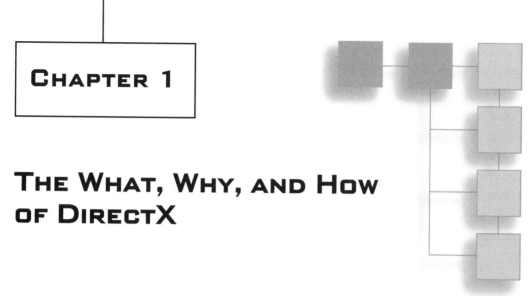

CHAPTER 1

THE WHAT, WHY, AND HOW OF DIRECTX

Prior to DirectX, game makers were struggling with problems stemming from hardware incompatibilities, making it almost impossible for everyone to enjoy the same games due to the sheer volume of hardware configurations that existed. As the industry faced the need for standardization, Microsoft introduced the Windows Game SDK for Windows 95, which became DirectX 1. DirectX provided game makers with a single set of APIs that would almost guarantee compatibility across different sets of PC hardware. Since DirectX's release, the number of games running under Windows has increased dramatically. This is still true almost 15 years later.

In this chapter:

- Understanding what DirectX is
- Why DirectX is useful
- How data flows through the Direct3D 11 pipeline
- What's new for Direct3D 11

WHAT IS DIRECTX?

DirectX, Microsoft's collection of application programming interfaces (APIs), is designed to give developers a low-level interface to the PC hardware running Windows-based operating systems. Each component provides access to different aspects of the hardware, including graphics, sound, GPU general purpose computing, and input devices, all through a standard interface.

This ideology allows developers to write their games using standard APIs without having to worry about the low-level interfacing with the different pieces of hardware a customer might have. Imagine the difficulty developers once faced by trying to write code paths for the many different hardware configurations a player might have. What if the player had a different input device? What about a different operating system—even an upgraded version like the difference between DOS and Windows 95? What about audio hardware and drivers? What about different types and models of graphics hardware?

Having one standard API that hardware manufacturers must adhere to is much more ideal than writing code paths for every possible device on the market, especially since newer devices released after a game has shipped could possibly not be recognized by the game, whereas using a standard solves this issue. DirectX is a collection of APIs used primarily by video game developers to address this need for standardization on the Windows and Xbox platforms. It is up to the hardware manufacturers to provide the driver layer for their devices.

Note

The Xbox 360 uses a variation of DirectX 9.

DirectX 10 versus DirectX 9

In 2006, DirectX 10 presented a major leap forward in the DirectX SDK. Usually when discussing DirectX we are discussing Direct3D, which is the API within DirectX that receives the most overhauls. Most other APIs in DirectX are either deprecated (meaning they are up for removal and it's recommended that new software not use them), are the same or have minor changes, or have been removed completely from the SDK.

The Direct3D 10 API is very lightweight when compared to its predecessors, and the API is much easier to use than past versions. In fact, early versions of DirectX were notoriously difficult to learn and use, but Microsoft has made changes and improvements to the API over many years. Direct3D 10 was not just an upgrade but, in many respects, an API that started fresh. And it indeed felt like a fresh start with the launch of Windows Vista, DirectX 10-class hardware, and a powerful API that was being hyped by one of the most influential software giants in the world.

The most apparent removal in Direct3D 10 was the fixed-function pipeline, which is essentially a set of rendering states and algorithms built into the API that allowed for the rendering of objects using common effects. The fixed-function pipeline was removed in favor of programmable shaders within graphics hardware. Graphics shaders, which will be discussed throughout this book, are code written specifically to customize how the graphics hardware processes geometry. Graphics shaders were first introduced in DirectX 8, but since then graphics hardware and the Shader Models that they run have evolved to a point where they have become the star of the API.

In Direct3D 9 we can render geometry, enable lighting by setting a few properties and rendering states, have the API transform our geometry, and so forth by calling a few Direct3D function calls. In Direct3D 10 we can do all of that ourselves and much more in shaders. The key thing for beginners to keep in mind if this is their first time learning graphics programming is that the fixed-function pipeline was limited to whatever was built into the API, whereas shaders allow us to create any effect, limited only by the frame-rate we deem desirable in our games. Want lighting? Call a Direct3D function to enable it and set its properties (up to eight lights). Want to render surfaces with more than one image? Just enable it. If, however, you wish to perform pixel-based motion blur and depth-of-field, you are out of luck using the fixed-function pipeline.

Often if the fixed-function pipeline does not explicitly support it and you are not using shaders, you cannot create the effect you want. Although some coders have found tricks and workarounds to getting some effects created without shaders, it was often a very difficult and inefficient workaround. I remember these times well and do not miss them.

Today, if we want to perform bump mapping, we can write a pixel shader that takes the light direction, performs a calculation using it and the pixel-level surface direction loaded from a special image known as a normal map, and combine that with the shading of the final pixel's color. In the days before shaders, or even when shaders were limited in the features they provided (such as the dark ages of register combiners for early versions of OpenGL), this was impossible, and doing even simple effects like normal mapping back then was only made possible through inefficient and often poor-quality tricks and approximations. Of course what is considered an easy effect to one person depends on his experience level.

The leap from DirectX 9 to DirectX 10 was a huge one. DirectX 10 went through two iterations as the market's acceptance caught up.

DirectX 11 versus DirectX 10

Direct3D 11 builds upon Direct3D 10.1 to add a new set of features for rendering next-generation graphics. The new additions to DirectX 11 include the following:

- General-purpose computing on the GPU using the new API DirectCompute
- True multi threaded rendering support
- New hardware tessellation
- Shader Model 5.0 and object-oriented programming concepts for shaders
- BC6 (sometimes called BC6H) and BC7 for texture compression of HDR and LDR images, respectively
- Increased texture resolution sizes
- And much more

Note

An image resource applied to a shape's surface is called a *texture*. Most often this refers to color images that are mapped to a surface to give it more detail.

DirectX 11 is more of an incremental update to DirectX 10.1 rather than the major update DirectX 10 was to DirectX 9. Microsoft took a risk by starting fresh with Direct3D 10 and requiring not only new hardware but Windows Vista as a minimum requirement. That was a few years ago, and today Microsoft's gamble is working out because not only is hardware support widespread, but also the majority of Windows users now are spanning Windows Vista and Windows 7. DirectX has always taken the future into consideration, and with the number of years it takes next-generation games to be developed, DirectX 11 will be very important to gaming for many years to come.

DirectX 11 versus OpenGL 4.0

OpenGL has long been considered a rival graphics API to Direct3D. OpenGL supports platforms outside of Windows-based operating systems, such as Mac computers, Linux OSs, Apple's iPhone and iPad, Sony's Playstation 3 (an implementation at least), and a variety of mobile devices such as cell phones and PDAs, along with other platforms. Although the native device creation of OpenGL can differ from one platform to another, the rest of the API is considered platform independent, not including the long history of hardware-specific extensions and features from competing entities within the OpenGL camp. DirectX, on the other hand, is available on the various Windows OSs and the Xbox game consoles. To be considered DirectX 10 or 11 compatible, hardware must adhere to a strict compatibility list, whereas prior to DirectX 10 this was not always the case. In the case of OpenGL this often led to vendor-specific extensions that worked on limited hardware. Incompatibilities within the hardware market caused rework when trying to achieve the same result on all supported devices.

The whole Direct3D versus OpenGL debate can often seem like a religious one, but the fact is that for many years OpenGL has lagged behind Direct3D. Microsoft has done a great job evolving Direct3D and improving it throughout the years, but OpenGL has only lagged behind, not keeping its promises as each new version is released, and time and time again has suffered from the same problems of yesteryear. When OpenGL 3.0 was first announced, it was thought that OpenGL would finally move back into a position to rival Direct3D. Unfortunately, the world of OpenGL has gone through its share of ups and downs, both within the group behind it and with how the API stacked against Direct3D, and Direct3D has continued to dominate.

OpenGL 4.0 catches up to many of the publicized features of DirectX 11, most notably through the support of general-purpose computing using OpenCL and tessellation, and is positioning itself to be a step closer to the promises that were never delivered in the past, most notably with OpenGL 2.0 and OpenGL 3.0. Although OpenGL is not out of the race yet, it unfortunately needs a lot of work to not only truly rival DirectX but also to win back the hearts and minds of many of us who turned to Direct3D once OpenGL's faults became too numerous. Even if the API catches up, the graphics API race is a lot like high school where the popular kid wins the election.

WHY IS DIRECTX NEEDED?

Before the release of the Windows operating system, developers were writing games for DOS. This single-threaded, non-GUI operating system provided developers with a direct path between their application code and the hardware it was running on. This had both its advantages and problems. For instance, because there was a direct path between the game code and the hardware, developers could pull every ounce of power out of the machine, giving them complete control over how their game performed. The downside included the need to either write directly to the hardware or use a variety of third-party libraries for any hardware they wanted their game title to support, including even common hardware such as video and sound cards.

Video cards were especially confusing because not all video cards followed the same standard. Even though most video cards supported a series of common resolutions, developers were forced to access video memory directly. This made even drawing to the screen difficult. Developers were definitely looking for a better and easier way.

When Windows 3.1 was released, it carried with it the same limitations that DOS had. Since Windows ran on top of DOS, it severely limited the resources available to games and took away the direct access developers had enjoyed for so long. Most games written to support Windows at the time consisted mainly of card and board games, while most games continued to support DOS only. Microsoft released DX1 as a way of enticing developers to make games for Windows to prove that the OS wasn't slow and move people away from DOS-based systems.

Microsoft's release of Windows 95 didn't eliminate any of these problems until the release of DirectX 1, also known as the Windows Games SDK. It gave developers a single library to write to, placing a common layer between their game and the PC hardware; drawing graphics to the screen had just become a whole lot easier. The first version of DirectX still didn't provide support for all the hardware out there, but it was a great starting point in giving game developers what they had been waiting for. Over the years, there have been multiple releases of DirectX, each one improving and adding support for new technologies such as network play, streaming audio, and new kinds of input devices. The latest version of DirectX includes Direct3D 11, which is compatible with Microsoft Windows Vista and Windows 7 operating systems.

How DirectX Is Put Together

DirectX is based on a collection of code libraries, each providing a common set of functionality needed for games and multimedia applications. To make sure that your game only has to link to the necessary functionality, DirectX is separated into multiple components.

The Components of DirectX 11

The DirectX API is split into multiple components, each representing a different aspect of the system. Each API can be used independently of one another, thereby allowing the addition of only the functionality your game requires. In the latest version of DirectX, some of the components were updated, such as Direct3D, while others are now being maintained at their previous levels by Microsoft until their removal (if they are deprecated). The components within DirectX can be upgraded individually as new functionality is required.

Direct2D

Direct2D is used for 2D graphics within Win32 applications. It is capable of rendering high-performance vector graphics.

DirectWrite

DirectWrite is used for fonts and text rendering within a Direct2D application.

DXGI

The DirectX Graphics Infrastructure, also known as DXGI, is used for the creation of Direct3D swap chains and the enumeration of device adapters.

Direct3D

Direct3D is used for all 3D graphics in DirectX. It is also the API that receives the most attention and updates. Throughout this book we will largely focus on Direct3D.

XAudio2

XAudio2 is a lower-level audio processing API that is part of the XDK (Xbox Development Kit) and, now, the DirectX SDK. XAudio2 is the replacement for DirectSound. The original XAudio was used on the first Xbox video game console.

XACT3

XACT3 is a higher-level audio processing API built on top of XAudio2. XACT3 allows developers to use the Cross-Platform Audio Creation Tool to author sounds in their applications. Developers would use XAudio2 if they needed low-level control of their audio system or if they wanted to build their own higher-level audio system similar to XACT3. XACT3, as discussed in Appendix B, "Audio in DirectX" from the companion website, is a powerful and incredible easy tool to use for game audio.

XInput

XInput is the input API for the XDK and the DirectX SDK and is used for processing of input from all Xbox 360 controllers. Essentially any controller you can use with your Xbox 360 can be used with the PC, and XInput is the API you use for working with these devices. These devices include not only Xbox gamepad controllers but also *Rock Band* and *Guitar Hero* instrument controllers (e.g., guitars, drums, and so forth), Big Button controllers (shipped with the game *Scene It*), arcade sticks (e.g., the Tekken 6 arcade stick), and so much more. XInput is the replacement for DirectInput.

Note

XAudio is the sound API used only on Xbox game consoles. XAudio2, its successor, can be used on both Xbox game consoles and Windows-based PCs.

XNA Math

The new XNA Math is not an API but rather a math library that implements optimized math operations that are common to video games. XNA Math uses SIMD (Single Instruction Multiple Data) to perform multiple operations with a single instruction call. The XNA Math library is available to the Xbox 360 and to Windows PCs. We'll discuss game math in general as well as XNA Math in more detail in Chapter 6.

Note

XNA Game Studio is a game development tool built on top of DirectX that allows developers to create games for both the Xbox 360 and Windows PCs using C# and .NET. XNA Math is the name of the math library in the new DirectX SDK and can be used outside of the XNA Game Studio. You do not need to download the XNA Game Studio SDK.

DirectCompute

DirectCompute is a new API added to DirectX 11 that allows for general-purpose multi threading computing using the GPU. The GPU has the ability to process many tasks in parallel, such as physics, video compression and decompression, audio processing, and much more. Not all tasks are suited for the GPU, but for those that are, the possibilities are tremendous.

For more information on DirectCompute, check out the book *Game Development with Microsoft's DirectCompute for Beginners*.

DirectSetup

Once your game is complete, you'll want to show it to others. DirectSetup gives you the functionality to install the latest version of DirectX on the user's computer. It also has the ability to check the latest installed version of DirectX.

Windows Games Explorer

The Games Explorer is a feature of Windows Vista and Windows 7 that allows developers to present their games on those OSs. The Games Explorer handles things such as the game's display, title, rating, description, region-specific box art, content ratings (e.g., M for Mature, T for Teens, etc.), game statistics and notifications, parental controls, and more. The DirectX SDK provides plenty of information on how to use the Games Explorer for your own games and could be very useful when it comes time to ship a game. An example of the Games Explorer can be seen in Figure 1.1.

DirectInput

DirectInput is an API for detecting input with keyboards, mice, and joysticks. Today XInput is used for all game controllers. For keyboards and mice we can use Win32 functions or we can use DirectInput, which we'll examine later in the book in Chapter 5. According to the DirectX SDK, DirectInput will remain in its current form until new technologies replace it.

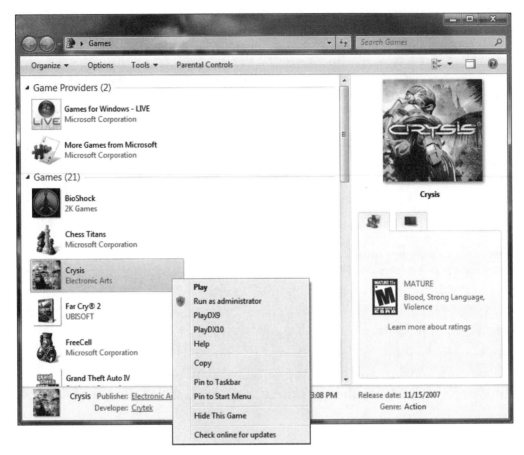

Figure 1.1
An example of the Games Explorer in Windows 7.

Obsolete DirectX Components

The following components are either deprecated or removed from the DirectX SDK:

DirectDraw

Once used for 2D rendering, today we can use either Direct2D or Direct3D for 2D graphics. DirectDraw was merged with Direct3D into what was called DirectX Graphics in DirectX 8.

Note

In previous versions of DirectX, 2D drawing functionality was provided by a component called DirectDraw. Because DirectDraw is no longer being updated, you should perform all drawing using Direct3D or Direct2D.

DirectPlay

DirectPlay was used for networking capabilities for online games. It was built on top of the UDP protocol (User Datagram Protocol) and served as a higher-level abstraction for network communication. Today the API has been removed and is no longer part of the DirectX SDK. DirectPlay was deprecated in favor of Games for Windows Live on the PC and Xbox Live on Xbox consoles.

DirectShow

DirectShow was used for multimedia rendering and recording. This meant DirectShow was able to display video files in multiple common formats, provide DVD navigation, and much more. Today DirectShow is part of the Windows SDK and is no longer part of the DirectX SDK. Alternatively, Windows Vista and Windows 7 users can use Microsoft's Media Foundations for media content, which is also part of the Windows SDK. This is useful for video games if they need to display CG cut-scenes and video files.

DirectMusic

DirectMusic is now a deprecated API from the DirectX 7 and earlier days for playing audio content in applications. DirectMusic offers low-level access to audio and hardware and has been a topic in DirectX books and tutorials for many years. Today we use XAudio2 (low-level) or XACT3 (high-level) for audio in games and media applications.

DirectSound

DirectSound is another deprecated audio API used to give low-level access to developers for their audio needs. XAudio2 is its replacement. We discuss audio in detail in Appendix B, "Audio in DirectX," located on the companion website.

The Components Object Model

The DirectX API is based on the Component Object Model (COM). COM objects consist of a collection of interfaces that expose methods that developers use to access DirectX. COM objects are normal DLL files that have been registered with the system to provide support for specific hardware in the machine. For DirectX COM objects, registration happens during the installation of DirectX. While similar to C++ objects, COM objects require the use of an interface to access the methods within them. This is actually an advantage over standard objects because multiple versions of an interface can be present within a COM object, allowing for backward compatibility.

For instance, each version of DirectX included a new DirectDraw interface accessible through the API, while still containing the previous version so as not to break existing code. Therefore, games created using DirectX 7 are able to work with DirectX 9. In other words, older games can be installed and played using the latest version of the DirectX runtime.

An additional advantage to COM objects is their ability to work with multiple languages, not just C++. Developers can use Visual Basic, C++, or C# and still use the same DirectX libraries. As Microsoft updates and adds new functionality to DirectX, the version numbers of each updated component will increase. You'll find that not all the included components exist at the same version level. For instance, DirectInput remains at version 8.0, while Direct3D is now at version 11.

Introducing Direct3D 11

The release of Windows 7 has brought with it the release of Direct3D 11. Direct3D 11 is compatible with Windows Vista and Windows 7, along with DirectX 10-class hardware. Certain features of DirectX 11, such as tessellation and Shader Model 5.0, require DirectX 11-class hardware. But most of the API can be used with DirectX 10-class hardware.

Stages of Direct3D 11

Direct3D is more than just an API; it's a tool for transforming geometric shapes and images into a living, breathing world. Even though you can treat many pieces of Direct3D as a black box and not have to worry about the implementation details, it is a good idea to understand at least an overview of how it works.

Direct3D processes your scene in multiple stages, with each stage performing a specific set of tasks resulting in a final image. These stages are known as Direct3D's rendering pipeline, and a screenshot of each can be seen in Figure 1.2.

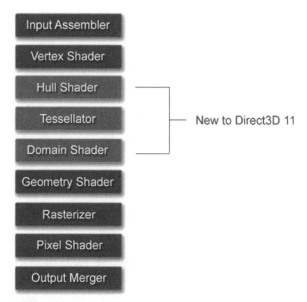

Figure 1.2
The stages of Direct3D 11.

The first stage of Direct3D's pipeline, called the Input-Assembler (IA) stage, can be thought of as the building-block stage. In this stage we set the geometry we are going to render along with the necessary information Direct3D needs to perform that task.

The second stage is the vertex shader (VS) stage. A vertex is a single point that makes up a shape, such as a triangle. In a vertex shader we can run code that operates on each vertex, much of which depends on the effect we are setting up for. Shaders will be discussed more throughout this entire book. A vertex shader always takes a single vertex as input and outputs a single vertex. This vertex data was supplied by the data set using the input assembler.

The third, fourth, and fifth stages are optional stages that deal with tessellation. Tessellation is an advanced topic that uses two new shaders to Direct3D called the hull and domain shaders. Hardware tessellation, in a nutshell, is the process of taking input geometry and increasing or decreasing its level of detail. This allows for very high polygonal models to be rendered in real time with polygon counts in the hundreds of thousands or even the millions. By having the hardware create the detail of the geometry, the application only has to submit a small amount of data that defines the low-level model. This model can be in the form of patches, which is a 3D modeling. The hardware takes this low-level model and makes it higher level. Subdividing polygons means to take a polygon and divide it into smaller pieces.

The hull shader takes its input from the output of the vertex shader, which is operating on control points and data versus traditional vertices, and produces output control points for what are known as patches. The tessellation stage, which appears between the hull shader and domain shader stages, is a fixed-function stage that takes the output from the hull shader and subdivides the data on hardware. The domain shader is responsible for generating the vertex of a subdivided point.

The sixth stage, the geometry shader (GS), is also an optional shader stage. If there is no tessellation being performed, the geometry shader stage occurs after the vertex shader stage. Geometry shaders operate on entire shapes such as triangles, whereas the vertex shader operates on a single point of a shape. The geometry shader has the ability to essentially create or destroy geometry as needed, which depends largely on the effect you are trying to create. One common example of geometry shaders is generating shadowing geometry from a model by creating what is known as a shadow volume. Another example is the generation of particles used to create particle effects such as rain or explosions by taking a list of points that act as the center of the particles and generating polygons around them.

The seventh stage, the Rasterizer, has the job of determining what pixels are visible through clipping and culling geometry (we'll discuss this in Chapter 6), setting up the pixel shaders, and determining how the pixel shaders will be invoked.

The eighth stage is the pixel shader (PS) stage. In the pixel shader stage, the shader receives the geometric data from all previous stages and is used to shade the pixels (sometimes referred to as fragments) that comprise that shape. The output of the pixel shader is a single color value that will be used by the final stage to build the final image displayed to the screen. If there are no tessellation or geometry shaders, the pixel shader receives its input from the vertex shader directly. The input to the pixel shader is technically interpolated data—that is, data that is generated between the points (vertices) of a shape. We'll discuss this more in the next chapter.

The final stage, the output merger (OM) stage, is where it all comes together. The OM takes all of the output pieces from the other stages of the pipeline and builds up the final image to send to the screen.

DIRECT3D 11 CONSIDERATIONS

Some of you may already be familiar with writing games using DirectX, and if so, there are a few things you need to be aware of when converting your game to the latest version of Direct3D. If updating from Direct3D 10 to Direct3D 11, the process is fairly straightforward, and most of the work will be to replace Direct3D 10 calls with their Direct3D 11 equivalent. Direct3D 11 is more of a superset of Direct3D 10 and 10.1, so there is not a lot that will need to be done. Going from Direct3D 9.0 to 11.0 is another story.

When coming to Direct3D 11 from Direct3D 9, the biggest change is the removal of the fixed-function pipeline. Previously you could choose one of the default ways to process your 3D scene, and Direct3D would handle the clipping, lighting, and the shading. Today, with D3D10 and D3D11, all this functionality needs to be specifically handled using the programmable pipeline. Chapter 7 is about shaders, and its purpose is to bring you fully up to speed with all that is included in Direct3D 11. Throughout the entire book we'll be using shaders and discussing them as necessary before we reach the comprehensive discussion in Chapter 7.

Another of the more major changes is the removal of the CAPS bits. In previous versions of Direct3D, you had to check the capabilities of the underlying video hardware to make sure that certain functionality like pixel shaders was available to use. Now, any features not provided by the hardware are emulated by the system in software, ensuring you always have the full range of functionality to play with. This will greatly simplify the initialization code for games using D3D10. It is also much needed, since in the past some hardware vendors supported only a subset of features, which caused issues when dealing with supporting different pieces of hardware. To be considered DirectX 10- or 11-compatible today, hardware must strictly follow guidelines for compliance.

Direct3D 9.0 is close to having a completely different API. It is not possible to do massive copy and paste on function names like you could get away with changing code from Direct3D 10.0 to 11.0. In this situation you'll most likely be better off creating a new rendering layer for your game and working off the strengths of Direct3D 11 instead of trying to do a line-by-line search and replace.

DirectX Tools

The DirectX SDK contains a wealth of information and tools for many DirectX-related topics. The SDK itself should be explored by all developers using DirectX because there are tremendously well documented and well developed tools that aid in the learning and/or developing of DirectX applications. In this section we will briefly take a look at some of the tools available in the DirectX SDK.

Sample Browser and Documentation

The DirectX SDK Sample Browser is a tool that displays all of the example demos, technical papers, tutorials, articles, and tools that come with the DirectX SDK. The Sample Browser lists dozens of entries that include DirectX 11, DirectX 10, and DirectX 9. Whenever a new version of the SDK is released, it is recommended that you check out the Sample Browser. You might find the implementation to a new technology or effect, a useful tutorial, or technical information about everything DirectX.

A screenshot of the Sample Browser can be seen in Figure 1.3. The sample browser can be found on the Start menu inside the subfolder for your DirectX SDK installation.

Also of valuable use are the DirectX documentation and the Graphics documentation. The graphics area of the SDK has its own documentation, which is important to know if you are looking for something graphics related and happen to open the wrong documentation file. Also, Microsoft's MSDN website has all of this documentation and more available online.

PIX

PIX is a tool used for the debugging and analysis of Direct3D applications as they are executing. PIX can give valuable information such as API calls, timing statistics, and mesh information before and after transformation, to name a few. PIX can also be used for the debugging of shader code on the GPU, along with breakpoints and the ability to step through code.

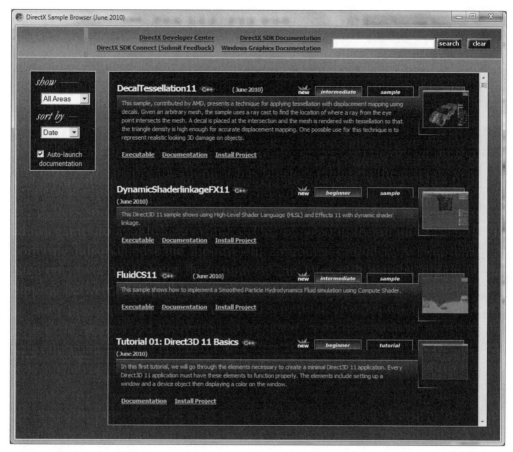

Figure 1.3
The DirectX SDK Sample Browser.

Caps Viewer

The DirectX Caps Viewer shows information about the hardware's capabilities by way of detailing its support for Direct3D, DirectDraw, DirectSound, and DirectInput. Every piece of information about what the hardware supports and its version are displayed by this tool. A screenshot of the Caps Viewer can be seen in Figure 1.4.

Diagnostic Tools

The DirectX Diagnostic tool is used to test various components of DirectX to see if they are working properly. The diagnostic tool is used to create diagnostic

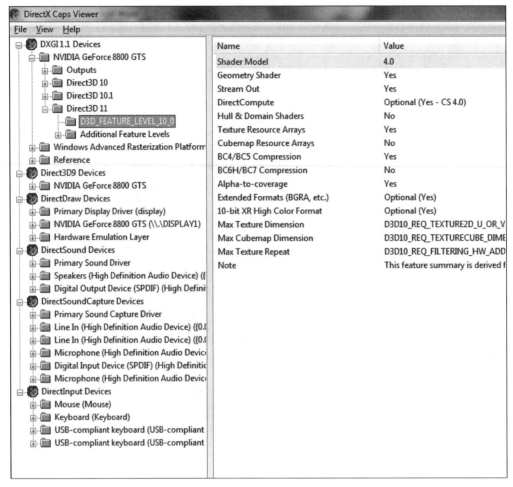

Figure 1.4
The Caps Viewer.

reports that can be saved to a file and/or sent to Microsoft. Sending the report to Microsoft is done via the Report button on the More Help tab of the tool. If you suspect some components are not working properly on a specific machine, running this tool can provide some insight.

Texture Tool

The DirectX Texture Tool is used to convert images to Direct3D texture formats that use DXTn compression. This tool is deprecated since it only supports texture formats supported by DirectX 9, not DirectX 10 or 11. If you are looking to create images compressed with DXT1 through DXT5, this tool can do the job.

Note

BC6 and BC7 are the new formats not supported by this tool. The "BC" has replaced the "DXT" in these compression formats.

The DirectX SDK also includes the Texture Converter. The Texture Converter is included with the TXVIEW.dll, which is installed as part of the DirectX SDK installation. The purpose of the Texture Converter is to convert an image from one format to another. The file formats that can be seen include:

- BMP
- JPEG
- DDS
- TGA
- PNG
- DIB
- HDR
- PMF

The Texture Converter works by right-clicking on an image (or multiple images) in the Windows Explorer and selecting Convert to File Format from the drop-down list. Once the dialog box appears, set the properties of the image you are converting by setting its output size, format, and output filename, to name a few. You could also use the texture conversion command-line tool called TexConv. exe or TexConvEx.exe for Direct3D 10 and 11 textures. The Texture Converter extension was last compatible with DirectX 9.

Error Lookup

The DirectX Error Lookup tool displays a description of any error code received while running your DirectX applications. You can enter the error code into this application, hit the Lookup button, and it will describe the error to you. Not all errors are clear, and this tool can be useful. The Error Lookup tool can be found in the Utilities folder of your DirectX SDK installation.

Control Panel

The DirectX Control Panel, located in the Utilities folder of the DirectX SDK, is used to examine and modify the properties of various DirectX components. With the Control Panel tool you can do the following:

- Enable the debug layer of Direct3D 10/11
- Change the debug output level and settings for use during development
- View driver information
- View hardware support information
- View version information for the various components

Cross-Platform Audio Creation Tool

The Cross-Platform Audio Creation tool is a GUI tool (also available with the DirectX SDK is a command-line alternative) for creating audio files used by XACT3, which is DirectX's high-level audio API/component. This tool is what we'll use to take our audio clip files and organize them into various banks, a process that is discussed in more detail in Appendix B (online).

A screenshot of the Cross-Platform Audio Creation tool can be seen in Figure 1.5. The XACT3 tool can be used to create audio files for Windows PC and the Xbox 360. For those doing game development using XNA, you can deploy a version of the audio files that matches the byte-ordering format of the processor within the 360. Since the Xbox 360 uses an architecture based on PowerPC, the same output files for the PC cannot be used interchangeably with the Xbox 360. This will not affect us in this book since this book assumes game development on an x86 processor using DirectX 11 on Windows Vista or a Windows 7 PC.

Game Definition File Editor

The Game Definition File Editor is used to create localized game definition files for Windows Vista and Windows 7. The information for a game definition file is displayed on the Games Explorer, which was discussed during the section titled

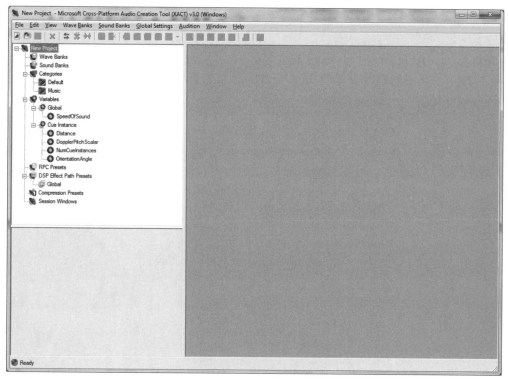

Figure 1.5
The Cross-Platform Audio Creation tool.

"The Components of DirectX 11." A screenshot of the editor can be seen in Figure 1.6.

The Game Definition File Editor allows you to create properties for the game's release date, its Games Explorer icon and box art, its rating (e.g., Teen, Mature, etc.), its name and description, and a host of other properties. There is a detailed tutorial of using the Game Definition File Editor that comes with the DirectX SDK documentation. You can also find this tutorial on the MSDN website by searching for "Game Definition File Editor: Tool Tutorial."

Down-Level Hardware

DirectX 11 supports a concept known as down-level hardware. When DirectX 10 and Windows Vista were released, they were built for a new driver model and hardware. Although DirectX 11 is its own version, it has the ability to target the

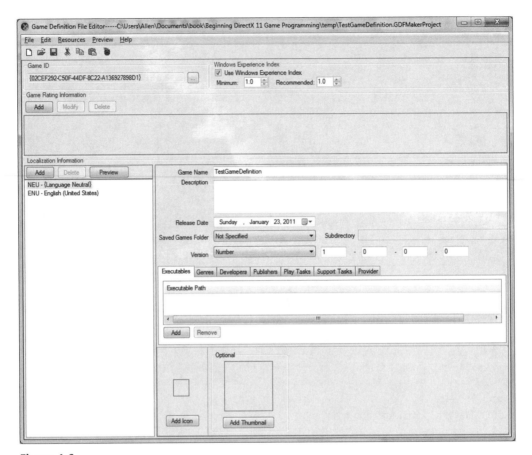

Figure 1.6
The Game Definition File Editor.

DirectX 10.0 and 10.1 class of hardware with a single set of functions. We'll see this in Chapter 2 when we build the first demos to check for compatibility with DirectX 11 first, and then for DirectX 10.1 and 10.0 if support for 11 isn't there. Even if the application does choose DirectX 10.1 or 10.0, the same API calls apply, and as long as we are using Shader Model 4.0 and features not required by DirectX 11, the application will work just fine on that hardware. If you do not have DirectX 11.0 hardware it's OK, since DirectX 10.0 hardware will work for all samples in this book.

Summary

As you go through the process of learning DirectX, don't worry if things seem overwhelming at times. If this is your first time with video game graphics programming, then DirectX, or OpenGL for that matter, will naturally have a steep learning curve. If you have experience with DirectX, you'll find things are much easier and much cleaner with Direct3D 10/11. If you are coming from OpenGL, you'll already have a handle on the more difficult and involved general graphics programming concepts, and you can focus on learning the specifics of the API itself.

When learning DirectX, it is useful to pick a system and write as many samples with it as you can. The goal is to start small and work your way up. By starting small you allow yourself a realistic goal that you can build upon until you reach your goal of DirectX mastery. As you code demo by demo, before you know it things start to make sense and fall into place. If you ever get stuck, remember you're not alone; sites like UltimateGameProgramming.com, GameDev.net, and Microsoft's MSDN are great places to find help. Like many things in life, the best way to learn is to do it again and again until you've mastered the craft.

Chapter Questions

Answers to all chapter review questions can be found in Appendix A on this book's companion website (**www.ultimategameprogramming.com/Beginning-DirectX11/**) or at **www.courseptr.com/downloads**.

1. What was the original name for the first version of DirectX?
   A. XNA
   B. Games SDK
   C. Direct3D
   D. Windows Foundations SDK

2. Which is *not* a feature of DirectX 11?
   A. Fixed-function rendering pipeline
   B. Multithreaded GPU
   C. Offers HDR texture compression
   D. None of the above

3. Which version of DirectX does the Xbox 360 use?
   A. A modified version of DirectX 10
   B. A modified version of DirectX 11

C. A modified version of DirectX 9
D. A modified version of DirectX 8

4. DirectCompute was introduced in which version of DirectX?
   A. DirectX 11
   B. DirectX 10
   C. DirectX 9
   D. DirectX on the Xbox 360

5. DirectX 11 introduces which shader model?
   A. Shader Model 4.0
   B. Shader Model 4.1
   C. Shader Model 5.0
   D. None of the above

6. Which stage appears after the pixel shader?
   A. The geometry shader
   B. Output merger
   C. Hull and domain shaders (for tessellation)
   D. Vertex shader

7. The DirectX Control Panel is?
   A. There is no Control Panel in the DirectX SDK
   B. Used to install/uninstall DirectX
   C. An extension to the Windows 7 Control Panel
   D. Used to examine component properties

8. The Game Definition File is used for what purpose?
   A. To edit the game's resources, such as images and models
   B. To create a game's help manual
   C. To create a game installer
   D. For creating localization files for the Games Explorer

9. PIX is what type of tool within the DirectX SDK?
   A. Used for performance analysis
   B. Used for texture viewing
   C. Used for texture converting
   D. None of the above

10. How many stages did we discuss for Direct3D 11?
    A. 12
    B. 7
    C. 9
    D. 11

11. Geometry shaders are used for tessellation (true or false).
    A. True
    B. False

12. The geometry shader stage occurs before the vertex stage and after the pixel stage (true or false).
    A. True
    B. False

13. DirectX 11 requires Windows Vista or higher (true or false).
    A. True
    B. False

14. The Xbox 360 uses a variation of DirectX 10 (true or false).
    A. True
    B. False

15. Compute shaders is a new shader type in DirectX 11 for general-purpose computing (true or false).
    A. True
    B. False

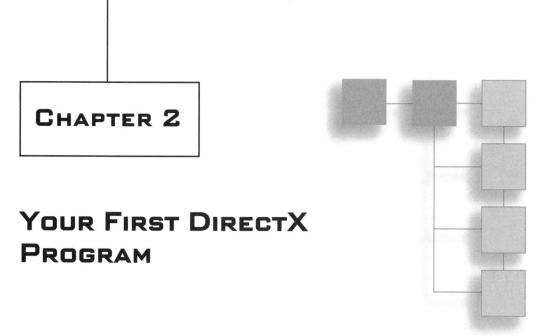

CHAPTER 2

YOUR FIRST DIRECTX PROGRAM

The best way to begin learning DirectX is to start at the beginning by creating simple demo applications. In this chapter we'll take you step-by-step through the process of creating your very first DirectX application, specifically focusing on Direct3D. By the end of this chapter you will have a firm understanding of the setup of Direct3D from start to finish.

In this chapter:

- How to create a project
- How to set up a Windows application
- How to initialize DirectX
- How to clear the screen
- How to display a scene

CREATING THE PROJECT

This book assumes you've already had experience creating C++ projects and working within Visual Studio. In this section and the one to follow we'll briefly cover the initial setup of a Win32 application. We'll modify this code throughout the chapter to include Direct3D initialization and basic rendering. By the end of the chapter we'll have a set of code used to create and initialize Direct3D that we can use for all demos throughout this book.

27

The first step to any application is the creation of the Visual Studio project. Start by running Visual Studio .NET with no project loaded. Throughout this book we are using Visual Studio C++ 2010 Express, which can be freely downloaded from Microsoft's website (www.microsoft.com/express/downloads/).

Note

You should already have Visual Studio .NET and the DirectX SDK installed. Read the Introduction if you have not performed this step.

We'll start by creating a new project called Blank Win32 Window by performing the following steps:

1. Within Visual Studio, select New > Project from the File menu to bring up the New Project dialog box, shown in Figure 2.1.

2. Enter "BlankWindow" as the project name and select Empty Project from the list of project templates. Click on the OK button when this is complete. This dialog box is shown in Figure 2.2.

3. Click the Finish button.

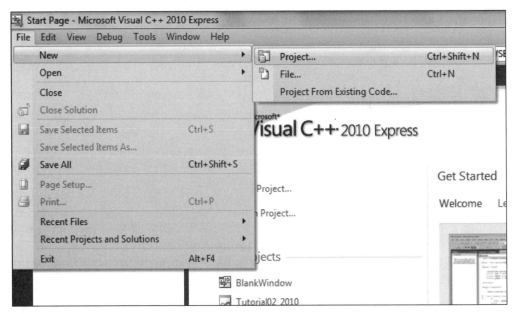

Figure 2.1
Visual Studio's New Project dialog box.

Figure 2.2
Creating an empty project.

The empty project is now created. In the next section we'll add code to the project that will serve as a template for all the demos throughout this book.

ADDING WINDOWS CODE

At this point, Visual Studio will have created an empty project. The next step is to create the source code to initialize the main application window. You start off by adding a blank source file to the project. This file will become our main source file that we'll name main.cpp. The steps to create the main.cpp file are:

1. Right-click the Source folder in the Solution Explorer section of Visual Studio and select Add New Item (see Figure 2.3).

2. In the New Item dialog box select the C++ source file and name it main.cpp (see Figure 2.4).

3. Click OK to finish.

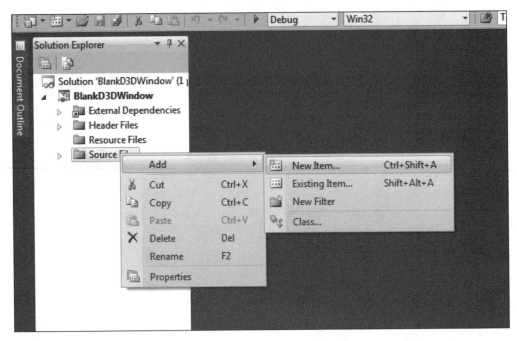

Figure 2.3
Creating a new item within the project.

With the main.cpp source file created within the project, we can now fill it with the Win32-specific code to create a blank window. Once we have our main entry point coded we'll initialize Direct3D 11 and use Direct3D to render the window's canvas.

The Main Entry Point

The first task of the main.cpp source file is to include the necessary Win32 header files and to define the main entry point. As you should be aware, the main entry point for Win32 applications is the WinMain function. As of now we'll only need to include the windows.h header file to the top of the source file. Both the empty WinMain function and the header section of the main.cpp source file can be seen in Listing 2.1.

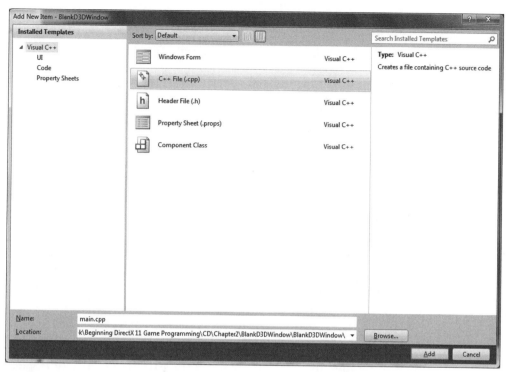

Figure 2.4
Creating the main.cpp source file.

Listing 2.1 The empty `WinMain` function (Blank Win32 Window Step 1).

```
#include<Windows.h>


int WINAPI wWinMain( HINSTANCE hInstance, HINSTANCE prevInstance,
                LPWSTR cmdLine, int cmdShow )
{
    return 0;
}
```

In Listing 2.1 you can see that we are using `wWinMain` instead of `WinMain`. The difference between the two is that `wWinMain` is used to handle Unicode parameters, specifically the third parameter `cmdLine`, while `WinMain` performs the conversion for you between Unicode and ANSI. Since this could lead to missing characters in a Unicode string, using `wWinMain` allows us to properly handle Unicode arguments if they are passed to the application.

The (w)WinMain function takes four parameters. Those parameters are defined as follows:

- HINSTANCE hInstance. The handle of the application's current instance.

- HINSTANCE prevInstance. The handle of the previous instance of the application. This will always be NULL according to the MSDN documentation. Since this will always be NULL, if you need a way to determine whether a previous instance of the application is already running, the documentation recommends creating a uniquely named mutex using CreateMutex. Although the mutex will be created, the CreateMutex function will return ERROR_ALREADY_EXISTS.

- LPSTR cmdLine (or LPWSTR in Unicode). The command line for the application without the program's name. This allows you to pass commands to the application, such as from the command prompt, by use of a shortcut with the command string provided, etc.

- int cmdShow. An ID that specifies how the window should be shown.

The current instance handle and command show parameters are the only ones we'll use throughout this book. The instance handle is needed by Direct3D's initialization, as well as window creation, and the command show ID is used after the window's creation when it is time to show the window, which we'll see throughout this chapter.

Windows Initialization

Although the application will run, it will not display anything since there is no actual window created. So the next step is to create the Win32 window. This is done by first registering the Window's class and then creating the window itself. This can be seen in Listing 2.2. Applications must register its windows with the system.

Listing 2.2. Window class registration and creation (Blank Win32 Window Step 2).

```
int WINAPI wWinMain( HINSTANCE hInstance, HINSTANCE prevInstance,
                LPWSTR cmdLine, int cmdShow )
{
```

```
    UNREFERENCED_PARAMETER( prevInstance );
    UNREFERENCED_PARAMETER( cmdLine );

    WNDCLASSEX wndClass = { 0 };
    wndClass.cbSize = sizeof( WNDCLASSEX ) ;
    wndClass.style = CS_HREDRAW | CS_VREDRAW;
    wndClass.lpfnWndProc = WndProc;
    wndClass.hInstance = hInstance;
    wndClass.hCursor = LoadCursor( NULL, IDC_ARROW );
    wndClass.hbrBackground = ( HBRUSH )( COLOR_WINDOW + 1 );
    wndClass.lpszMenuName = NULL;
    wndClass.lpszClassName = "DX11BookWindowClass";

    if( !RegisterClassEx( &wndClass ) )
        return -1;

    RECT rc = { 0, 0, 640, 480 };
    AdjustWindowRect( &rc, WS_OVERLAPPEDWINDOW, FALSE );

    HWND hwnd = CreateWindowA( "DX11BookWindowClass", "Blank Win32 Window",
        WS_OVERLAPPEDWINDOW, CW_USEDEFAULT, CW_USEDEFAULT, rc.right - rc.
left,
        rc.bottom - rc.top, NULL, NULL, hInstance, NULL );

    if( !hwnd )
        return -1;

    ShowWindow( hwnd, cmdShow );

    return 0;
}
```

The Win32 macro UNREFERENCED_PARAMETER can be used to avoid compiler warnings about parameters that are unused by a function's body. Although it technically is not necessary, it is good programming practice to strive for 0 warnings when building source code. Since this specific macro does not do anything, the compiler within Visual Studio will optimize it out.

Following the handling of the unused parameters is the description of the window class. The window class, defined by WNDCLASSEX, contains various properties of the Win32 window, which include the window's icon, its menu, the application instance the window belongs to, the look of the cursor, and other properties we'll briefly review. The WNDCLASSEX can be found in Winuser.h, which is included within windows.h and has the following definition:

```
typedef struct tagWNDCLASSEX {
    UINT      cbSize;
    UINT      style;
    WNDPROC   lpfnWndProc;
    int       cbClsExtra;
    int       cbWndExtra;
    HINSTANCE hInstance;
    HICON     hIcon;
    HCURSOR   hCursor;
    HBRUSH    hbrBackground;
    LPCTSTR   lpszMenuName;
    LPCTSTR   lpszClassName;
    HICON     hIconSm;
} WNDCLASSEX, *PWNDCLASSEX;
```

The members of the WNDCLASSEX structure are defined as:

- **cbSize.** The size of the structure in bytes.

- **style.** Style flags used to define the window's look.

- **lpfnWndProc.** A callback function that is called whenever an event notification comes from the operating system. There will be a function in our demos called WndProc that will be discussed later in this chapter, which is why we are setting this property. This property is a function pointer.

- **cbClsExtra.** Number of extra bytes to allocate for the window structure.

- **cbWndExtra.** Number of extra bytes to allocate for the window's instance.

- **hInstance.** The application instance that contains the windows procedure (callback) for this window class.

- **hIcon.** The resource ID for the icon graphic to be displayed for the application. If NULL, the default icon is used (e.g., Microsoft Word has an icon of a W on top of a document graphic).

- **hCursor.** The resource ID for the graphic that will act as the cursor. We'll usually stick with the standard arrow cursor throughout this book.

- **hbrBackground.** A handle to the background brush that will be used for painting the window's background.

- **lpszMenuName.** A null-terminated string of the resource name for the menu.

- **lpszClassName.** A null-terminated string for what you wish to name your window class. The maximum length is 256 characters.

- **hIconSm.** Handle to the window's small icon (i.e., like those seen on running applications on the task bar).

Most members of the window structure deal with Win32 programming that is beyond the scope of this book, such as creating menus (outside of an editor, we'll most likely not want to create a Win32 menu in a game). Many of these members we'll set to a value of 0.

With the WNDCLASSEX structure created we can send it to RegisterClassEx() to register the window class. The RegisterClassEx() must be called before we attempt to create the window, and it takes as a parameter the address of the window class structure to register. If a value of 0 is returned by this function, then the registration failed, and you'll likely need to check the values specified for the window class to ensure they are all valid, assuming there is not a bigger problem.

The next step is to create the actual window. First we call AdjustWindowRect to calculate the size required of the window based on our desired dimensions and style. The type of window will determine how much true size we'll need. If you look at most Win32 applications, there is space for non-client areas such as the title bar, a border around the application, etc. If we are going for a specific window size, we'll have to keep in mind that we have both a client area and a non-client area.

The AdjustWindowRect function first takes a rectangle (lpRect) that defines the bottom left, bottom right, upper left, and upper right areas of the window. The left and top properties represent the starting location of the window, while the right and bottom represent the width and height. The AdjustWindowRect function also takes as parameters the window style flag of the window being created and a Boolean flag indicating whether or not the window has a menu, which affects the non-client area.

The window is created next by calling the Win32 function CreateWindow. In Listing 2.2 we call a variation of it called CreateWindowA. The main difference is that CreateWindowA accepts ANSI string parameters, while CreateWindow accepts Unicode. If using the Unicode version, we can always prefix the letter L before the quotes of the string to indicate we are providing Unicode characters.

The Win32 function CreateWindow(A) takes as parameters:

- lpClassName (optional)—The window class name (same name used for the window class structure).

- lpWindowName (optional)—The window title bar text.

- dwStyle—The window's style flags.

- X—The window's horizontal position.

- Y—The window's vertical position.

- nWidth—The window's width.

- hHeight—The window's height.

- hWndParent (optional)—Handle to the parent window's handle (optional if this new window is a pop-up or child window).

- hMenu (optional)—Resource handle to the window's menu.

- hInstance (optional)—The application instance ID (first parameter of wWinMain).

- lpParam (optional)—Data to be passed to the window and made available via the lpParam parameter of the windows proc callback function (discussed in the section titled "Windows Callback Procedures").

The return value of the CreateWindow(A) function is a non-null handle. If CreateWindow(A) succeeds, we can show the window by calling the Win32 function ShowWindow, which takes as parameters the window handle returned by CreateWindow(A) and the command show flag (cmdShow, which is the wWinMain's last parameter).

With the window created, the application can begin doing its job. Win32 GUI applications are event-based applications. This essentially means that when an event happens, the application is notified of it, and some action then occurs.

This continues until the event for quitting the application is encountered. For example, when Microsoft Word launches, a "create" event is fired and the application loads. Whenever the user clicks the mouse on a toolbar button, menu item, etc., an event is triggered and sent to the application for processing. If the mouse-click event over the open file button is triggered, then a dialog box is displayed that allows users to visually select the file they wish to open. Many applications work using an event-based approach.

In video games, the applications are real time, meaning that whether or not some event or action takes place will not keep the application from performing many tasks throughout its lifetime. If the user presses buttons on the game-pad controller, usually it is detected during an update step of the game loop, and the game responds to it appropriately. If there are no events, the game still must process constantly by rendering the current game state (e.g., rendering the menu, cinematic, game world, etc.), performing logic updates, looking for and responding to networking data, playing audio, and so much more.

Either way, both real-time and event-based programs must run until the user decides to quit. This introduces the concept of the application loop. The application loop is literally an infinite loop that continues until it is somehow broken by a user's action. This can be done by receiving a WM_QUIT (Win32 quit message) event, the user pressing the Escape key at a point in the main menu where it makes sense to close the application (e.g., hitting Escape while the game is being played might bring up a pause screen but shouldn't just quit the application, unless you design it that way), or any number of other ways you design it to quit. Later on in this book, the demos will quit only when the user presses the Escape key, clicks the close "X" button on the window, or press the Back button on an Xbox 360 game-pad controller.

Listing 2.3 shows an example of the application loop we'll use throughout this book, minus anything related to Direct3D or the demos themselves. The comments within Listing 2.3 are placeholders for where we'll place function calls for our demo and Direct3D-related code later on. If we've implemented a state management system, which is useful for game menus, in-game interfaces, and more, we could have the demo's one-time initialize and shutdown in the loop itself. Since the state management would never allow the initialization and shutdown states to occur more than once per run, this would work fine. There are a number of game menu tutorials at www.UltimateGameProgramming.com for those of you interested in more advanced topics beyond the scope of this book.

Listing 2.3 The application loop.

```
int WINAPI wWinMain( HINSTANCE hInstance, HINSTANCE prevInstance,
                     LPWSTR cmdLine, int cmdShow )
{
    UNREFERENCED_PARAMETER( prevInstance );
    UNREFERENCED_PARAMETER( cmdLine );


    ...

    // Demo Initialize

    MSG msg = { 0 };

    while( msg.message != WM_QUIT )
    {
        if( PeekMessage( &msg, 0, 0, 0, PM_REMOVE ) )
        {
            TranslateMessage( &msg );
            DispatchMessage( &msg );
        }
        else
        {
            // Update
            // Draw
        }
    }

    // Demo Shutdown

    return static_cast<int>( msg.wParam );
}
```

As a quick reference, the static_cast<> operator is a C++ operator used to perform casts. The old C-style casts, for example int a = (int)floatVar, are not recommended in C++ even though it is legal to do. It is good programming practice to use C++ casting keywords over C-style casts. The static_cast<>

operator is best used when casting numerical data, like we are doing in Listing 2.3 by casting the `wParam` to an integer. But beware when trying to cast pointers of base classes to derived class and vice-versa, as these are not always going to be safe. In such a case it would be better to use `dynamic_cast<>`. Also, `static_cast<>` does not do run-time checking like `dynamic_cast<>`. The `dynamic_cast<>` is safer but only works on pointers. Although C-style casts are legal, here are some general thoughts to keep in mind:

- C++ style casts are clear in their intent (`dynamic_casts` for pointers, `const_cast` for handling `const-ness`, etc).

- If you try to perform illegal casts with C++ style casts, the compiler will give an error.

- It's easier to spot casts within code when using C++ style casts versus C-style (although the syntax highlighting in Visual Studio can sometimes help when spotting them).

- C-style casts on objects with multiple inheritance or casting object addresses to `char*` and using pointer arithmetic on them can cause undefined behavior.

- C-style casts are easy to misuse.

In Listing 2.3, MSG is a Win32 structure used to hold window messages, some of which come from the operating system, and it is up to the application to respond to these messages. If this does not happen after a certain amount of time has passed, the operating system will report the application as not responding. Usually we assume this means the application has frozen or has had some error occur, but generally it means the application has not talked back to the operating system in a while. If the application is designed to respond to the OS, after a while it can be safe to assume the program froze whenever Windows displays the "Not Responding" message next to the window's title on the title bar or next to the application's name on the Task Manager. There have been times when I've run really complex and long queries over a network in Microsoft Access and had the operating system report the program as not responding, although it was just busy doing some task and not processing events.

With window messages we need to do two things. First we need to get new messages and process them, and second we need to dispatch (respond) to these messages. The PeekMessage Win32 function retrieves a message for the associated window (the window we've created using CreateWindow). The first parameter is the structure that will hold the message (its address), the window handle (optional), min and max message filter flags (optional), and the remove flag. Specifying PM_REMOVE as the remove flag like we've done removes it from the queue. Since we are processing this message, it will not need to stay on the queue once we've handled it.

If there is a message obtained by PeekMessage, we can respond to that message by calling TranslateMessage and DispatchMessage. The Win32 function TranslateMessage translates the messages from virtual-key messages to character messages, and the DispatchMessage function dispatches the message to the Windows procedure callback function, which will be covered in the next section. The Windows procedure function will actually perform actions based on the message it receives.

If there are no messages, the only thing to do is to perform game updates and rendering. In the demos throughout this book this boils down to performing any demo-specific updates, which can be detecting and responding to user input, physics calculations, animations, updating audio buffers, etc., and to render the scene geometry.

This is a simplified look at the game loop, which is a series of game-specific steps taken for each rendered frame. One frame in a game is a single iteration of the game loop. Most games strive to reach 30 or 60 frames per second, or in other words 30 to 60 game loop iterations for each second of real-world time. As games become more complex, this is harder to achieve. The frames per second of a game is usually viewed as how fast the game can render, but games are more than just rendering code, and often the game's physics, collisions, artificial intelligence, audio, streaming, and so forth affect the game's overall frames per second.

Within the application loop we can perform one iteration of the game loop. In Listing 2.3 we have comment placeholders for where we will add the update and render functions in a later demo. Since we are not at the Direct3D section yet, this will come later.

The last line of code in the wWinMain function of the Blank Win32 Window demo returns 0. Generally you are returning an exit code, which would only matter if you launched one application from another application, and the results of that application's exit status mattered. Later on, once we add Direct3D, we'll return the exit code message, although for our purposes the value we return doesn't matter as much. Even in C++ console applications it is common for coders to just return 0 all the time.

The entire Blank Win32 Window wWinMain function with all the information we've discussed can be seen in Listing 2.4.

Listing 2.4 The Blank Win32 Window demo's wWinMain in its entirety.

```
#include<Windows.h>

LRESULT CALLBACK WndProc( HWND hwnd, UINT message,
    WPARAM wParam, LPARAM lParam );


int WINAPI wWinMain( HINSTANCE hInstance, HINSTANCE prevInstance,
                 LPWSTR cmdLine, int cmdShow )
{
    UNREFERENCED_PARAMETER( prevInstance );
    UNREFERENCED_PARAMETER( cmdLine );

    WNDCLASSEX wndClass = { 0 };
    wndClass.cbSize = sizeof( WNDCLASSEX ) ;
    wndClass.style = CS_HREDRAW | CS_VREDRAW;
    wndClass.lpfnWndProc = WndProc;
    wndClass.hInstance = hInstance;
    wndClass.hCursor = LoadCursor( NULL, IDC_ARROW );
    wndClass.hbrBackground = ( HBRUSH )( COLOR_WINDOW + 1 );
    wndClass.lpszMenuName = NULL;
    wndClass.lpszClassName = "DX11BookWindowClass";

    if( !RegisterClassEx( &wndClass ) )
        return -1;

    RECT rc = { 0, 0, 640, 480 };
    AdjustWindowRect( &rc, WS_OVERLAPPEDWINDOW, FALSE );
```

```
    HWND hwnd = CreateWindowA( "DX11BookWindowClass", "Blank Win32 Window",
        WS_OVERLAPPEDWINDOW, CW_USEDEFAULT, CW_USEDEFAULT, rc.right - rc.
left,
        rc.bottom - rc.top, NULL, NULL, hInstance, NULL );

    if( !hwnd )
        return -1;

    ShowWindow( hwnd, cmdShow );

    // Demo Initialize

    MSG msg = { 0 };

    while( msg.message != WM_QUIT )
    {
        if( PeekMessage( &msg, 0, 0, 0, PM_REMOVE ) )
        {
            TranslateMessage( &msg );
            DispatchMessage( &msg );
        }
        // Update
        // Draw
    }

    // Demo Shutdown

    return static_cast<int>( msg.wParam );
}
```

Windows Callback Procedure

The last piece of the puzzle before we can compile and build our application is to provide the windows procedure, often called windows proc function. Throughout the previous code listing (Listing 2.4) there was a forward declaration for this function, and in the wWinMain function it was passed to the WNDCLASSEX structure to one of its function, pointer members. The windows proc function is a callback function, meaning that it is called whenever messages are being obtained and processed by our application. The Blank Win32 Window demo's window proc function can be seen in Listing 2.5.

Listing 2.5 The Blank Win32 Window demo's window proc function.

```
LRESULT CALLBACK WndProc( HWND hwnd, UINT message, WPARAM wParam, LPARAM lParam )
{
    PAINTSTRUCT paintStruct;
    HDC hDC;

    switch( message )
    {
        case WM_PAINT:
            hDC = BeginPaint( hwnd, &paintStruct );
            EndPaint( hwnd, &paintStruct );
            break;

        case WM_DESTROY:
            PostQuitMessage( 0 );
            break;

        default:
            return DefWindowProc( hwnd, message, wParam, lParam );
    }

    return 0;
}
```

The windows proc function has a return type of LRESULT and uses the CALLBACK attribute. The function itself can be named whatever you like, but throughout this book it happens to be named WndProc. The callback function takes as parameters the handle of the window dispatching this message, the message as an unsigned integer, and two parameters specifying additional information (wParam and lparam). The last two parameters are used to supply data to the callback function for messages that require more data to perform some type of action. This topic goes deeper into Win32 programming than what we will need throughout this book, and we will not make use of those last two parameters.

In the Blank Win32 Window demo we respond to the paint message, and we respond to the quit message. The paint message is handled by calling Win32 functions to draw the window's background, which is handled by calling BeginPaint and EndPaint. Since Direct3D will be doing all of our rendering, this will be all we'll have to do for this message throughout this book. We won't have Direct3D-specific code with this message. but it is still a required message to respond to.

The quit message is handled by calling the Win32 PostQuitMessage function, which will cause the MSG object in our application loop to retrieve a WM_QUIT message, which causes the application loop to end and the application to quit as we've intended. Since there are situations where we don't want to just flat-out quit, we can use this to only post a quit message if we really want to quit. For example, in Microsoft Word if you try to quit without saving, a dialog pop-up appears asking you if you wish to save before exiting, exit without saving, or cancel exiting altogether.

The final part of the windows proc function is the calling of DefWindowProc, which takes the same parameters as the windows proc function. This function is only called on messages for which we are not writing custom response code. In this demo we are responding to paint requests from the operating system and quit messages but there is a ton of other events we could also look for, such as key presses, mouse clicks, mouse movements, timers, and much more. The DefWindowProc function is a Win32 function that processes every message sent to it with default processing behavior and is used to ensure that we at least respond to every message, even if we don't actually care about them.

At this point you can compile and build the demo. There should be 0 warnings and 0 errors and, if so, you can run the application to be greeted to an empty white window. To close this application you can click on the close "X" button on the upper right corner of the window, which will cause the quit message to be processed, the application loop to break, and the program to exit successfully. A screenshot from the Blank Win32 Window demo can be seen in Figure 2.5.

The Blank Win32 Window demo code and project can be found on the book's companion website in the Chapter 2/BlankWindow folder.

Time for Direct3D

We are now ready to add Direct3D 11 to the code we've written in the Blank Win32 Window demo to create a new demo called Blank Direct3D Window.

The Blank Direct3D Window demo can be found on the companion website in the Chapter2/BlankD3DWindow folder.

Figure 2.5
The Blank Win32 Window demo running.

In this section we'll first discuss all of the Direct3D functions and objects necessary to get started with Direct3D 11. In the next section we'll cover the Blank Direct3D Window demo in detail. Discussing everything needed to start Direct3D first outside of the specific chapter demo will make implementing the Blank Direct3D Window demo as a chapter tutorial much easier for beginners.

If you wish to follow along with the creation of the Blank Direct3D Window demo, create a new project titled BlankD3DWindow and copy the main.cpp source file from the Blank Win32 Window demo over to this one. This new demo will build off of that code.

Adding the DirectX Libraries

Before we begin we must include the DirectX 11 libraries that we'll be using. To link the DirectX libraries, click on the Project menu item and select [project name] Properties from the drop-down list, where [project name] is, in this case,

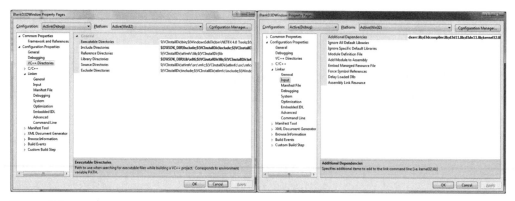

Figure 2.6
The Linker (left) and the VC++ Directories (right).

BlankD3DWindow. The project properties dialog box will appear and looks similar to what is seen in Figure 2.6.

On the left side of the properties dialog you'll see a list of property categories. Click on the Configuration Properties tab and then click on the arrow next to the Linker tab to reveal the Linker properties. From the Configuration drop-down list on the upper left of the window, switch from Debug to All Configurations so that we can apply the same data to both debug and release builds.

On the Linker tab, click Input to display the input properties of the project. From there, in the Additional Dependencies text box add to the linked libraries the files d3d11.lib, d3dx11.lib, and dxerr.lib. Keep in mind that when adding each library, end the library's name with a semi-colon (;).

If the DirectX SDK installation did not add the DirectX directory paths, you can do so yourself by going to the VC++ Directories option under the Configuration Properties tab and add to the Include Directories text box "$(DXSDK_DIR) Include;" and add to the Library Directories text box "$(DXSDK_DIR)Lib\x86;". In Figure 2.6 you can see where the Configuration Properties are, where the Linker tab is located, where the VC++ Directories tab is located, and which text boxes to fill in.

Before continuing to build the project, make sure no errors are reported with finding the libraries. If there are errors, make sure you've installed the DirectX SDK and make sure you don't have any typos in the library name or the path directories that you've just entered.

Initializing Direct3D

To set up Direct3D we need to complete the following four steps:

1. Define the device types and feature levels we want to check for.
2. Create the Direct3D device, rendering context, and swap chain.
3. Create the render target.
4. Set the viewport.

In this section we'll discuss each of these steps one at a time and cover in detail the various Direct3D objects and functions used.

Driver Types and Features Levels

In Direct3D 11 we can have a hardware device, a WARP device, a software driver device, or a reference device.

A hardware device is a Direct3D device that runs on the graphics hardware and is the fastest of all devices. This is the type of device you should be able to create if you have graphics hardware that supports the feature level we are aiming for, which will be discussed momentarily.

A reference device is used for users without hardware support by performing the rendering on the CPU. In other words, the reference device completely emulates hardware rendering on the CPU within software. This process is very slow, inefficient, and should only be used during development if there is no other alternative. This is useful when new versions of DirectX are released, but there is no hardware on the market that can run it with a hardware device.

A software driver device allows developers to write their own software rendering driver and use it with Direct3D. This is called a pluggable software driver. Usually this option is not recommended for high-performance, demanding applications where hardware, or maybe even WARP, would be the better option.

The WARP device is an efficient CPU-rendering device that emulates the full feature set of Direct3D. WARP uses the Windows Graphic runtime found in Windows Vista and Windows 7 and uses highly optimized instructions and code, which makes it a better choice than reference mode. This device is said to be on par with lower-end machines, which can be useful if we wish to see how a game performs with limited performance. This is a good real-time alternative if hardware support is not available, whereas the reference device is usually too slow for real-time applications. WARP is still not as fast as hardware since it is still emulation.

Note

There are also unknown and null device types where a null device is a reference device without rendering capabilities.

The feature levels of Direct3D allow us to specify which feature set we want to target, which eliminates the need for device caps (capabilities) from DirectX 9.0 and below. Throughout this book there are three devices we will target, with the first being a Direct3D 11.0 device, the second being a Direct3D 10.1 device, and the third being a Direct3D 10.0 device. If you do not have DirectX 11–class hardware, then we can code our demos to use Direct3D 10.1 or 10.0 as a fallback if those devices exist in hardware without any additional code. If no hardware option exists for the feature levels we want, we'll have to try to find support for one of the feature levels in a WARP or reference mode.

Listing 2.6 shows the driver type and feature levels declaration we'll use later on. By creating an array of each type, we can use that to loop through and try to create the most desired device first before continuing to the other types if the process failed. On a side note, the Win32 macro ARRAYSIZE can be used to return the size of an array, and the GetClientRect Win32 function allows us to calculate the client area of the application, which we'll use for setting the Direct3D device's rendering width and height later on in this section. Remember that Win32 applications have client areas as well as non-client areas, but we can only render to the client area.

Listing 2.6 Specifying the driver type and feature levels.

```
RECT dimensions;
GetClientRect( hwnd, &dimensions );

unsigned int width = dimensions.right - dimensions.left;
unsigned int height = dimensions.bottom - dimensions.top;
```

```
D3D_DRIVER_TYPE driverTypes[] =
{
    D3D_DRIVER_TYPE_HARDWARE, D3D_DRIVER_TYPE_WARP, D3D_DRIVER_TYPE_SOFTWARE
};

unsigned int totalDriverTypes = ARRAYSIZE( driverTypes );

D3D_FEATURE_LEVEL featureLevels[] =
{
    D3D_FEATURE_LEVEL_11_0,
    D3D_FEATURE_LEVEL_10_1,
    D3D_FEATURE_LEVEL_10_0
};

unsigned int totalFeatureLevels = ARRAYSIZE( featureLevels );
```

Device and Swap Chain Creation

The next step is the creation of the swap chain. A swap chain in Direct3D is a collection of rendering destinations for a device. Each device has at least one swap chain, but multiple swap chains can be created for multiple devices. A rendering destination can be a color buffer that is rendered to and displayed to the screen, a depth buffer (discussed in Chapter 3, "The 2D Resurgence"), a stencil buffer (also discussed in Chapter 3), and so forth.

Usually in games we have two color buffers that are being rendered onto called the primary buffer and the secondary buffer, as well as being known as the front and back buffers. The primary buffer (front buffer) is the one that is displayed to the screen, while the secondary buffer (back buffer) is being drawn to for the next frame.

Rendering can occur so fast that parts of the screen can be drawn on top of the previous results before the monitor has finished updating the display. When this happens it causes rendering artifacts and undesirable issues. Switching between the buffers so that one is being written onto and the other is being displayed allows games to avoid these artifacts. This ping-pong technique is called double buffering (also called page flipping) in computer graphics. A swap chain can have one, two, or more of these buffers, and Direct3D handles the buffer page flipping between them all.

Listing 2.7 shows the creation of a swap chain description. A swap chain description is used to define how we want the swap chain created. It has a member for:

- The buffer count (primary/secondary buffer for page flipping).
- The width and height of the buffers.
- The buffer's format (describe in the section titled "Formats" later in this chapter).
- The refresh rate, which is used to determine how often the display is refreshed in Hertz (by using 60/1 we are specifying a 60 Hertz refresh rate).
- The window handle (same window created by CreateWindow(A)).
- A Boolean flag called Windowed that is used to specify whether Direct3D should stay windowed or resize into full-screen mode.
- The sample count and quality for the sample description.

Listing 2.7 The swap chain description.

```
DXGI_SWAP_CHAIN_DESC swapChainDesc;
ZeroMemory( &swapChainDesc, sizeof( swapChainDesc ) );
swapChainDesc.BufferCount = 1;
swapChainDesc.BufferDesc.Width = width;
swapChainDesc.BufferDesc.Height = height;
swapChainDesc.BufferDesc.Format = DXGI_FORMAT_R8G8B8A8_UNORM;
swapChainDesc.BufferDesc.RefreshRate.Numerator = 60;
swapChainDesc.BufferDesc.RefreshRate.Denominator = 1;
swapChainDesc.BufferUsage = DXGI_USAGE_RENDER_TARGET_OUTPUT;
swapChainDesc.OutputWindow = hwnd;
swapChainDesc.Windowed = true;
swapChainDesc.SampleDesc.Count = 1;
swapChainDesc.SampleDesc.Quality = 0;
```

The sample description defines the multisampling properties of Direct3D. Multisampling is a technique used to sample and average rendered pixels to create smoother transitions between sharp color changes. The artifacts we are attempting to reduce with multisampling are called jagged edges, also known as the staircase effect. Figure 2.7 shows an example of this effect on the left, as well

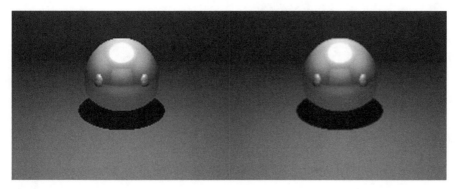

Figure 2.7
Jagged edges versus a smoother display.

as the desired smoothing we are looking to achieve with multiple sampling on the right. If these artifacts are bad, it can be unsightly to look at in a game.

The buffer usage and description of the swap chain has the most members to set, which are all pretty straightforward. The buffer usage for our swap chain is set to DXGI_USAGE_RENDER_TARGET_OUTPUT so that the swap chain is able to be used for output, or in other words it can be rendered to.

The next step is to create the rendering context, device, and swap chain now that we have the swap chain description. The Direct3D device is the device itself and communicates with the hardware. The Direct3D context is a rendering context that tells the device how to draw. It also includes rendering states and other drawing information. The swap chain as we've already discussed is the rendering destinations that the device and context will draw to. The creation of the device, rendering context, and swap chain can be seen in Listing 2.8. The Direct3D device is of type ID3D11Device, the rendering context is of type ID3D11Context, and the swap chain is of type IDXGISwapChain. The code clip from Listing 2.8 is an example setup from the upcoming Blank Direct3D Window demo code we'll look at later in this chapter.

Listing 2.8 Create the Direct3D device, context, and swap chain.

```
ID3D11Device device_;
ID3D11Context d3dContext_;
IDXGISwapChain swapChain_;
```

```
unsigned int creationFlags = 0;

#ifdef _DEBUG
    creationFlags |= D3D11_CREATE_DEVICE_DEBUG;
#endif

HRESULT result;
unsigned int driver = 0;

for( driver = 0; driver < totalDriverTypes; ++driver )
{
    result = D3D11CreateDeviceAndSwapChain( 0, driverTypes[driver], 0,
        creationFlags, featureLevels, totalFeatureLevels,
        D3D11_SDK_VERSION, &swapChainDesc, &swapChain_,
        &d3dDevice_, &featureLevel_, &d3dContext_ );

    if( SUCCEEDED( result ) )
    {
        driverType_ = driverTypes[driver];
        break;
    }
}

if( FAILED( result ) )
{
    DXTRACE_MSG( "Failed to create the Direct3D device!" );
    return false;
}
```

The swap chain, device, and rendering context can be created with a single Direct3D function call or by object-specific Direct3D calls (e.g., CreateSwapChain to create just a swap chain). This function is called D3D11CreateDeviceAndSwap-Chain. In Listing 2.8 we loop through each driver type and attempt to create a hardware device, a WARP device, or a reference device. If all fail, we can't initialize Direct3D. The D3D11CreateDeviceAndSwapChain function also takes our feature levels, so if at least one of those feature levels exists, and if our device type exists, then this function will succeed.

The D3D11CreateDeviceAndSwapChain takes as parameters the following values:

- A pointer to the video adapter to use to create the device. Passing null causes Direct3D to use the default device. This can be useful if there is more than one device installed in the machine.

- The driver type we wish to create (i.e., hardware, WARP, software, or reference).

- A handle to a DLL that implements a software rendering device. If our driver type is software (D3D_DRIVER_TYPE_SOFTWARE), then this parameter CANNOT be null.

- The creation flags. In Direct3D a creation flag of 0 can be used in release builds of our games, while a creation flag of D3D11_CREATE_DEVICE_DEBUG allows us to create a device with debugging capabilities, which is useful for development.

- The feature levels we wish to target, ordered from the most desired to the least desired. In this book we are concerned with Direct3D 11 or Direct3D 10, but we could also target Direct3D 9 through D3D_FEATURE_LEVEL_9_3, D3D_FEATURE_LEVEL_9_2, or D3D_FEATURE_LEVEL_9_1.

- Number of feature levels in the feature levels array.

- The SDK version, which will always be D3D11_SDK_VERSION since we are using the DirectX 11 SDK.

- The swap chain description object.

- The address for the device object (with the device being of type ID3D11-Device).

- The address of the feature level that was selected. Earlier we supplied a list of features we want but only one is chosen, which is stored in this address.

- The address for the rendering context (with the context being of the type ID3D11Context).

Render Target View Creation

A render target view is a Direct3D resource written to by the output merger stage. In order for the output merger to render to the swap chain's back buffer (secondary buffer), we create a render target view of it.

In Chapter 3 we'll discuss textures in detail, but for now understand that a texture is often an image. The primary and secondary rendering buffers of the swap chain are color textures, and to obtain a pointer to it we call the swap chain function GetBuffer. GetBuffer takes as parameters:

- The buffer index (a value of 0 gives us the first buffer).

- The type of interface we are trying to manipulate. The type of a 2D texture is ID3D11Texture2D.

- The address of the buffer we are obtaining. We must cast to LPVOID.

With a pointer to the buffer, we call CreateRenderTargetView, which is a function of the Direct3D device object, to create the render target view. Render target views have the type of ID3D11RenderTargetView, and the CreateRender TargetView function takes as parameters the 2D texture we are creating the view for, the render target description, and the address of the ID3D11RenderTarget View object we are creating. Setting the render target description parameter to null gives us a view of the entire surface at mip level 0. Mip-map levels will be discussed in more detail in Chapter 3.

Once we are done creating the render target view, we can release our pointer to the back buffer of the swap chain. Since we obtained a reference via a COM object, we must call the COM's Release function to decrement the reference count. This must be done to avoid memory leaks, because we don't want the system holding onto it once the application quits.

Each time we want to render to a specific render target, we must set it first before any drawing calls. This is done by calling OMSetRenderTarget, which is a function that is part of the output merger (hence the OM in OMSetRenderTarget). The OMSetRenderTarget function takes as parameters the number of views we are binding in this function call, the list of render target views, and the depth/stencil views. We'll discuss depth and stencils in Chapter 3. Listing 2.9 shows the creation and binding of the render target view.

Listing 2.9 The creation and binding of the render target view.

```
ID3D11RenderTargetView* backBufferTarget_;
ID3D11Texture2D* backBufferTexture;
```

```
HRESULT result = swapChain_->GetBuffer( 0, __uuidof( ID3D11Texture2D ),
    ( LPVOID* )&backBufferTexture );

if( FAILED( result ) )
{
    DXTRACE_MSG( "Failed to get the swap chain back buffer!" );
    return false;
}

result = d3dDevice_->CreateRenderTargetView( backBufferTexture, 0,
    &backBufferTarget_ );

if( backBufferTexture )
    backBufferTexture->Release( );

if( FAILED( result ) )
{
    DXTRACE_MSG( "Failed to create the render target view!" );
    return false;
}

d3dContext_->OMSetRenderTargets( 1, &backBufferTarget_, 0 );
```

You'll notice in Listing 2.9 that we are using a macro called DXTRACE_MSG. This macro is used for debugging purposes, and we'll discuss it in more detail at the end of this chapter, along with the other DirectX Error Handling Library.

The Viewport

The last piece of the Direct3D 11 puzzle is the creation and setting of the viewport. The viewport defines the area of the screen we are rendering to. In single player or non-split-screen multiplayer games this is often the entire screen, and so we set the viewport's width and height to the Direct3D swap chain's width and height. For split-screen games we can create two viewports, with one defining the upper portion of the screen and one for the lower portion. In order to render split-screen views we would have to render the scene once for player 1's perspective, once for player 2's perspective, etc. Although multiplayer games are beyond the scope of this book, an example of creating a split-screen demo can be found at www.UltimateGameProgramming.com.

Viewports are created by filling out a D3D11_VIEWPORT object and setting it to the rendering context by calling the context's RSSetViewports function. RSSetView ports takes the number of viewports we are setting with this function call and the list of viewport objects. The creation and setting of our full-screen viewport can be seen in Listing 2.10, where the X and Y positions mark the left and top screen positions, and min and max depths are values between 0 and 1 that mark the min and max depths of the viewport.

Listing 2.10 The creation and setting of a full-screen viewport.

```
D3D11_VIEWPORT viewport;
viewport.Width = static_cast<float>(width);
viewport.Height = static_cast<float>(height);
viewport.MinDepth = 0.0f;
viewport.MaxDepth = 1.0f;
viewport.TopLeftX = 0.0f;
viewport.TopLeftY = 0.0f;


d3dContext_->RSSetViewports( 1, &viewport );
```

Clearing and Displaying the Screen

Rendering to the screen takes place in a few different steps. The first step is usually to clear any necessary render target surfaces. In most games this includes buffers such as the depth buffer, which we'll discuss in Chapter 3. In the Blank Direct3D Window demo we'll implement later in this chapter, we clear the color buffer of the render target view to a specified color. This is done by calling the Direct3D content's ClearRenderTargetView function. ClearRenderTargetView has the following function prototype:

```
void ClearRenderTargetView( ID3D11RenderTargetView* pRenderTargetView,
    const FLOAT ColorRGBA[4] );
```

Note

It is not necessary to clear the color buffer before rendering in most commercial games because the sky and environment geometry ensures every pixel will be overridden in the color buffer anyway, making the clearing step unnecessary.

The ClearRenderTargetView function takes as parameters the render target view we are clearing and a value to clear it to. To clear the screen, we are specifying the color as the color we want the background shaded to. This color is a red, green, blue, and alpha array with color values specified in the 0.0 to 1.0 range. In this case 0.0 is nonintensity, and 1.0 is full intensity. In byte terms, 1.0 would be equivalent to a value of 255. If the red, green, and blue components of the color are 1.0, then we have a pure white color. Colors are discussed more in Chapter 3.

The next step is to draw the scene's geometry. In this chapter we won't be drawing any geometry, but in Chapter 3 we'll cover this in more detail.

The last step is to display the rendered buffer to the screen by calling the swap chain's `Present` function. `Present` has the following function prototype:

```
HRESULT IDXGISwapChain::Present( UINT SyncInterval, UINT Flags );
```

The parameters of the `Present` function are the sync interval and the presentation flags. The sync interval can be 0 for immediate display or 1, 2, 3, or 4 to present after the *n*th vertical blank. A vertical blank is the time difference between the last line of the frame update for the current frame and the first line update for the next frame. Devices such as computer monitors update the pixels of the display vertically line-by-line.

The `Present` function flags can be 0 to output each buffer, `DXGI_PRESENT_ TEST` to not output anything for testing purposes, or `DXGI_PRESENT_DO_ NOT_SEQUENCE` for presenting the output without sequencing to exploit the vertical blank synchronization. For our purposes we can just pass 0 and 0 to the `Present` function to display our rendered results.

Listing 2.11 shows an example of clearing the screen and presenting it to the viewer. In Chapter 3 we'll dive more into rendering buffers for color, depth, double buffering for smooth animations, and much more. In this chapter the focus is learning the setup of Direct3D 11. Listing 2.11 would display a dark blue background color if this were executed in a program.

Listing 2.11 Clearing the rendering target and displaying the new rendered scene.

```
float clearColor[4] = { 0.0f, 0.0f, 0.25f, 1.0f };
d3dContext_->ClearRenderTargetView( backBufferTarget_, clearColor );

swapChain_->Present( 0, 0 );
```

Cleaning Up

The final thing to do in any Direct3D application is to clean up and release the objects that you've created. For instance, at the beginning of a program, you would have created a Direct3D device, a Direct3D rendering context, a swap chain, and a render target view at the least. When the application closes, you need to release these objects so the resources are returned to the system for reuse.

COM objects keep a reference count that tells the system when it's safe to remove objects from memory. By using the Release function, you decrement the reference count for an object. When the reference count reaches 0, the system reclaims these resources.

An example of releasing our Direct3D objects can be seen in Listing 2.12. The if-statements in Listing 2.12 first check to make sure that the objects is not null and then calls their Release functions. It's a good idea to release the objects in the reverse order in which they were created.

Listing 2.12 Releasing the main Direct3D 11 objects.

```
if( backBufferTarget_ ) backBufferTarget_->Release( );
if( swapChain_ ) swapChain_->Release( );
if( d3dContext_ ) d3dContext_->Release( );
if( d3dDevice_ ) d3dDevice_->Release( );
```

Tip

Always check to make sure that DirectX objects are not null before calling Release on them. Attempting to release an invalid pointer can cause your game to crash due to undefined behavior.

Formats

Occasionally you'll be required to specify a DXGI format. Formats can be used to describe the layout of an image, the number of bits used for each color, or the layout of vertices for a vertex buffer (Chapter 3). Most commonly, DXGI formats are used to describe the layout of the buffers in the swap chain. DXGI formats are not specific to any type of data, only the format in which it comes.

An example DXGI format, DXGI_FORMAT_R8G8B8A8_UNORM says that the data coming in will use 8 bits for each of the RGBA components. When defining

Table 2.1 Common Direct3D Formats

Format	Description
DXGI_FORMAT_R32G32B32A32_TYPELESS	128-bit format consisting of four typeless RGBA components.
DXGI_FORMAT_R32G32B32A32_FLOAT	128-bit format consisting of four float RGBA components.
DXGI_FORMAT_R32G32B32A32_UINT	128-bit format consisting of four unsigned integer RGBA components.
DXGI_FORMAT_R32G32B32A32_SINT	128-bit format consisting of four signed integer RGBA components.
DXGI_FORMAT_R8G8B8A8_TYPELESS	32-bit format consisting of four typeless RGBA components.
DXGI_FORMAT_R8G8B8A8_UINT	32-bit format consisting of four unsigned integer RGBA components.
DXGI_FORMAT_R8G8B8A8_SINT	32-bit format consisting of four signed integer RGBA components.

vertices, formats like DXGI_FORMAT_R32G32B32_FLOAT are used where 32 bits are available for the three components. Even though a format may specify RGB, it's only a description of how the data is laid out, not what the data is used for.

Occasionally you'll see formats that specify the same number of bits for each component but have a different extension to them. For instance, both DXGI_FORMAT_R32G32B32A32_FLOAT and DXGI_FORMAT_R32G32B32A32_UINT reserve the same number of bits for each component but also specify the type of data contained in those bits. These are considered fully typed formats.

Formats that don't declare a type are called typeless formats. They reserve the same number of bits for each component but don't care what type of data is contained, such as DXGI_FORMAT_R32G32B32A32_TYPELESS. The list of common formats can be seen in Table 2.1.

THE BLANK D3D WINDOW

The companion website includes a demo in the Chapter 2 folder called Blank D3D Window (the folder is Chapter2/BlankD3DWindow/). In this section we will create this demo step-by-step using the knowledge gained about Direct3D 11 up to this point. What we will accomplish here we'll be able to use as the base for all demos throughout the book.

Design of the Template Framework

The setup, shutdown, and initialization of non-demo–specific Direct3D objects are fairly straightforward, and rewriting essentially the same thing each time we want to write a new demo can prove unnecessary. Sometimes we want to get straight to the demo itself without having to write the standard Win32 and Direct3D startup code. Although it is not a big deal, it is at times an inconvenience without resorting to copy-and-paste methods.

To resolve this we will write all the Direct3D startup and cleanup code in one source file and reuse that code throughout the book. To facilitate this we will create a class called DX11DemoBase. To create our specific demos, we'll derive from this base class and override virtual functions necessary for us to create our demos.

In this section we'll cover the Blank Direct3D Window demo in its entirety and use the code created here as the basis for all demos to follow.

The Direct3D Class

But why use a class? Why not use global variables and functions to act on them like many other books, tutorials, and resources? There are many answers to this, and most of them stem from good versus bad programming practices.

Global variables are looked down upon in programming for many reasons. In general it is just bad programming to use them, and they should be avoided. Alternatively, we could also pass objects as parameters, but there are too many objects that would need to be passed to nearly every function in our application. Of course we could create a class or structure to store them and pass that object around, but in the end it makes sense to have a demo class that demo-specific classes derive from; it makes little sense to return to the C way of doing things.

In our setup, a demo is its own object. It can load the content it needs, render what needs to be rendered, and update what needs to be updated. It has a solitary purpose and exists to perform a single job. The question now is what will we need from our base class? For starters, we'll need functions to do the following:

- Initialize Direct3D
- Release Direct3D objects created during startup
- Store member variables for our Direct3D objects that are not demo-specific

- Provide a way to load demo-specific content
- Provide a way to unload demo-specific content
- Provide the ability to perform demo-specific updates once per frame
- Provide the demo-specific rendering code

Judging by the list of needs that we've just identified, it makes sense to create a base class with public initialize and shutdown functions, virtual functions for the loading and unloading of content, and virtual functions for the rendering and updating steps of the game loop. By making these demo-specific functions virtual, the demo classes that derive from this base class can implement their custom logic and behaviors. The DX11DemoBase class definition can be seen in Listing 2.13.

Listing 2.13 The Demo Bases definition.

```
#ifndef _DEMO_BASE_H_
#define _DEMO_BASE_H_

#include<d3d11.h>
#include<d3dx11.h>
#include<DxErr.h>


class Dx11DemoBase
{
    public:
        Dx11DemoBase( );
        virtual ~Dx11DemoBase( );

        bool Initialize( HINSTANCE hInstance, HWND hwnd );
        void Shutdown( );

        virtual bool LoadContent( );
        virtual void UnloadContent( );

        virtual void Update( float dt ) = 0;
        virtual void Render( ) = 0;
    protected:
        HINSTANCE hInstance_;
```

```
        HWND hwnd_;

        D3D_DRIVER_TYPE driverType_;
        D3D_FEATURE_LEVEL featureLevel_;

        ID3D11Device* d3dDevice_;
        ID3D11DeviceContext* d3dContext_;
        IDXGISwapChain* swapChain_;
        ID3D11RenderTargetView* backBufferTarget_;
};
```

#endif

In Listing 2.13 we can see that all of the minimum Direct3D objects we'll need are included as protected class members. If a demo needs objects specific to that demo, such as additional rendering targets, then it is up to that demo-specific class to declare those as members of the derived class. The base class is just for objects that are common across all demos.

Taking a look at the member functions of the demo base class, we see that we need only a few methods to give us the ability to create a wide range of demos. The job of the constructor is to set the member objects to default values like null. To do this we'll use the constructor's member initialize list, which is a method of initializing member variables outside the body of the constructor. Doing this is often good programming practice and can be more efficient than letting a default constructor call occur before a copy constructor on objects. In the case of our Direct3D objects, they have no constructors, so this is done largely for consistency. But in general when working with initializing objects, it is a good idea to avoid unnecessary constructor calls. Although built-in types can be initialized during the member initialize list or through assignment within the constructor, the result will be the same either way, since they are built-in types and not objects.

The class's destructor is tasked with calling the Shutdown function to ensure that all Direct3D objects are properly released when the demo is either deleted or falls out of scope.

The Shutdown function calls Release on all of our COM-based Direct3D objects. In the Shutdown function it is important to release our demo-specific content;

therefore Shutdown first calls the UnloadContent function before releasing its own member objects.

The UnloadContent function releases any demo-specific data and is overridden by the derived class. Since not all demos will necessarily have content, such as this Blank Window demo, this function does not need to be purely virtual. The same goes with the LoadContent function that loads all demo-specific content such as geometry, texture images, shaders, audio files, and so forth.

Note

XNA Game Studio uses a slightly similar idea where each game derives from the Game base class and overrides specific functions to implement game-specific behavior. If you're not already aware of it, XNA Game Studio is a game development framework built on top of DirectX to create Windows-PC and Xbox 360 games.

The Dx11DemoBase class's constructor, destructor, LoadContent, UnloadContent, and Shutdown functions can be seen in Listing 2.14.

Listing 2.14 Some Dx11DemoBase functions.

```
#include"Dx11DemoBase.h"


Dx11DemoBase::Dx11DemoBase( ) : driverType_( D3D_DRIVER_TYPE_NULL ),
    featureLevel_( D3D_FEATURE_LEVEL_11_0 ), d3dDevice_( 0 ), d3dContext_( 0 ),
    swapChain_( 0 ), backBufferTarget_( 0 )
{

}


Dx11DemoBase::~Dx11DemoBase( )
{
    Shutdown( );
}


bool Dx11DemoBase::LoadContent( )
{
    // Override with demo specifics, if any...
```

```
        return true;
}


void Dx11DemoBase::UnloadContent( )
{
    // Override with demo specifics, if any...
}


void Dx11DemoBase::Shutdown( )
{
    UnloadContent( );

    if( backBufferTarget_ ) backBufferTarget_->Release( );
    if( swapChain_ ) swapChain_->Release( );
    if( d3dContext_ ) d3dContext_->Release( );
    if( d3dDevice_ ) d3dDevice_->Release( );
    d3dDevice_ = 0;
    d3dContext_ = 0;
    swapChain_ = 0;
    backBufferTarget_ = 0;
}
```

The last function in the Dx11DemoBase class is the Initialize function. The Initialize function performs the Direct3D initialization as we've described throughout this chapter. The function begins by declaring our driver types for hardware, WARP, or software, and our feature levels for Direct3D 11.0, 10.1, or 10.0. The setup of this code is to attempt to create a hardware device in Direct3D 11. If that fails, we'll try other driver types and feature levels until we find one that is supported. This also means that if you're using Direct3D 10 hardware you can still run this demo in hardware, since the 10.1 or 10.0 feature level will be chosen.

The next step is to create the swap chain description and use that information to attempt to find a supported device type and feature level. If that passes, we create the render target view out of the swap chain's back buffer, create the viewport, and call LoadContent to load any demo-specific game content. Since our Direct3D initialization must occur before demo-specific initialization, LoadContent must be called last. By including it here we don't have to call it manually outside of the class. The same can be said for having to manually call UnloadContent before the application quits since Shutdown calls UnloadContent itself.

The full Direct3D 11 initialization can be seen in Listing 2.15 for the Blank Direct3D Window demo. Most of the code deals with error checking and setting property values.

Listing 2.15 The Dx11DemoBase Initialize function.

```
bool Dx11DemoBase::Initialize( HINSTANCE hInstance, HWND hwnd )
{
    hInstance_ = hInstance;
    hwnd_ = hwnd;

    RECT dimensions;
    GetClientRect( hwnd, &dimensions );

    unsigned int width = dimensions.right - dimensions.left;
    unsigned int height = dimensions.bottom - dimensions.top;

    D3D_DRIVER_TYPE driverTypes[] =
    {
        D3D_DRIVER_TYPE_HARDWARE, D3D_DRIVER_TYPE_WARP, D3D_DRIVER_TYPE_-
SOFTWARE
    };

    unsigned int totalDriverTypes = ARRAYSIZE( driverTypes );

    D3D_FEATURE_LEVEL featureLevels[] =
    {
        D3D_FEATURE_LEVEL_11_0,
        D3D_FEATURE_LEVEL_10_1,
        D3D_FEATURE_LEVEL_10_0
    };

    unsigned int totalFeatureLevels = ARRAYSIZE( featureLevels );

    DXGI_SWAP_CHAIN_DESC swapChainDesc;
    ZeroMemory( &swapChainDesc, sizeof( swapChainDesc ) );
    swapChainDesc.BufferCount = 1;
```

```
    swapChainDesc.BufferDesc.Width = width;
    swapChainDesc.BufferDesc.Height = height;
    swapChainDesc.BufferDesc.Format = DXGI_FORMAT_R8G8B8A8_UNORM;
    swapChainDesc.BufferDesc.RefreshRate.Numerator = 60;
    swapChainDesc.BufferDesc.RefreshRate.Denominator = 1;
    swapChainDesc.BufferUsage = DXGI_USAGE_RENDER_TARGET_OUTPUT;
    swapChainDesc.OutputWindow = hwnd;
    swapChainDesc.Windowed = true;
    swapChainDesc.SampleDesc.Count = 1;
    swapChainDesc.SampleDesc.Quality = 0;

    unsigned int creationFlags = 0;

#ifdef _DEBUG
    creationFlags |= D3D11_CREATE_DEVICE_DEBUG;
#endif

    HRESULT result;
    unsigned int driver = 0;

    for( driver = 0; driver < totalDriverTypes; ++driver )
    {
        result = D3D11CreateDeviceAndSwapChain( 0, driverTypes[driver], 0,
            creationFlags, featureLevels, totalFeatureLevels,
            D3D11_SDK_VERSION, &swapChainDesc, &swapChain_,
            &d3dDevice_, &featureLevel_, &d3dContext_ );

        if( SUCCEEDED( result ) )
        {
            driverType_ = driverTypes[driver];
            break;
        }
    }

    if( FAILED( result ) )
    {
        DXTRACE_MSG( "Failed to create the Direct3D device!" );
        return false;
    }
    ID3D11Texture2D* backBufferTexture;
```

```
    result = swapChain_->GetBuffer( 0, __uuidof( ID3D11Texture2D ),
       ( LPVOID* )&backBufferTexture );

    if( FAILED( result ) )
    {
        DXTRACE_MSG( "Failed to get the swap chain back buffer!" );
        return false;
    }

    result = d3dDevice_->CreateRenderTargetView( backBufferTexture, 0,
       &backBufferTarget_ );

    if( backBufferTexture )
        backBufferTexture->Release( );

    if( FAILED( result ) )
    {
        DXTRACE_MSG( "Failed to create the render target view!" );
        return false;
    }

    d3dContext_->OMSetRenderTargets( 1, &backBufferTarget_, 0 );

    D3D11_VIEWPORT viewport;
    viewport.Width = static_cast<float>(width);
    viewport.Height = static_cast<float>(height);
    viewport.MinDepth = 0.0f;
    viewport.MaxDepth = 1.0f;
    viewport.TopLeftX = 0.0f;
    viewport.TopLeftY = 0.0f;

    d3dContext_->RSSetViewports( 1, &viewport );

    return LoadContent( );
}
```

The Blank Window Demo Class

Currently we have everything needed to run the Blank Direct3D Window demo. To do this we'll derive a class from the Dx11DemoBase class and call it BlankDemo. The BlankDemo class definition can be seen in Listing 2.16.

Listing 2.16 The BlankDemo class header.

```
#ifndef _BLANK_DEMO_H_
#define _BLANK_DEMO_H_

#include"Dx11DemoBase.h"


class BlankDemo : public Dx11DemoBase
{
    public:
        BlankDemo( );
        virtual ~BlankDemo( );

        bool LoadContent( );
        void UnloadContent( );

        void Update( float dt );
        void Render( );
};

#endif
```

The Update function takes a single parameter called dt. We'll look at this value more closely in Chapter 3, but for now understand that in games we often need to update logic based on real time. The dt parameter will represent the time delta that has passed since the last frame, and we'll use it for time-based updates. For now we'll ignore it until we discuss animation.

Since the demo does not do anything special but clears the screen using Direct3D, all of the overridden functions are empty, with the exception of the Render function. In the Render function we only call two Direct3D functions. We first call ClearRenderTargetView to clear the screen to a specified color, and then we call Present to display that newly rendered scene (or lack thereof, since the render was just a uniform color). It is all pretty basic and made even easier to understand since all of the Direct3D functions used throughout this demo have already been discussed in great detail earlier in the chapter. The BlankDemo implemented member functions can be seen in Listing 2.17, in case you're following along by writing code as you read.

Listing 2.17 The implementation of the BlankDemo class.

```cpp
#include"BlankDemo.h"


BlankDemo::BlankDemo( )
{

}


BlankDemo::~BlankDemo( )
{

}


bool BlankDemo::LoadContent( )
{
    return true;
}


void BlankDemo::UnloadContent( )
{

}


void BlankDemo::Update( float dt )
{

}


void BlankDemo::Render( )
{
    if( d3dContext_ == 0 )
        return;

    float clearColor[4] = { 0.0f, 0.0f, 0.25f, 1.0f };
```

```
    d3dContext_->ClearRenderTargetView( backBufferTarget_, clearColor );

    swapChain_->Present( 0, 0 );
}
```

Updating the Application Loop

Currently we have everything needed to bring the Blank Direct3D Window demo to life. The last and final step is updating the wWinMain function we created in the first demo of this chapter (the Blank Win32 Window demo) to use our demo class. Remember when we only had comments set as placeholders where we would add our Direct3D code? In Listing 2.18 you get to see where those comments were removed and replaced with their corresponding function calls.

Listing 2.18 The main source file of the Blank Direct3D Window demo.

```
#include<Windows.h>
#include<memory>
#include"BlankDemo.h"


LRESULT CALLBACK WndProc( HWND hwnd, UINT message, WPARAM wParam, LPARAM lParam
);


int WINAPI wWinMain( HINSTANCE hInstance, HINSTANCE prevInstance,
                LPWSTR cmdLine, int cmdShow )
{
    UNREFERENCED_PARAMETER( prevInstance );
    UNREFERENCED_PARAMETER( cmdLine );

    WNDCLASSEX wndClass = { 0 };
    wndClass.cbSize = sizeof( WNDCLASSEX ) ;
    wndClass.style = CS_HREDRAW | CS_VREDRAW;
    wndClass.lpfnWndProc = WndProc;
    wndClass.hInstance = hInstance;
    wndClass.hCursor = LoadCursor( NULL, IDC_ARROW );
    wndClass.hbrBackground = ( HBRUSH )( COLOR_WINDOW + 1 );
    wndClass.lpszMenuName = NULL;
    wndClass.lpszClassName = "DX11BookWindowClass";
```

```
    if( !RegisterClassEx( &wndClass ) )
        return -1;

    RECT rc = { 0, 0, 640, 480 };
    AdjustWindowRect( &rc, WS_OVERLAPPEDWINDOW, FALSE );

    HWND hwnd = CreateWindowA( "DX11BookWindowClass", "Blank Direct3D 11
Window",
        WS_OVERLAPPEDWINDOW, CW_USEDEFAULT, CW_USEDEFAULT, rc.right - rc.left,
        rc.bottom - rc.top, NULL, NULL, hInstance, NULL );

    if( !hwnd )
        return -1;

    ShowWindow( hwnd, cmdShow );

    std::auto_ptr<Dx11DemoBase> demo( new BlankDemo( ) );

    // Demo Initialize
    bool result = demo->Initialize( hInstance, hwnd );

    // Error reporting if there is an issue
    if( result == false )
        return -1;

    MSG msg = { 0 };

    while( msg.message != WM_QUIT )
    {
        if( PeekMessage( &msg, 0, 0, 0, PM_REMOVE ) )
        {
            TranslateMessage( &msg );
            DispatchMessage( &msg );
        }
        else
        {
            // Update and Draw
            demo->Update( 0.0f );
            demo->Render( );
        }
```

```
    }

    // Demo Shutdown
    demo->Shutdown( );

    return static_cast<int>( msg.wParam );
}


LRESULT CALLBACK WndProc( HWND hwnd, UINT message, WPARAM wParam, LPARAM lParam )
{
    PAINTSTRUCT paintStruct;
    HDC hDC;

    switch( message )
    {
        case WM_PAINT:
            hDC = BeginPaint( hwnd, &paintStruct );
            EndPaint( hwnd, &paintStruct );
            break;

        case WM_DESTROY:
            PostQuitMessage( 0 );
            break;

        default:
            return DefWindowProc( hwnd, message, wParam, lParam );
    }

    return 0;
}
```

We've added seven lines of code to the wWinMain function. First we've created the
demo instance by using the C++ standard smart pointer auto_ptr<>. The
auto_ptr<> smart pointer is one that automatically deletes the memory it is
pointing to when the scope it is in ends or when it is copied to another
auto_ptr<>. The scope can be function level, within an if-statement, inside a
loop, and within a pair of curly braces arbitrarily placed to create a new scope.

The benefit to this is that we don't need to manually delete the allocated data.
The true benefit that goes beyond that (since it would not be hard or even

unlikely to just call delete on the demo object) is that using `auto_ptr<>` is exception safe. This means that even if an exception is triggered and your application halts, the `auto_ptr<>` will still release its data during stack unwinding. This means no leaks, even when the application crashes. If we manually had to delete this pointer and if execution did halt, we'd be left with leaked memory. There are tons of benefits to using memory objects such as `auto_ptr<>`. If you are unfamiliar with them it is important to read up on smart pointers and other standards offered by the C++ programming language that are beyond the scope of this book. If you have not brushed up on the recent standard of C++ (C++0x), it is recommended you do so.

The last thing to note in the `wWinMain` function is that we are returning the `wParam` member of the `MSG` object in order to return the application's exit code. Since `wWinMain` returns an integer, we cast this object to an integer by using C++'s `static_cast<>` operator.

A screenshot of the Blank Direct3D Window can be seen in Figure 2.8. The demo is using a dark color to clear the screen, which should be reflected in the screenshot when compared to the earlier Blank Win32 Window demo.

The completion of the Blank Direct3D Window demo marks the completion of the template files we'll use throughout this book to create future demos. To create the future demos, we just need to derive new classes from Dx11DemoBase and implement the demo-specific logic we need by overriding `LoadContent`, `UnloadContent`, `Update`, and `Render`.

DirectX Error Handling Library

The DirectX SDK comes with a series of utility functions and macros that aid in the debugging of DirectX applications. To gain access to these utilities, projects must link to Dxerr.lib and include the Dxerr.h header file. In this section we will discuss the various error handling functions and macros that exist.

Error Handling Functions

There are three functions in the DirectX Error Handling library:

- `TCHAR* DXGetErrorDescription( HRESULT hr )`
- `TCHAR* DXGetErrorString( HRESULT hr )`

Figure 2.8
The Blank D3D Window demo screenshot.

■ HRESULT DXTrace(CHAR * strFile, DWORD dwline, HRESULT hr, CHAR * strMsg, BOOL bPopMsgBox)

The function DXGetErrorDescription takes any HRESULT return value and returns a string storing the description of that error.

The function DXGetErrorString also takes any HRESULT error value but returns a string holding the error code. For example, "D3DERR_DEVICELOST" will be returned for a value matching that error code, while DXGetErrorDescription returns the description of what that actually means.

The last function, DXTrace, will display a message with the error string from DXGetErrorString. This function takes as parameters the current file (you can use the Win32 __FILE__ macros for this parameter), the line number (you can use the Win32 macro __LINE__), the HRESULT holding the error value, a pointer to an optional string message that will be displayed along with the file and line, and a Boolean specifying if the trace should display a pop-up message box.

Error Handling Macros

There are three main error handling macros to be aware of, and to fully utilize them you must be running the application in the debugger. These error handling macros include the following, which are related to the DXTrace function:

- DXTRACE_ERR(str, hr)
- DXTRACE_ERR_MSGBOX(str, hr)
- DXTRACE_MSG(str)

The DXTRACE_ERR macro is used to output a message to the debugger, where str is a string you want displayed along with the tracing information and the HRESULT value of the error result. The DXTRACE_ERR_MSGBOX is essentially DXTRACE_ERR but will display the output using a message box pop-up. The final macro, DXTRACE_MSG, takes a single parameter, which is the string to display to the output debugger window. The file and line appear with the string parameter with each of these macros.

Throughout this chapter we've focused mostly on using DXTRACE_MSG to display errors when they occur during our Direct3D setup. It is important to be aware of these macros, as they can be very useful when building and debugging DirectX applications.

SUMMARY

This chapter covered how to set up and create a Direct3D 11 window using Visual Studio 2010. We've ended this chapter with a set of template files that we can use for the rest of the demos throughout this book. If you're coming to Direct3D 11 from Direct3D 9 or below, you can appreciate how easy it is to get Direct3D up and running. Although it took a number of lines of code, those lines of code were fairly straightforward and easy to digest.

In the next chapter we will begin rendering 2D geometry to the screen, along with discussing the topic of texture mapped images. We will build off the code developed throughout this chapter; therefore it is important to have a solid understanding of each of the Win32 and DirectX functions as well as how the code template works.

CHAPTER QUESTIONS

Answers to the following chapter review questions can be found in Appendix A on this book's companion website.

1. Which of the following is a Direct3D device type?

    A. Hardware

    B. Software

    C. WARP

    D. Both A and B

    E. All of the above

2. The viewport does what?

    A. Draws to the monitor

    B. Defines the area of the window that is drawn to

    C. Is a 3D camera

    D. None of the above

3. What are swap chains?

    A. Another name for a Direct3D device

    B. Another name for a Direct3D context

    C. Both A and B

    D. A collection of rendering destinations displayed to the screen

4. Presenting the rendered scene is done with the `Present` method. Which object does `Present` belong to?

    A. Swap chains

    B. Direct3D device

    C. Direct3D context

    D. Render target view

5. What are render targets?

    A. An object used to render geometry

    B. A texture that is the destination of a rendering output

    C. Another name for a swap chain

    D. None of the above

6. What feature levels did the Blank Window demo support?

    A. Direct3D 11

    B. Direct3D 10

    C. Direct3D 9

    D. Both A and B

    E. Both A and B and Direct3D 10.1

    F. All of the above

7. What is a WARP device?

    A. A fast hardware-rendering device.

    B. A down-level hardware-rendering device

    C. A fast software-rendering device

    D. None of the above

8. How are Direct3D objects freed?

    A. Calling delete on them like C++ dynamically located objects

    B. Calling the COM object's `Release` method

    C. They are automatically released upon the application's exit

    D. Use an `auto_ptr<>`

9. How can we create a full-screen Direct3D window?

    A. Setting the window's width and height to a resolution larger than the screen

B. Can only be done in hardware device mode

C. Must use a special Direct3D context creation device for full-screen applications

D. Set the `Windowed` property of the swap chain description to false

10. What is the purpose of the DirectX Error Handling Library?

A. Debug output

B. Used to create exception-safe code

C. Fixes errors at run-time

D. Similar to C++ try/catch but for the graphics card

11. True or False: `auto_ptr<>` is exception safe

A. True

B. False

12. True or False: `WinMain` has Unicode parameters

A. True

B. False

13. True or False: The operator `dynamic_cast<>` offers run-time safety

A. True

B. False

14. True or False: The operator `static_cast<>` is used to cast static variables

A. True

B. False

15. True or False: `DXTRACE_MSG` displays a string to a message box

A. True

B. False

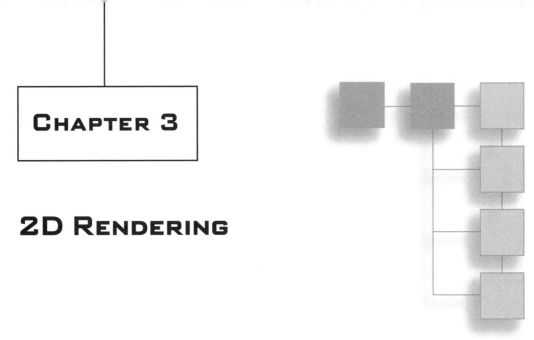

CHAPTER 3

2D RENDERING

Two-dimensional (2D) games, immensely popular in the early days of video games, have had a huge revival in recent years. Due to the relative ease of development, thousands of independent (indie) and professional games are being brought to life using 2D rendering techniques. Using Microsoft's Xbox Live Arcade as an example, a number of the most popular games available are strictly 2D, such as *Geometry Wars 2* and *Scott Pilgrim vs. The World*. In addition, web games based on Adobe Flash, Microsoft Silverlight, and the HTML 5 standard, along with mobile devices such as the iPhone and Android-based phones, are also home to many 2D games. Developers are quickly being reminded that games don't have to have the most expensive budgets or the latest 3D technology; they just have to be fun. 2D games are as relevant today as they always were.

In this chapter:

- How to take advantage of 2D techniques needed to build a game
- What textures are and how they can be used
- An easy way to load in a texture image
- How to create and use sprites

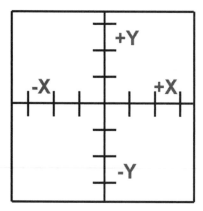

Figure 3.1
An example of a 2D grid.

2D Game Development

2D games take place in a grid-like area whose space is comprised of only width and height. Using a real-world example of a grid, it is like a piece of grid paper used during math classes in most elementary and middle schools. In game graphics, objects are placed on this invisible grid by specifying their X and Y axis locations, but in the 2D game universe this space is infinite. Figure 3.1 shows an example of this 2D grid and objects placed within it. The 2D area of a grid is also known as the grid's *plane*, where a plane is a 2D area that stretches to infinity.

In 3D games the grid still exists, but instead of just the X and Y axes, there is also the Z axis for depth. Visually we can think of this grid as a cube instead of a square, where the cube has an infinite number of 2D planes stacked on top of each other for its depth. These planes are infinitely thin slices of space that make up the virtual universe. A visual example of a 3D grid can be seen in Figure 3.2.

Mathematically, the requirements of a 2D game and a 3D game are like night and day, due mostly to both the simulation (e.g., physics, collisions, animations, etc.) and the rendering techniques used to shade the surfaces. In addition to having more complex math operations for the various effects, animations, and geometric objects, 3D games also have a ton more assets such as textures and geometry that far surpass what is seen in 2D games in terms of numbers and memory requirements. But even though 2D games tend to have different requirements in general (e.g., development manpower, storage, CPU cycles,

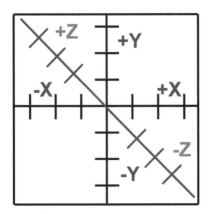

Figure 3.2
An example of a 3D grid.

hardware requirements, etc.), it is still challenging to create a professional-quality 2D game.

In 2D games we generally have the following pieces of information common to the rendering portions of a game, each of which will be highlighted throughout this chapter:

- Textures
- Sprites

Textures

A texture is a core piece of any game, be it 2D or 3D. A texture is another name for an image that is mapped over a surface, usually to give that surface the appearance of having a more complex makeup than it really has.

Take for example a brick wall. Instead of modeling out a brick wall with all its nooks and crannies, chips, and other defects that make the look of bricks in an environment realistic, it is far more efficient to use a simple square shape and have the image of a brick wall displayed over it. This is, after all, why textures exist, and their purpose in computer graphics is to simulate complex surfaces where this complexity does not actually exist in the geometric sense.

A square with the image of a brick wall does not have anywhere near the geometric complexity of a 3D wall with modeled bricks. In fact, we can be talking about two triangles versus several thousand or even millions. To take it a step further, we can even simulate the change of light as it interacts with this small simulated detail by combining texture mapping with another technique known as *normal mapping.*

Note

Video game graphics are all about shading and simulating effects. Textures are used to simulate complexity on the per-pixel level that does not actually exist for the surface.

There are many different types of textures common in video games, most of which are found in 3D games. These types of textures commonly include the following:

- Color maps (sometimes referred to as decal maps and used for coloring surfaces).

- Specular maps (also known as gloss maps and used for masking highlights).

- Light maps (prerendered lights and/or shadows stored in textures).

- Ambient occlusion maps (advanced lighting topic that moves toward the realm of global illumination).

- Shadow maps (used during real-time shadow generation and rendering).

- Height maps (used for a variety of reasons, usually displacement of geometry to deform its shape).

- Normal maps (used during per-pixel lighting to simulate high-complexity geometry on low-resolution geometry as far as lighting and the view's perspective is concerned).

- Alpha maps (used for transparency).

- Cube maps (commonly used for reflections and environment lighting).

- And many more.

An example of a color texture image being created in Photoshop can be seen in Figure 3.3. As you can see in the list of texture types, most textures are not used for color information, and a lot of them have to do with lighting and shadowing.

Figure 3.3
An example of a texture created in Photoshop.

Technically, even those used for lighting are actually what we would call a look-up texture, where the texture is used to store values on the per-pixel level that is used for some algorithm that takes place during the rendering pipeline—which is not necessarily lighting but can be for any purpose. For example, a height map being used for displacement is used to deform the geometry, not shade it. A color map is used to shade the surface with a solid color, whereas the look-up textures used during lighting are used to alter this solid color based on lighting properties in the environment.

Note

A look-up texture allows us to store values for a pixel that can be used for "some" algorithm, whether it is to look up the color value of the pixel, some value used during the lighting calculations, etc.

In 2D games, out of the list above, we'll mostly deal only with color map textures and alpha maps, since the rest of the items on the list deal mostly with lighting, which is a 3D topic. Since 32-bit images have an alpha channel, the alpha map does not need to be a separate image on today's hardware. We'll revisit textures later in this chapter during the section titled "Texture Mapping." The alpha channel of an image is used to specify the transparency (opacity) of each pixel in the image.

Sprites

A sprite is a special type of object. The word *sprite* is used to refer to a 2D graphical element that appears on the screen. Sprites are not just used in 2D games but also in 3D games. For 3D, sprites are used for the graphical elements of the heads-up display (e.g., the health bar, timers, armor levels, etc.) as well as particles and effects and more. An example of 2D elements being used in 3D games can be seen in Figure 3.4, Figure 3.5, and Figure 3.6.

In Figure 3.5 the particles from the ParticlesGS demo from the DirectX SDK uses sprites that are always facing the camera to hide the fact that they are flat. In Figure 3.6 multiple sprites are used together to create the smoke effect in the SoftParticles DirectX SDK demo. Since these sprites use composition and transparency, it is sometimes hard to see the individual elements with the naked eye, even if the camera has a close-up of the sprites. In Figure 3.6 the left

Figure 3.4
2D elements being rendered on top of the action in the DirectX SDK's Pipes GS demo.

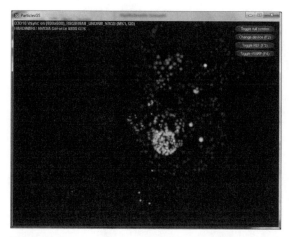

Figure 3.5
Sprites used within a particle system in the ParticlesGS DirectX SDK demo.

Figure 3.6
A close look at how transparent particles are used to create smoke in the SoftParticles DirectX SDK demo.

and right views show how the sprite smoke is always facing the camera, even as the camera moves around it. This is known as a billboard sprite.

Note

A billboard sprite is a sprite that is always facing the camera, regardless of changes in the camera's orientation.

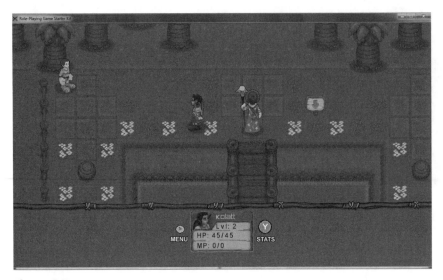

Figure 3.7
A 2D game made of sprites (XNA's Role Player Game Starter Kit).

A sprite is essentially a textured 2D shape, like a rectangle or square. In 2D games, sprites are used not only for characters but also for backgrounds, game objects, weapons, and every single element or item that can be drawn. An example can be seen in the Role Playing Game Starter Kit sample, available for Microsoft's XNA Game Studio Express (Figure 3.7) where the characters, props, backgrounds, etc. are all sprites that come together to create the scene.

Animations in 2D are performed by taking a series of sprites and displaying them one at a time in rapid succession. This is similar to a flip book or how cartoon animations operate by displaying frames of animation where each frame shows an instance of the animation being displayed. Developers of 2D games often use what are known as *sprite sheets*, which are large images that contain all frames of animation for a particular sprite.

2D GEOMETRY

Understanding how to create and manipulate geometry is critical to mastering video game graphics. What we see on the screen is a fine combination of art and math that works together to create the simulation our gamers enjoy. For newcomers to game graphics, this section will serve as a brief introduction to

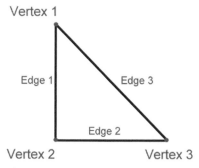

Figure 3.8
The breakdown of a triangle.

the basics of 2D geometry and Direct3D rendering. Although Direct3D is largely associated with 3D graphics, it is also capable of rendering 2D graphics via the graphics hardware.

What Is a Vertex?

Shapes are defined in game graphics as a collection of points connected together via lines whose insides are shaded in by the graphics hardware. These points are referred to as vertices (the plural term for a vertex), and these lines are referred to as edges. A shape is referred to as lines if it has two connected points or as polygons if it has three or more connected points. As you move on to more advanced rendering topics (beyond the scope of this book), you'll undoubtedly come across each of these terms often. See Figure 3.8 for an example of each of these terms.

Vertices are not technically drawn but instead provide the graphics hardware with information necessary to mathematically define a surface for rendering. Of course, it is possible to render points with the Direct3D API and use the position of a vertex as the point's position, but in reality a vertex is a unit of data used by the graphics card, along with other data, to define attributes of a larger shape. Although a vertex and a point are not the same thing, they both share having a position in common.

A vertex is more than a point. A vertex is actually a series of attributes that defines a region of the shape. In fact, the points in Figure 3.8 could actually refer to vertices of a triangle being passed to Direct3D for rendering where each vertex has a host of information the shaders will need to produce an effect. We use vertices to mathematically define the shape, and the graphics hardware uses these properties to draw the shape being specified, where all of the properties provided depend on the graphics effect being shaded. Common properties of a vertex that we will discuss throughout this book include:

- Position
- Color
- Normal vector
- Texture coordinate(s)

Other properties that are common in video games include but are not limited to the following:

- S-tangent (usually used during normal mapping)
- Bi-normal (also often used for normal mapping)
- Bone weights and indices (used for skeleton animation)
- Light map coordinates
- Per-vertex ambient occlusion factor
- And much more

The position of a vertex is the only property of a vertex that is not optional. Without a position we cannot define a shape, which means Direct3D cannot draw anything to any of its buffers. A 2D vertex has X and Y values for its position, whereas a 3D vertex has X, Y, and Z values. Most of the time we define the position first and all other properties after it. These properties ultimately depend on what per-vertex data is needed to create a specific rendering effect. For example, texture coordinates are necessary for producing a UV texture mapping effect just like bone animation information is necessary for performing animations within the vertex shader.

Many rendering effects work from per-pixel data instead of per-vertex data, such as per-pixel lighting and normal mapping. But remember that we don't specify per-pixel data in the form of geometry, so this per-pixel data is calculated using interpolation. Interpolation is the generation of intermediate values between one point and the next. Taking the pixel shader as an example: It receives interpolated data from the vertex shader (or geometry shader if one is present). This interpolated data includes positions, colors, texture coordinates, and all other attributes provided by the previous shader stage. As the pixel shader is invoked by the graphics hardware, the pixels that fall within the shape are shaded.

When we do specify per-pixel data, it is often in the form of texture images, such as a normal map texture used to provide per-pixel level normal vectors to alter lighting on a more micro-level to simulate higher amounts of detail across a shape. Another example is the classic texture mapping, which is used to provide per-pixel color data used to shade the surface of a shape.

On a side note, a normal vector (which we'll dive deeper into in Chapter 6) is a direction. Keep in mind that a vertex is a collection of attributes for a point of a shape, whereas a vector is an X and Y axis direction for 2D vectors and an X, Y, and Z direction for 3D vectors. Sometimes you'll see the terms used interchangeably, but it is important to know that they are not the same. This happens mostly because, code-wise, a vertex defines just a position, and a vector is essentially the same and is only different in what it represents in the context you are using it. An example is as follows:

```
struct Vertex2D
{
    float X;
    float Y;
};
```


```
struct Vector2D
{
    float X;
    float Y;
};
```

In some cases the difference between a vertex with only a position attribute and a vector really lies in our interpretation of the data, and either structure can be used for either purpose as long as we are being consistent. For example a vector pointing in the direction a bullet is traveling is different from the bullet's actual position at any point in time, but in code both a 3D vertex's position and a 3D vector are both X, Y, and Z floating-point values. Also, a vector with a magnitude of 1 is known as a unit-length vector, which we'll discuss more in Chapter 6.

In Direct3D we even have vector structures that we can use with the XNA Math library. Usually most programmers will use the vector structure to define the position of the vertex, even though a vector is not necessarily a position *per se*. This is very common, and it is important to be aware of this little tidbit. A vector used in this manner can be considered a direction from the virtual world's origin (or even another frame of reference) at which the vertex is located. Since the origin is usually 0 for the X, Y, and Z in 3D space, this vector direction happens to equal the relative or absolute position of the point and hence can be used interchangeably. An example of using vectors to define attributes of a vertex that uses X, Y, and Z values is as follows:

```
struct Vector2D
{
    float X;
    float Y;
};


struct Vector3D
{
    float X;
    float Y;
    float Z;
};


struct Vertex3D
{
    Vector3D position;
    Vector3D normal;
    Vector2D textureCoordinate;
};
```

As you can see, even though a vector is not a point, it can be used as if it were a position, since the direction from the origin located at (0, 0, 0) will equal a vector with the same values as a point's position. In other words, the context in which a vector is used determines what it ultimately represents.

Definition of a Triangle

If we define a polygon as a shape with three or more vertices, then the polygon with the smallest number of vertices is a triangle. Traditionally we think of a triangle as a shape being made up of three points, such as what is shown in Figure 3.8.

In game graphics we can define an array of these triangles where each triangle is its own independent shape. A collection of triangles is what we use to define meshes, where a mesh is defined as an object made up of a bunch of polygons. A collection of meshes creates a model, where a model is defined as one or more meshes. An example of a mesh can be a head shape of a 3D character, whereas the head, torso, legs, and other body parts (meshes) make up the entire character model. These terms are highly important to understand when learning game graphics. An example can be seen in Figure 3.9 (a mesh being a collection of triangle polygons) and Figure 3.10 (several meshes together forming a model).

An array of individual triangles is known as a triangle list, but there are other types of triangles, known as a triangle strip and triangle fan. A triangle strip is an array, where the first three vertices define the first triangle and the fourth vertex,

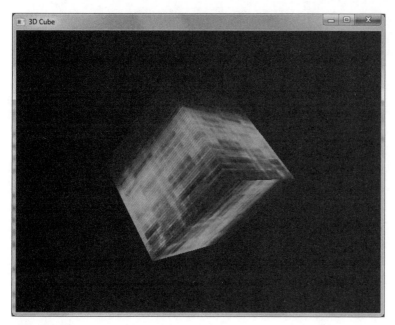

Figure 3.9
A mesh.

Figure 3.10
Several meshes forming one model.

along with the two vertices that came before the fourth vertex (i.e., second and third vertices) define the second triangle. This means that adding another triangle to the list is a matter of adding one more vertex instead of three vertices as with a triangle list. This can allow us to save on memory because we don't need as much memory to represent higher polygon shapes, but it also means that all triangles must be connected (whereas since a triangle list has individual triangles independent of one another, they don't technically have to touch). An example of a triangle strip can be seen in Figure 3.11.

A triangle fan is similar to a triangle strip, but a triangle fan uses the first vertex and the previous vertex along with the new vertex to create the next shape. For example (see Figure 3.12), the first triangle is the first three vertices, the second

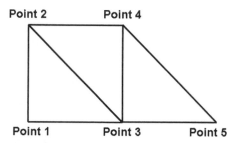

Figure 3.11
An example of a triangle strip.

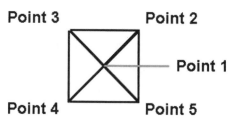

Figure 3.12
An example of a triangle fan.

triangle is the first vertex, the third vertex, and the fourth vertex, and the third triangle is the first vertex, the fourth vertex, and the fifth vertex.

Another representation we must discuss for polygons is the use of indexed geometry. Index geometry refers to using only unique vertices for the vertex list and using array indexes into that list to define which points make up which triangles. For example, the cube object in Figure 3.9 technically has only eight unique vertices, with one vertex appearing in each corner of the cube. If we used a triangle list we'd have many overlapping vertices along the end points of the cube, causing us to define a vertex list of 36 vertices (3 vertices per triangle × 2 triangles per side × 6 sides = 36).

The main benefit from using index geometry comes from models with hundreds, thousands, or more polygons. For these models there will usually be a very high number of triangles that share the same edges with one another. Remember that an edge is the line between two connecting vertices, and triangles have three edges in total. If our index geometry uses 16-bit values for the indices, then a triangle can be defined by using three 16-bit integers, which equals 48 bits (which equals 6 bytes). Compare this to a 3D vertex that has three floating-point values at 4 bytes per axis, giving us 12 bytes per vertex and 36 bytes per triangle. Since indexed geometry includes the vertex list of unique vertices, we won't see any savings until the polygon count has reached a high enough count to where adding more triangles is cheaper memory-wise using indices than it is by specifying more independent triangles. As the polygon count rises, so does the difference in memory consumed by a model using indexed geometry and one that uses triangle lists. We'll revisit this discuss in Chapter 6 when we discuss 3D geometry in more detail.

Vertex Buffers

A buffer is memory of a specific size. If you have an array of 100 chars, then you can say you have a buffer that is 100 bytes in size. If instead of chars we were talking about integers, then you could say you have a buffer of integers, where the buffer is 400 bytes in size (integer = 4 bytes × 100 integers = 400 bytes). When dealing with Direct3D, we create buffers for many different reasons, but the first reason we'll discuss is the creation of what are known as vertex buffers.

A vertex buffer is a Direct3D buffer of the type ID3D11Buffer that is used to store all the vertex data for a mesh. When we create a vertex buffer in Direct3D we are creating an object that resides in an optimal location of memory, such as video memory of the graphics hardware, which is chosen by the device driver. When Direct3D renders our objects, it transfers this information across the graphics bus and performs the necessary operations throughout the rendering pipeline that ultimately causes that geometry to be rendered onscreen or not. We say "or not" because geometry can ultimately be determined by Direct3D as not being visible. Attempting to render a ton of geometry that is not visible can lead to negative performance, and most advanced 3D commercial video games use techniques to determine what geometry is visible beforehand and only submit those that are either visible or potentially visible to the graphics hardware. This is an advanced topic and usually falls within scene management and deals with many topics known as culling and partitioning algorithms. The fastest geometry to draw is geometry you don't draw at all, and this is one of the keys for next-generation games.

Let's take a look at the creation of a vertex buffer. Let's assume we are defining vertices that specify only a positional attribute such as the following:

```
struct VertexPos
{
    XMFLOAT3 pos;
};
```

XMFLOAT3 is a structure with X, Y, and Z floating-point values within. The name defines what the structure represents, where the XM refers to XNA Math, FLOAT refers to the data type of the structure's members, and 3 refers to how many members the structure has. This structure can be used for 3D points, 3D vectors, etc., and again what it represents depends on the context in which you use it. Direct3D 11 uses the XNA Math library, whereas previous versions of Direct3D would have used D3DXVECTOR3 for this purpose. Direct3D has long since provided us with a highly optimized math library, so we don't have to write one ourselves, but we will cover the details and the math of these common structures and operations in Chapter 6.

Assuming we have a valid Direct3D device created, we could create a vertex buffer with a simple triangle using the following code as an example:

```
VertexPos vertices[] =
{
    XMFLOAT3(  0.5f,  0.5f, 0.5f ),
    XMFLOAT3(  0.5f, -0.5f, 0.5f ),
    XMFLOAT3( -0.5f, -0.5f, 0.5f )
};

D3D11_BUFFER_DESC vertexDesc;
ZeroMemory( &vertexDesc, sizeof( vertexDesc ) );

vertexDesc.Usage = D3D11_USAGE_DEFAULT;
vertexDesc.BindFlags = D3D11_BIND_VERTEX_BUFFER;
vertexDesc.ByteWidth = sizeof( VertexPos ) * 3;

D3D11_SUBRESOURCE_DATA resourceData;
ZeroMemory( &resourceData, sizeof( resourceData ) );
resourceData.pSysMem = vertices;

ID3D11Buffer* vertexBuffer;
HRESULT result = d3dDevice_->CreateBuffer( &vertexDesc, &resourceData,
    &vertexBuffer );
```

First you'll notice we define the vertex list, which has three vertices that define a single triangle. Next we create the buffer descriptor object. The buffer descriptor, of the type `D3D11_BUFFER_DESC`, is used to provide the details of the buffer we are creating, which is important since technically we could be creating another type of buffer other than a vertex buffer. The buffer description has the following structure and members:

```
typedef struct D3D11_BUFFER_DESC {
    UINT ByteWidth;
    D3D11_USAGE Usage;
    UINT BindFlags;
    UINT CPUAccessFlags;
    UINT MiscFlags;
    UINT StructureByteStride;
} D3D11_BUFFER_DESC;
```

Next we create a sub resource. Sub resources are used in this case for us to pass the vertex data to the buffer's creation function so that the buffer is filled with this data. We optionally can pass null for the data, which will create an empty buffer, but in this case we already know what data we want to store in the buffer, and the use of a `D3D11_SUBRESOURCE_DATA` object allows us to do that. The `D3D11_SUBRESOURCE_DATA` has the following structure and members:

```
typedef struct D3D11_SUBRESOURCE_DATA {
    const void* pSysMem;
    UINT SysMemPitch;
    UINT SysMemSlicePitch;
} D3D11_SUBRESOURCE_DATA;
```

The `pSysMem` member of the `D3D11_SUBRESOURCE_DATA` structure is the pointer to the initialized memory, or in our case the memory we are sending to fill the buffer with. The `SysMemPitch` and `SysMemSlicePitch` are used for texture images, where `SysMemPitch` is used to determine where the beginning of one line of a texture to the next line is, and `SysMemSlicePitch` is used to determine one depth line to the next, which is used for 3D textures.

With the buffer descriptor and the sub-resource data we can create the buffer by simply calling a single Direct3D device function called `CreateBuffer`. `CreateBuffer` has the following function prototype and takes as parameters the buffer description, the sub-resource data (optionally), and the pointer for the `ID3D11Buffer` object that will be created as our vertex buffer, as defined by the descriptor.

```
HRESULT CreateBuffer(
    const D3D11_BUFFER_DESC* pDesc,
    const D3D11_SUBRESOURCE_DATA* pInitialData,
    ID3D11Buffer** ppBuffer
);
```

If `CreateBuffer` succeeds, we can draw the geometry in the buffer at any point.

Input Layout

When we send geometry to the graphics card we are sending it a chunk of data. In order for Direct3D to know what the various attributes defined are, their ordering, and size, we use what is known as the input layout to tell the API about the data's vertex layout of the geometry we are about to draw.

In Direct3D we use an array of `D3D11_INPUT_ELEMENT_DESC` elements to describe the vertex layout of a vertex structure. The `D3D11_INPUT_ELEMENT_DESC` structure has the following elements:

```
typedef struct D3D11_INPUT_ELEMENT_DESC {
    LPCSTR SemanticName;
    UINT SemanticIndex;
    DXGI_FORMAT Format;
    UINT InputSlot;
    UINT AlignedByteOffset;
    D3D11_INPUT_CLASSIFICATION InputSlotClass;
    UINT InstanceDataStepRate;
} D3D11_INPUT_ELEMENT_DESC;
```

The first member, the semantic name, is a string that describes the purpose of the element. For example one element will be the vertex's position, and therefore its semantic will be `"POSITION"`. We could also have an element for the vertex's color by using `"COLOR"`, a normal vector by using `"NORMAL"`, and so forth. The semantic binds the element to an HLSL shader's input or output variable, which we'll see later in this chapter.

The second member is the semantic index. A vertex can have multiple elements using the same semantic name but store different values. For example, if a vertex can have two colors, then we can use a semantic index of 0 for the first color and 1 for the second. More commonly, a vertex can have multiple texture coordinates, which can occur when UV texture mapping and light mapping are being applied at the same time, for example.

The third member is the format of the element. For example for a position with X, Y, and Z floating-point axes, the format we would use for such a position would be DXGI_FORMAT_R32G32B32_FLOAT, where 32 bits (4 bytes) are reserved for the R, G, and B components. Although the format has R, G, and B in its name, it can be used as the X, Y, and Z. Don't let the color notation throw you off to the fact that these formats are used for more than just colors.

The fourth member is the input slot, which is used to specify which vertex buffer the element is found in. In Direct3D you can bind and pass multiple vertex buffers at the same time. We can use the input slot member to specific the array index of which vertex buffer this element is found in.

The fifth parameter is the aligned byte offset value, which is used to tell Direct3D the starting byte offset into the vertex buffer where it can find this element.

The sixth member is the input slot class, which is used to describe whether the element is to be used for each vertex (per vertex) or for each instance (per object). Per-object attributes deal with a more advanced topic known as *instancing*, which is a technique used to draw multiple objects of the same mesh with a single draw call—a technique used to greatly improve rendering performance where applicable.

The last member is the instance data step rate value, which is used to tell Direct3D how many instances to draw in the scene.

An input layout uses the type of ID3D11InputLayout. Input layouts are created with a call to the Direct3D device function CreateInputLayout. The CreateInputLayout function has the following function prototype:

```
HRESULT CreateInputLayout(
    const D3D11_INPUT_ELEMENT_DESC* pInputElementDescs,
    UINT NumElements,
    const void* pShaderBytecodeWithInputSignature,
    SIZE_T BytecodeLength,
    ID3D11InputLayout** ppInputLayout
);
```

The first parameter to the CreateInputLayout function is the array of elements in the vertex layout, while the second parameter is the number of elements in that array.

The third parameter is the compiled vertex shader code with the input signature that will be validated against the array of elements, and the fourth element is the size of the shader's bytecode. The vertex shader's input signature must match our input layout, and this function call will fail if it does not.

The final parameter is the pointer of the object that will be created with this function call.

A vertex shader is compiled code executed on the GPU. A vertex shader is executed for each vertex that's processed by the device. There are various types of shaders that Direct3D supports, each of which is discussed in more detail in Chapter 7. Direct3D requires shaders for rendering geometry, and therefore we must encounter them before we dive deep into their inner workings.

Below is an example of creating a vertex shader, which we'll need before we can create the input layout, since the vertex shader's signature must match the input layout:

```
ID3D11VertexShader* solidColorVS;
ID3D11PixelShader* solidColorPS;
ID3D11InputLayout* inputLayout;

ID3DBlob* vsBuffer = 0;

DWORD shaderFlags = D3DCOMPILE_ENABLE_STRICTNESS;

#if defined( DEBUG ) || defined( _DEBUG )
    shaderFlags |= D3DCOMPILE_DEBUG;
#endif

ID3DBlob* errorBuffer = 0;
HRESULT result;

result = D3DX11CompileFromFile( "sampleShader.fx", 0, 0, "VS_Main", "vs_4_0",
    shaderFlags, 0, 0, &vsBuffer, &errorBuffer, 0 );

if( FAILED( result ) )
{
    if( errorBuffer != 0 )
```

```
        {
            OutputDebugStringA( ( char* )errorBuffer->GetBufferPointer( ) );
            errorBuffer->Release( );
        }

        return false;
    }

if( errorBuffer != 0 )
    errorBuffer->Release( );

result = d3dDevice_->CreateVertexShader( vsBuffer->GetBufferPointer( ),
    vsBuffer->GetBufferSize( ), 0, &solidColorVS );

if( FAILED( result ) )
{
    if( vsBuffer )
        vsBuffer->Release( );

    return false;
}
```

To begin, we load the vertex shader from a text file and compile it into byte-code. You can optionally already have compiled byte code, or we can allow Direct3D to do it for us during startup, which is acceptable for the demos throughout this book. Compiling a shader is done with a call to the D3DX11Com-pileFromFile function. This function has the following prototype:

```
HRESULT D3DX11CompileFromFile(
    LPCTSTR pSrcFile,
    const D3D10_SHADER_MACRO* pDefines,
    LPD3D10INCLUDE pInclude,
    LPCSTR pFunctionName,
    LPCSTR pProfile,
    UINT Flags1,
    UINT Flags2,
    ID3DX11ThreadPump* pPump,
    ID3D10Blob** ppShader,
    ID3D10Blob** ppErrorMsgs,
    HRESULT* pHResult
);
```

The first parameter of the `D3DX11CompileFromFile` function is the path of the HLSL shader code to be loaded and compiled.

The second parameter is the global macros within the shader's code. Macros in a HLSL shader work the same way they do in C/C++. An HLSL macro is defined on the application side using the type `D3D_SHADER_MACRO` and an example of defining a macro called `"AGE"`, and giving it the value of 18 can be seen as follows:

```
const D3D_SHADER_MACRO defineMacros[] =
{
    "AGE", "18",
};
```

The third parameter of the `D3DX11CompileFromFile` is an optional parameter for handling `#include` statements that exist within the HLSL shader file. This interface mainly is used to specify behavior for opening and closing files that are included in the shader source.

The fourth parameter is the entry function name for the shader you are compiling. A file can have multiple shader types (e.g., vertex, pixel, geometry, etc.) and many functions for various purposes. This parameter is important for telling the compiler which of these potentially many functions serve as the entry point to the shader we are compiling.

The fifth parameter specifies the shader model. For our purposes we'll be using either `vs_4_0` or `vs_5_0` for vertex shader 4.0 or 5.0, respectively. In order to use shader model 5.0, you must have a DirectX 11–supported graphics unit, whereas to use shader model 4.0 you'll need a DirectX 10 and above graphics unit. We'll cover shaders and shader models in more detail in Chapter 7.

The sixth parameter of the `D3DX11CompileFromFile` is the compile flags for the shader code and is used to specify compile options during compilation. The compile flags are specified using the following macros:

- `D3D10_SHADER_AVOID_FLOW_CONTROL`—disables flow control whenever possible.

- `D3D10_SHADER_DEBUG`—inserts debugging information with the compiled shader.

- D3D10_SHADER_ENABLE_STRICTNESS—disallows legacy syntax.

- D3D10_SHADER_ENABLE_BACKWARDS_COMPATIBILITY—allows older syntax to compile to shader 4.0.

- D3D10_SHADER_FORCE_VS_SOFTWARE_NO_OPT—forces vertex shaders to compile to the next highest supported version.

- D3D10_SHADER_FORCE_PS_SOFTWARE_NO_OPT—forces pixel shaders to compile to the next highest supported version.

- D3D10_SHADER_IEEE_STRICTNESS—enables strict IEEE rules for compilation.

- D3D10_SHADER_NO_PRESHADER—disables the compiler from pulling out static expressions.

- D3D10_SHADER_OPTIMIZATION_LEVEL0 (level 0 through 3)—used to set the optimization level, where level 0 produces the slowest code and level 3 produces the most optimized.

- D3D10_SHADER_PACK_MATRIX_ROW_MAJOR—used to specify that matrices are declared using a row major layout.

- D3D10_SHADER_PACK_MATRIX_COLUMN_MAJOR—used to specify that matrices are declared using column major layout.

- D3D10_SHADER_PARTIAL_PRECISION—forces computations to use partial precision, which can lead to performance increases on some hardware.

- D3D10_SHADER_PREFER_FLOW_CONTROL—tells the compiler to prefer flow control whenever it is possible.

- D3D10_SHADER_SKIP_OPTIMIZATION—used to completely skip optimizing the compiled code.

- D3D10_SHADER_SKIP_VALIDATION—used to skip the device validation, which should only be used for shaders that have already passed the device validation process in a previous compilation.

- D3D10_SHADER_WARNINGS_ARE_ERRORS—used to treat warnings as errors.

The seventh parameter of the D3DX11CompileFromFile is the effect file flags. This is only set if we are compiling a shader using an effect file and will be discussed in Chapter 7. The effect file flags can be set to one or more of the following:

- D3D10_EFFECT_COMPILE_CHILD_EFFECT—allows us to compile to a child effect.

- D3D10_EFFECT_COMPILE_ALLOW_SLOW_OPS—disables performance mode.

- D3D10_EFFECT_SINGLE_THREADED—disables synchronizing with other threads loading into the effect pool.

The eighth parameter of the D3DX11CompileFromFile is a pointer to a thread pump. By specifying a value of null for this parameter, the function will return when the compilation is complete. This parameter deals with multithreading, which is a hot and advanced topic in game development. Using a thread allows us to load a shader asynchronously while we continue code execution.

The ninth parameter of the D3DX11CompileFromFile is the out address to memory where the compiled shader will reside. This includes any debug and symbol-table information for the compiled shader.

The tenth parameter of the D3DX11CompileFromFile is the out address to memory where any compilation errors and warnings will be stored. This object will be null if there are no errors, but if there are we can use this to report what the errors were so we can fix them.

The eleventh parameter of the D3DX11CompileFromFile is the return value for the thread pump. If the thread pump parameter (the eighth one) is not null, then this parameter must be a valid memory location until the asynchronous execution completes.

With the compiled shader code we can create a vertex shader with a call to the Direct3D device's CreateVertexShader, which takes as parameters the buffer for the compiled code, its size in bytes, a pointer to the class linkage type, and the pointer to the vertex shader object we are creating. The function prototype for the CreateVertexShader function is as follows:

```
HRESULT CreateVertexShader(
    const void* pShaderBytecode,
    SIZE_T BytecodeLength,
    ID3D11ClassLinkage* pClassLinkage,
    ID3D11VertexShader** ppVertexShader
);
```

Next is to specify the layout of the vertex elements. In our simple vertex structure we are just using a vertex position, so we specify this using the "POSITION" semantic at semantic index 0 (since it is the first and only element of this semantic), the format that specifies its X, Y, and Z values are 32 bits each, its input slot of 0 and a byte offset of 0, an input slot class of being per-vertex, since our positions are for each vertex, and an instance step rate of 0 since we are not using instancing.

The input layout itself is created with a call to CreateInputLayout, which we've discussed in a previously in this section. An example of using the created vertex shader to create the input layout can be seen as follows:

```
D3D11_INPUT_ELEMENT_DESC vertexLayout[] =
{
    { "POSITION", 0, DXGI_FORMAT_R32G32B32_FLOAT, 0, 0,
       D3D11_INPUT_PER_VERTEX_DATA, 0 }
};

unsigned int totalLayoutElements = ARRAYSIZE( vertexLayout );

HRESULT result = d3dDevice_->CreateInputLayout( vertexLayout,
       totalLayoutElements, vsBuffer->GetBufferPointer( ),
       vsBuffer->GetBufferSize( ), &inputLayout );

vsBuffer->Release( );

if( FAILED( d3dResult ) )
{
    return false;
}
```

Just to complete things, we also will usually need to load the pixel shader when working with Direct3D 10 and 11. An example of loading the pixel shader can be seen as follows, which looks much like what we've done with the vertex shader:

```
ID3DBlob* psBuffer = 0;
ID3DBlob* errorBuffer = 0;

HRESULT result;

result = D3DX11CompileFromFile( "sampleShader.fx", 0, 0, "PS_Main", "ps_4_0",
       shaderFlags, 0, 0, &psBuffer, &errorBuffer, 0 );
```

```
if( FAILED( result ) )
{
    if( errorBuffer != 0 )
    {
        OutputDebugStringA( ( char* )errorBuffer->GetBufferPointer( ) );
        errorBuffer->Release( );
    }

    return false;
}

if( errorBuffer != 0 )
    errorBuffer->Release( );

result = d3dDevice_->CreatePixelShader( psBuffer->GetBufferPointer( ),
    psBuffer->GetBufferSize( ), 0, &solidColorPS );

psBuffer->Release( );

if( FAILED( result ) )
{
    return false;
}
```

Drawing a 2D Triangle

Rendering is the heart of all that we've been working toward. To render geometry in Direct3D, we generally must set up the input assembly, bind our shaders and other assets (such as textures), and draw each mesh. To set the input assembly we'll start by examining Direct3D's `IASetInputLayout`, `IASetVertexBuffers`, and `IASETPrimitiveTopology`.

The `IASetInputLayout` function of the Direct3D context object is used to bind the vertex layout that we created when we called the device's `CreateInputLayout` function. This is done each time we are about to render geometry that uses a specific input layout, and the `IASetInputLayout` function takes as a single parameter that `ID3D11InputLayout` object.

The `IASetVertexBuffers` function is used to set one or more vertex buffers and has the following function prototype:

```
void IASetVertexBuffers(
    UINT StartSlot,
    UINT NumBuffers,
    ID3D11Buffer* const* ppVertexBuffers,
    const UINT* pStrides,
    const UINT* pOffsets
);
```

The first parameter of the IASetVertexBuffers function is the starting slot to bind the buffer. The first buffer in the array of buffers you are passing is placed in this slot while the subsequent buffers are placed implicitly after.

The second parameter of the IASetVertexBuffers function is the number of buffers that are being set, while the third parameter is an array of one or more buffers being set.

The fourth parameter is the vertex stride, which is the size in bytes of each vertex, while the last parameter is the offset in bytes from the start of the buffer to the start of the first element of a vertex. The third and fourth parameters must specify a value for each vertex buffer being set and therefore can be an array of values if there are multiple buffers.

The IASetPrimitiveTopology is used to tell Direct3D what type of geometry we are rendering. For example, if we are rendering a triangle list we would use the flag D3D11_PRIMITIVE_TOPOLOGY_TRIANGLELIST as the function's parameter, or if we wanted to use triangle strips we would use D3D11_PRIMITIVE_TOPOLOGY_ TRIANGLESTRIP. There are about 42 values that can be used, most of which deal with control points for more advanced geometry, and the full list can be found in the DirectX documentation.

After setting the input assembler we can set the shaders. Later in this book we'll look at how to apply other types of shaders (e.g., geometry shaders), but for now we'll focus on vertex and pixel shaders. A vertex shader is set by calling the Direct3D context's VSSetShader function, and a pixel shader is set by calling PSSetShader. Both functions take as parameters the shader being set, a pointer to an array of class instances, and the total number of class instances being set. We'll discuss class instance interfaces in Chapter 7.

Once we've set and bound all of the necessary data for our geometry, the last step is to draw it by calling the Draw function. The Draw function of the Direct3D context object takes as parameters the total number of vertices in the vertex array and the start vertex location, which can act as an offset into the vertex buffer where you wish to begin drawing.

An example of rendering geometry is as follows:

```
float clearColor[4] = { 0.0f, 0.0f, 0.25f, 1.0f };
d3dContext_->ClearRenderTargetView( backBufferTarget, clearColor );

unsigned int stride = sizeof( VertexPos );
unsigned int offset = 0;

d3dContext_->IASetInputLayout( inputLayout );
d3dContext_->IASetVertexBuffers( 0, 1, &vertexBuffer_, &stride, &offset );
d3dContext_->IASetPrimitiveTopology( D3D11_PRIMITIVE_TOPOLOGY_TRIANGLELIST );

d3dContext_->VSSetShader( solidColorVS, 0, 0 );
d3dContext_->PSSetShader( solidColorPS, 0, 0 );
d3dContext_->Draw( 3, 0 );

swapChain_->Present( 0, 0 );
```

Calling the swap chain's Present function allows us to present the rendered image to the screen. The Present function takes as parameters the sync interval and the presentation flags. The sync interval can be 0 to present immediately, or it can be a value that states after which vertical blank we want to present (for example, 3 means after the third vertical blank). The flags can be any of the DXGI_PRESENT values, where 0 means to present a frame from each buffer to the output, DXGI_PRESENT_DO_NOT_SEQUENCE to present a frame from each buffer to the output while using the vertical blank synchronization, DXGI_PRESENT_TEST to now present to the output (which can be useful for testing and error checking), or DXGI_PRESENT_RESTART to tell the driver to discard any outstanding request to Present.

In Chapter 6 we'll discuss how to draw indexed geometry when we move to the topic of 3D rendering. Indexed geometry doesn't serve much use in 2D scenes, but when we move to 3D it will be very important to cover it.

2D TRIANGLE DEMO

In this section we'll briefly cover the Triangle demo from the companion website located in the Chapter3/Triangle folder. The purpose of this demo is to use what was covered thus far to render a single triangle to the screen. This demo builds off of the Blank Direct3D Window demo from Chapter 2.

Loading the Geometry

In this chapter we've discussed that in order to render geometry we need a vertex buffer, an input layout describing the vertex layout used by the buffer, and a set of shaders. Since Direct3D 10, shaders are a base requirement for graphics rendering in Direct3D, and in this demo we'll be specifying vertex and pixel shaders that do nothing more than render a surface with a solid color. Later on in this chapter we'll see how to extend this effect to map a texture image across the surface.

The demo's class, `TriangleDemo` from the TriangleDemo.h header file, adds to the class members an `ID3D11VertexShader` called `solidColorVS_`, an `ID3D11 PixelShader` called `solidColorPS`, an `ID3D11InputLayout` called `inputLayout_`, and an `ID3D11Buffer` called `vertexBuffer_`. The `TriangleDemo` class from the TriangleDemo.h header file can be seen in Listing 3.1.

Listing 3.1 The `TriangleDemo` class header file.

```
#include"Dx11DemoBase.h"


class TriangleDemo : public Dx11DemoBase
{
    public:
        TriangleDemo( );
        virtual ~TriangleDemo( );

        bool LoadContent( );
        void UnloadContent( );

        void Update( float dt );
        void Render( );
```

```
private:
    ID3D11VertexShader* solidColorVS_;
    ID3D11PixelShader* solidColorPS_;

    ID3D11InputLayout* inputLayout_;
    ID3D11Buffer* vertexBuffer_;
};
```

The vertex structure we will be using is a simple three-component floating-point structure from the XNA Math library called XMFLOAT3. As for the TriangleDemo class members, at the end of the application these objects will need to be released by calling the Release method on each object. Releasing the memory used by these objects is performed in the UnloadContent function of the TriangleDemo class. Listing 3.2 shows the vertex structure and TriangleDemo class constructor and destructor, while Listing 3.3 shows the UnloadContent function.

Listing 3.2 TriangleDemo vertex structure, constructor, and destructor.

```
#include"TriangleDemo.h"
#include<xnamath.h>


struct VertexPos
{
    XMFLOAT3 pos;
};


TriangleDemo::TriangleDemo( ) : solidColorVS_( 0 ), solidColorPS_( 0 ),
                                inputLayout_( 0 ), vertexBuffer_( 0 )
{

}


TriangleDemo::~TriangleDemo( )
{

}
```

Listing 3.3 TriangleDemo's UnloadContent.

```
void TriangleDemo::UnloadContent( )
{
    if( solidColorVS_ ) solidColorVS_->Release( );
    if( solidColorPS_ ) solidColorPS_->Release( );
    if( inputLayout_ ) inputLayout_->Release( );
    if( vertexBuffer_ ) vertexBuffer_->Release( );

    solidColorVS_ = 0;
    solidColorPS_ = 0;
    inputLayout_ = 0;
    vertexBuffer_ = 0;
}
```

Next is the LoadContent function. This function begins by loading the vertex shader, which can be found in a file called SolidGreenColor.fx. The name of this file comes from the fact that the shaders within work together to shade a surface with a solid green color.

Once the vertex shader source is compiled and the shader created with a call to CreateVertexShader, we then create the vertex layout. Since the vertex layout is validated against the vertex shader signature, we need at least the vertex shader loaded into memory.

After the vertex shader and input layout are created we next create the pixel shader. This code makes up half of the LoadContent function and can be seen in Listing 3.4. The code for CompileD3DShader can also be seen in Listing 3.5 and was separated out due to the fact that loading multiple shaders for different effects can cause us to write a lot of redundant code that we can avoid by abstracting the behavior in a member function of the base class DX11DemoBase with the other high level Direct3D code.

Listing 3.4 LoadContent's shader loading code.

```
bool TriangleDemo::LoadContent( )
{
    ID3DBlob* vsBuffer = 0;

    bool compileResult = CompileD3DShader( "SolidGreenColor.fx",
```

```
            "VS_Main", "vs_4_0", &vsBuffer );

    if( compileResult == false )
    {
        MessageBox( 0, "Error loading vertex shader!", "Compile Error", MB_OK );
        return false;
    }

    HRESULT d3dResult;

    d3dResult = d3dDevice_->CreateVertexShader( vsBuffer->GetBufferPointer(
),
        vsBuffer->GetBufferSize( ), 0, &solidColorVS_ );

    if( FAILED( d3dResult ) )
    {
        if( vsBuffer )
            vsBuffer->Release( );

        return false;
    }

    D3D11_INPUT_ELEMENT_DESC solidColorLayout[] =
    {
        { "POSITION", 0, DXGI_FORMAT_R32G32B32_FLOAT,
            0, 0, D3D11_INPUT_PER_VERTEX_DATA, 0 }
    };

    unsigned int totalLayoutElements = ARRAYSIZE( solidColorLayout );

    d3dResult = d3dDevice_->CreateInputLayout( solidColorLayout,
        totalLayoutElements, vsBuffer->GetBufferPointer( ),
        vsBuffer->GetBufferSize( ), &inputLayout_ );

    vsBuffer->Release( );

    if( FAILED( d3dResult ) )
    {
        return false;
    }
```

```
ID3DBlob* psBuffer = 0;

compileResult = CompileD3DShader( "SolidGreenColor.fx",
    "PS_Main", "ps_4_0", &psBuffer );

if( compileResult == false )
{
    MessageBox( 0, "Error loading pixel shader!", "Compile Error", MB_OK );
    return false;
}

d3dResult = d3dDevice_->CreatePixelShader( psBuffer->GetBufferPointer( ),
    psBuffer->GetBufferSize( ), 0, &solidColorPS_ );

psBuffer->Release( );

if( FAILED( d3dResult ) )
{
    return false;
}


...
}
```

Listing 3.5 The implementation of the `CompileShader` function.

```
bool Dx11DemoBase::CompileD3DShader( char* filePath, char* entry, char*
shaderModel, ID3DBlob** buffer )
{
    DWORD shaderFlags = D3DCOMPILE_ENABLE_STRICTNESS;

#if defined( DEBUG ) || defined( _DEBUG )
    shaderFlags |= D3DCOMPILE_DEBUG;
#endif

    ID3DBlob* errorBuffer = 0;
    HRESULT result;

    result = D3DX11CompileFromFile( filePath, 0, 0, entry, shaderModel,
        shaderFlags, 0, 0, buffer, &errorBuffer, 0 );
```

```
if( FAILED( result ) )
{
    if( errorBuffer != 0 )
    {
        OutputDebugStringA( ( char* )errorBuffer->GetBufferPointer( ) );
        errorBuffer->Release( );
    }

    return false;
}

if( errorBuffer != 0 )
    errorBuffer->Release( );

return true;
}
```

The second half of the LoadContent function creates the vertex buffer. This code begins by defining a simple triangle that is half a unit in size along the X and Y axes. It is also 0.5f along the Z axis to make it visible on screen, because if the camera is too close or behind the surface, the surface won't render.

The vertex list is stored in an array called vertices, and it is provided as a sub-resource data that is used during the call to CreateBuffer to create the actual vertex buffer. The second half of the LoadContent function can be seen in Listing 3.6.

Listing 3.6 LoadContent's geometry loading code.

```
bool TriangleDemo::LoadContent( )
{
    ...

    VertexPos vertices[] =
    {
        XMFLOAT3(  0.5f,  0.5f, 0.5f ),
        XMFLOAT3(  0.5f, -0.5f, 0.5f ),
        XMFLOAT3( -0.5f, -0.5f, 0.5f )
    };

    D3D11_BUFFER_DESC vertexDesc;
    ZeroMemory( &vertexDesc, sizeof( vertexDesc ) );
```

```
vertexDesc.Usage = D3D11_USAGE_DEFAULT;
vertexDesc.BindFlags = D3D11_BIND_VERTEX_BUFFER;
vertexDesc.ByteWidth = sizeof( VertexPos ) * 3;

D3D11_SUBRESOURCE_DATA resourceData;
ZeroMemory( &resourceData, sizeof( resourceData ) );
resourceData.pSysMem = vertices;

d3dResult = d3dDevice_->CreateBuffer( &vertexDesc,
    &resourceData, &vertexBuffer_ );

if( FAILED( d3dResult ) )
{
    return false;
}

    return true;
}
```

Rendering the Geometry

The last two pieces of code comprise the code to render the geometry and the shaders themselves. The code to render the geometry is found in the Triangle-Demo's Render function. The Render function is nearly the same as the example rendering code we've examined earlier in this chapter when we discussed vertex buffers. The function has a conditional statement to ensure that the Direct3D context is valid.

Next we clear the rendering targets and set up the input assembler. Since the triangle does not move, we don't necessarily have to clear the rendering targets, but we'll definitely need to do so later on in the book. The input assembler stage is set by binding the input layout object we've created, providing the vertex buffer we are drawing out of, and setting the topology to triangle list.

The Render function from the TriangleDemo can be seen in Listing 3.7.

Listing 3.7 TriangleDemo's rendering function.

```
void TriangleDemo::Render( )
{
    if( d3dContext_ == 0 )
```

```
        return;

    float clearColor[4] = { 0.0f, 0.0f, 0.25f, 1.0f };
    d3dContext_->ClearRenderTargetView( backBufferTarget_, clearColor );

    unsigned int stride = sizeof( VertexPos );
    unsigned int offset = 0;

    d3dContext_->IASetInputLayout( inputLayout_ );
    d3dContext_->IASetVertexBuffers( 0, 1, &vertexBuffer_, &stride, &offset );
    d3dContext_->IASetPrimitiveTopology( D3D11_PRIMITIVE_TOPOLOGY_
TRIANGLELIST );

    d3dContext_->VSSetShader( solidColorVS_, 0, 0 );
    d3dContext_->PSSetShader( solidColorPS_, 0, 0 );
    d3dContext_->Draw( 3, 0 );

    swapChain_->Present( 0, 0 );
}
```

The last piece of code to view is the shaders. The vertex shader is as basic as they get; it works by passing along the incoming vertex position to the output. Later we'll have to manipulate this data to correctly draw our objects, but for this simple demo it is enough to just pass along the values we've provided.

The pixel shader is also as basic as a pixel shader can be by returning a solid green color value for any pixel shaded using this shader. Colors from a pixel shader are specified using four floating-point values for the red, green, blue, and alpha color channels. In shaders we specify colors in the range of 0.0 to 1.0 where 0.0 equals 0 and 1.0 equals 255 when using an unsigned char color buffer for the rendering target (which we set up in the demo's base class startup function).

The output of a vertex shader is the input to the pixel shader unless we have a geometry shader bound to the input assembler, which we do not. The output of the pixel shader is the color value that is written to the output buffer. This buffer is eventually displayed to the user when the swap chain's Present function is called.

The vertex and pixel shaders from TriangleDemo can be seen in Listing 3.8. A screenshot of the demo can also be seen in Figure 3.13.

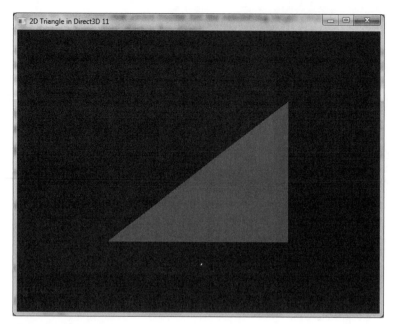

Figure 3.13
Screenshot of the Triangle demo.

Listing 3.8 The Triangle demo's shaders.

```
float4 VS_Main( float4 pos : POSITION ) : SV_POSITION
{
    return pos;
}


float4 PS_Main( float4 pos : SV_POSITION ) : SV_TARGET
{
    return float4( 0.0f, 1.0f, 0.0f, 1.0f );
}
```

TEXTURE MAPPING

As mentioned earlier in this chapter, a texture is data that is mapped to the surface of our shapes and solids. Usually this data is color values that are used to map an image onto the surface via a process called texture mapping. This data could also be other pieces of information such as a normal map used for normal mapping, alpha values used to control transparency levels, and so forth.

Textures, like other data your game needs, will usually be loaded at runtime. Since textures are an integral part of Direct3D, a few built-in functions are available to you for handling textures. For starters, the function D3DX11Create-TextureFromFile is used to load in textures from a disk. This function supports a variety of popular graphics formats, such as BMP, PNG, and DDS. The D3DX11CreateTextureFromFile function takes six parameters and has the following function prototype:

```
HRESULT D3DX11CreateTextureFromFile(
    ID3D11Device* pDevice,
    LPCTSTR pSrcFile,
    D3DX11_IMAGE_LOAD_INFO* pLoadInfo,
    ID3DX11ThreadPump* pPump,
    ID3D11Resource** ppTexture,
    HRESULT* pHResult
);
```

The first parameter to the D3DX11CreateTextureFromFile is the Direct3D device. This parameter must be a valid Direct3D device.

The second parameter of the D3DX11CreateTextureFromFile is the path and file name of the file being loaded.

The third parameter of the D3DX11CreateTextureFromFile is the image information structure. This is an optional parameter and allows the function to control how the texture image is loaded by allowing us to specify values for the CPU access flags, internal format, width and height, and so forth.

The fourth parameter of the D3DX11CreateTextureFromFile function is used for the thread pump, which is used when loading the texture asynchronously via multi threading.

The fifth parameter of the D3DX11CreateTextureFromFile function is the out address to the texture object being created by this function call. If this function is successful, this parameter will have a ready-to-go texture.

The last parameter is a pointer to the return value for the thread pump. If the thread pump parameter is not null, this parameter must be a valid location of memory.

In Direct3D we can use the Direct3D functions to load many different image file formats, which are listed below:

- Windows Bitmap (BMP)

- Joint Photographic Expert Group—i.e., JPEG (JPG)

- Portable Network Graphics (PNG)

- Tagged Image Format (TIFF)

- Graphics Interchange Format (GIF)

- DirectDraw Surface (DDS)

- Windows Media Player (WMP)

Texture Interfaces

Texture interfaces are used to manage image data of a certain type. Within Direct3D there are three main types of texture interfaces:

- ID3D11Texture1D—Handles a 1D or image strip type of texture.

- ID3D11Texture2D—2D image data. This is the most common type of texture resource.

- ID3D11Texture3D—Image data used to represent volume textures (3D textures).

Each of these texture resources contains one or more subresources. The subresources represent the different MIP levels of the texture, which will be discussed in the next section. Most of the textures you use in your game will be of the 2D variety and will need to be converted to ID3D11Texture2D resources. Editors such as Adobe's Photoshop are commonly used to create 2D textures, whereas oftentimes 1D textures are arrays of data that are used as look-up tables within a shader. Usually the effects performed that often use 1D or 3D textures are advanced special effects and rendering techniques that go beyond simple texture mapping.

A 2D texture uses a single value for its texture coordinate. A texture coordinate can be thought of as an array index into the texture image. Therefore, a 2D texture uses two values for the texture coordinates, also known as the TU and TV coordinates (or simply U and V), and 3D textures use three values (TU, TV, and TR). Cube maps, which we'll briefly discuss in the section titled "Texture Details," also uses three texture coordinates since a cube map creates a much more simplistic volume than a 3D texture.

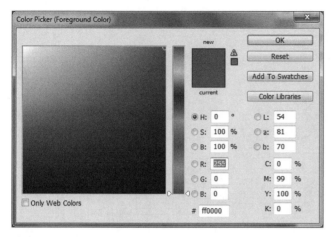

Figure 3.14
Selecting a 32-bit color in Adobe Photoshop.

MIP Maps

Each pixel in a texture is known as a texel. A texel in a color map is a color value, usually between the values of 0 and 255 in common image formats. A 32-bit image is made up of four 8-bit values, with one for the red, one for the green, one for the blue, and one for the alpha. In other words each component is a single byte in size, and a 32-bit color is four bytes in size. On the other hand, an RGB image, where each component is stored in a single byte, is 24 bits in size.

Most image editors use color values in the range of 0 and 255 by default. For example, in Adobe Photoshop you can select colors from the color picker when creating images, and each component of the color can be a value between 0 and 255 (see Figure 3.14).

An image's resolution describes its size along the width and height of the image. An image with the resolution of 1024 × 768 has a width of 1024 texels by 768 texels. This is the same as saying an image of this size has 1,024 columns and 768 rows in a table. That means for this resolution 1,024 times 768 equals 786,432 texels in total. If each texel is 4 bytes each (32-bits), then the size of the image is 786,432 times 4, which equals 3,145,728 bytes. This equates to 3072 kilobytes, which is 3 megabytes of uncompressed data.

So what are MIP maps? MIP levels are decreasingly lower resolution versions of the same texture. MIP levels allow the system to swap in the proper texture

Figure 3.15
MIP Levels.

Figure 3.16
An object close and far from the viewer.

resolution based on a surface's distance. Objects further away need a lower texture applied to them because they are not close enough to see all the detail anyway. An example can be seen in Figure 3.15 of various MIP levels.

Figure 3.16 shows an example of an object close to the viewer as well as far from the viewer. For objects that are far away from the viewer, the number of pixels that are shaded on the screen becomes less and less as the object moves away from the viewer. This means that, in order to preserve high quality, we'll often need to use high-resolution images for close objects. But if objects are far away, or if they can move far away, high-resolution images do not need to be passed along the rendering pipeline; instead, a lower-resolution version of the image can be used.

This is important because the less data we need to move, the faster our performance can potentially be. If there are many objects that are away from the camera, then using a texture resolution that is high enough to cause no noticeable difference in appearance from the high-level version is one of the keys to improving performance. This process is known as mipmapping, and the D3DX11CreateTextureFromFile will create the full MIP level chain by default. Another benefit to using MIP maps comes from their ability to help reduce aliasing artifacts.

This also brings forth two new terms called MIN and MAG. Minification occurs as the textured surface moves away from the viewer. As the surface moves away, more texels from the texture are combined to color a single screen pixel. This is because multiple textures occupy the same pixel for surfaces as they move away from the view. Magnification of the texture occurs when the textured surface gets closer to the camera, causing more pixels to render the same texels. If each texel is being applied to a single pixel, then MIN and MAG do not occur, but in 3D games the reality is that these are pretty much always present for all textured surfaces.

Texture Details

Occasionally you'll need to get certain information from a loaded texture such as its dimensions or pixel format. This information is available using the ID3D11-Texture2D::GetDesc function. This function fills in a D3D11_TEXTURE2D_DESC structure with all the details.

D3D11_TEXTURE2D_DESC is just one of the texture description structures available and is specifically for 2D textures. Direct3D also has the structures D3D11_TEX TURE1D_DESC and D3D11_TEXTURE3D_DESC available for 1D and 3D textures, respectively. The D3D11_TEXTURE2D_DESC structure will give you additional information of a texture and can be seen as follows:

```
typedef struct D3D11_TEXTURE2D_DESC {
    UINT            Width;
    UINT            Height;
    UINT            MipLevels;
    UINT            ArraySize;
```

```
DXGI_FORMAT       Format;
DXGI_SAMPLE_DESC  SampleDesc;
D3D11_USAGE       Usage;
UINT              BindFlags;
UINT              CPUAccessFlags;
UINT              MiscFlags;
} D3D11_TEXTURE2D_DESC;
```

Each of the members of the D3D11_TEXTURE2D_DESC structure has been seen in one context or another, with the exception of ArraySize. Before we describe what this is, we'll discuss cube maps. A cube map texture is a collection (array) of six 2D texture images that, together, usually form the various views of an environment. A cube map usually maps to the up, down, left, right, forward, and back directions. The ArraySize of the D3D11_TEXTURE2D_DESC will be 6 for cube map, images since there are six images in the array. An example of a cube map can be seen in Figure 3.17.

Texture Mapping Demo

In this section we've covered nearly enough information to implement texture mapping. The details that have not been covered we'll discuss along the way. The

Figure 3.17
An example of a cube map.

Texture Mapping demo can be found on the website in the Chapter 3/ TextureMapping folder.

To start we'll be building from the `TriangleDemo` code from earlier in this chapter. In the `TextureDemo` class we'll add a shader resource view called `colorMap_` (`ID3D11ShaderResourceView`) and a sampler state called `color-MapSampler_` (`ID3D11SamplerState`).

A shader resource view is an object shaders use to access resources. When we load the texture into memory we must create a shader resource view in order to access that data via a shader, and that is what we will be binding to the input assembler. Shader resource views have other uses, such as providing general purpose data to DirectCompute for parallel computing, but in this chapter we will focus only on textures. The `ID3D11Texture2D` is a buffer of data, while the shader resource view allows us to view that buffer in a shader.

A sampler state allows us to access sampling state information of a texture. We'll discuss this more when we look at how to create the object, but in general, note that the sampler state allows us to set properties such as the texture filtering and addressing—topics we'll also discuss soon.

The `TextureDemo` class can be seen in Listing 3.9.

Listing 3.9 The `TextureDemo` class from the TextureDemo.h header file.

```
class TextureDemo : public Dx11DemoBase
{
    public:
        TextureDemo( );
        virtual ~TextureDemo( );

        bool LoadContent( );
        void UnloadContent( );

        void Update( float dt );
        void Render( );

    private:
        ID3D11VertexShader* solidColorVS_;
        ID3D11PixelShader* solidColorPS_;
```

```
    ID3D11InputLayout* inputLayout_;
    ID3D11Buffer* vertexBuffer_;

    ID3D11ShaderResourceView* colorMap_;
    ID3D11SamplerState* colorMapSampler_;
};
```

Since we are performing texture mapping, we need to update the vertex structure to include two floating-point variables for the TU and TV texture coordinates. This can be done with the XMFLOAT2 structure.

When we create the input layout, we must also add to the D3D11_INPUT_ELE MENT_DESC array in the LoadContent function an element for the texture coordinate. The semantic name is "TEXCOORD", and its format will be DXGI_FOR-MAT_R32G32_FLOAT (since we are using only two float values). Also, for the offset we must use 12 because in the beginning of our vertex structure layout is a XMFLOAT3 for the position. Since an XMFLOAT3 is 12 bytes in size, our texture coordinates won't appear in the vertex until after the 12th byte. Listing 3.10 shows the vertex structure, LoadContent, and UnloadContent functions for this demo.

Listing 3.10 The vertex structure and the Texture demo's LoadContent and UnloadContent.

```
struct VertexPos
{
    XMFLOAT3 pos;
    XMFLOAT2 tex0;
};


bool TextureDemo::LoadContent( )
{
    ... Load vertex Shader ...


    D3D11_INPUT_ELEMENT_DESC solidColorLayout[] =
    {
        { "POSITION", 0, DXGI_FORMAT_R32G32B32_FLOAT,
          0, 0, D3D11_INPUT_PER_VERTEX_DATA, 0 },
        { "TEXCOORD", 0, DXGI_FORMAT_R32G32_FLOAT,
```

```
            0, 12, D3D11_INPUT_PER_VERTEX_DATA, 0 }
};

unsigned int totalLayoutElements = ARRAYSIZE( solidColorLayout );

d3dResult = d3dDevice_->CreateInputLayout( solidColorLayout,
    totalLayoutElements, vsBuffer->GetBufferPointer( ),
    vsBuffer->GetBufferSize( ), &inputLayout_ );


... Load Pixel Shader ...


VertexPos vertices[] =
{
    { XMFLOAT3(  1.0f,  1.0f, 1.0f ), XMFLOAT2( 1.0f, 1.0f ) },
    { XMFLOAT3(  1.0f, -1.0f, 1.0f ), XMFLOAT2( 1.0f, 0.0f ) },
    { XMFLOAT3( -1.0f, -1.0f, 1.0f ), XMFLOAT2( 0.0f, 0.0f ) },

    { XMFLOAT3( -1.0f, -1.0f, 1.0f ), XMFLOAT2( 0.0f, 0.0f ) },
    { XMFLOAT3( -1.0f,  1.0f, 1.0f ), XMFLOAT2( 0.0f, 1.0f ) },
    { XMFLOAT3(  1.0f,  1.0f, 1.0f ), XMFLOAT2( 1.0f, 1.0f ) },
};


... Create Vertex Buffer ...


d3dResult = D3DX11CreateShaderResourceViewFromFile( d3dDevice_,
    "decal.dds", 0, 0, &colorMap_, 0 );

if( FAILED( d3dResult ) )
{
    DXTRACE_MSG( "Failed to load the texture image!" );
    return false;
}

D3D11_SAMPLER_DESC colorMapDesc;
ZeroMemory( &colorMapDesc, sizeof( colorMapDesc ) );
colorMapDesc.AddressU = D3D11_TEXTURE_ADDRESS_WRAP;
```

```
colorMapDesc.AddressV = D3D11_TEXTURE_ADDRESS_WRAP;
colorMapDesc.AddressW = D3D11_TEXTURE_ADDRESS_WRAP;
colorMapDesc.ComparisonFunc = D3D11_COMPARISON_NEVER;
colorMapDesc.Filter = D3D11_FILTER_MIN_MAG_MIP_LINEAR;
colorMapDesc.MaxLOD = D3D11_FLOAT32_MAX;

d3dResult = d3dDevice_->CreateSamplerState( &colorMapDesc,
    &colorMapSampler_ );

if( FAILED( d3dResult ) )
{
    DXTRACE_MSG( "Failed to create color map sampler state!" );
    return false;
}

return true;
}


void TextureDemo::UnloadContent( )
{
    if( colorMapSampler_ ) colorMapSampler_->Release( );
    if( colorMap_ ) colorMap_->Release( );
    if( solidColorVS_ ) solidColorVS_->Release( );
    if( solidColorPS_ ) solidColorPS_->Release( );
    if( inputLayout_ ) inputLayout_->Release( );
    if( vertexBuffer_ ) vertexBuffer_->Release( );

    colorMapSampler_ = 0;
    colorMap_ = 0;
    solidColorVS_ = 0;
    solidColorPS_ = 0;
    inputLayout_ = 0;
    vertexBuffer_ = 0;
}
```

The UnloadContent function releases our new objects, and the remainder of the LoadContent function loads our texture image. To load a texture and create a shader resource view in one call, we can use the Direct3D utility function D3DX11CreateShaderResourceViewFromFile. This function is useful when we want to both load a texture and create a new shader resource view conveniently at once. The D3DX11CreateShaderResourceViewFromFile function has the following prototype, whose parameters closely match the D3DX11CreateTextureFromFile function:

```
HRESULT D3DX11CreateShaderResourceViewFromFile(
    ID3D11Device* pDevice,
    LPCTSTR pSrcFile,
    D3DX11_IMAGE_LOAD_INFO* pLoadInfo,
    ID3DX11ThreadPump* pPump,
    ID3D11ShaderResourceView** ppShaderResourceView,
    HRESULT* pHResult
);
```

The last new section of code in the LoadContent function is the creation of the sampler state. To create a sampler state object, we call CreateSamplerState of the Direct3D device, which takes as parameters the sampler description and the out address to the sampler state object that will store the results. The sampler description has the following structure:

```
typedef struct D3D11_SAMPLER_DESC {
    D3D11_FILTER                Filter;
    D3D11_TEXTURE_ADDRESS_MODE AddressU;
    D3D11_TEXTURE_ADDRESS_MODE AddressV;
    D3D11_TEXTURE_ADDRESS_MODE AddressW;
    FLOAT                       MipLODBias;
    UINT                        MaxAnisotropy;
    D3D11_COMPARISON_FUNC       ComparisonFunc;
    FLOAT                       BorderColor[4];
    FLOAT                       MinLOD;
    FLOAT                       MaxLOD;
} D3D11_SAMPLER_DESC;
```

The first member of the D3D11_SAMPLER_DESC is a D3D11_FILTER member that specifies how the texture being sampled will be filtered. Texture filtering refers to the way values are read and combined from the source and made available to the shader. Filtering can be used to improve quality but at the cost of more expensive texture sampling, since some filtering types can cause more than one value to be read and combined to produce a single color value that the shader sees. The various filtering types available in Direct3D 11 include the following:

```
typedef enum D3D11_FILTER {
  D3D11_FILTER_MIN_MAG_MIP_POINT
  D3D11_FILTER_MIN_MAG_POINT_MIP_LINEAR
  D3D11_FILTER_MIN_POINT_MAG_LINEAR_MIP_POINT
  D3D11_FILTER_MIN_POINT_MAG_MIP_LINEAR
  D3D11_FILTER_MIN_LINEAR_MAG_MIP_POINT
  D3D11_FILTER_MIN_LINEAR_MAG_POINT_MIP_LINEAR
  D3D11_FILTER_MIN_MAG_LINEAR_MIP_POINT
  D3D11_FILTER_MIN_MAG_MIP_LINEAR
  D3D11_FILTER_ANISOTROPIC
  D3D11_FILTER_COMPARISON_MIN_MAG_MIP_POINT
  D3D11_FILTER_COMPARISON_MIN_MAG_POINT_MIP_LINEAR
  D3D11_FILTER_COMPARISON_MIN_POINT_MAG_LINEAR_MIP_POINT
  D3D11_FILTER_COMPARISON_MIN_POINT_MAG_MIP_LINEAR
  D3D11_FILTER_COMPARISON_MIN_LINEAR_MAG_MIP_POINT
  D3D11_FILTER_COMPARISON_MIN_LINEAR_MAG_POINT_MIP_LINEAR
  D3D11_FILTER_COMPARISON_MIN_MAG_LINEAR_MIP_POINT
  D3D11_FILTER_COMPARISON_MIN_MAG_MIP_LINEAR
  D3D11_FILTER_COMPARISON_ANISOTROPIC
  D3D11_FILTER_TEXT_1BIT
} D3D11_FILTER;
```

The various numerations in the D3D11_FILTER enumeration account for different combinations of the texture's MIN, MAG, and MIP levels. The comparison versions of these values are used to tell Direct3D to interpolate using the Boolean result of a comparison value with the value being fetched.

Point sampling, also known as nearest-neighbor sampling, for the filter is the fastest type of sampling. It works by fetching a single value from the texture with no further modifications. The value chosen is the texel closest to the pixel's center.

Bilinear sampling, on the other hand, will perform bilinear interpolation on the value sampled at that texture coordinate as well as several samples surrounding it. The interpolated value (combined results) is what the shaders will see. The samples selected by this filtering are the four texels closest to the pixel's center. This combination of multiple nearby values can smooth the results a bit, which can cause a reduction in rendering artifacts.

Trilinear filtering works by performing bilinear sampling around the texel for the two closest MIP levels and interpolating the results. When a surface goes from using one MIP level to another, there can be a noticeable change in the appearance of that surface at that moment of change. Interpolating between the closest MIP levels, after bilinearly filtering both levels, can greatly help to reduce these rendering artifacts.

Anisotropic filtering works by trilinearly sampling in a trapezoid area instead of a square area. Bilinear and trilinear filtering work best when looking directly at the surface because of the square area of sampling, but when viewing a surface at an angle, such as a floor or terrain in a 3D game, a noticeable amount of blurriness and rendering artifacts can appear. Anisotropic filtering takes angles into consideration and samples using a different shaped area.

The next three members of the D3D11_SAMPLER_DESC structure are used for texture address modes. Texture coordinates are specified in the range of 0.0 and 1.0 for each dimension of the texture. The texture address mode tells Direct3D how to handle values outside of this range. The texture address mode for the U, V, and R can be one of the following values:

```
typedef enum D3D11_TEXTURE_ADDRESS_MODE {
    D3D11_TEXTURE_ADDRESS_WRAP,
    D3D11_TEXTURE_ADDRESS_MIRROR,
    D3D11_TEXTURE_ADDRESS_CLAMP,
    D3D11_TEXTURE_ADDRESS_BORDER,
    D3D11_TEXTURE_ADDRESS_MIRROR_ONCE,
} D3D11_TEXTURE_ADDRESS_MODE;
```

WRAP for the texture address will cause the texture to wrap around and repeat. For example, if you have a square shape and you want a texture to display twice on it along the horizontal direction, you just need to specify 2.0 for the U texture coordinates for the right most vertices, as seen in Figure 3.18. This can be used to tile a texture along a single surface, which has the benefit of giving the appearance of more detail while using less data.

The MIRROR texture address mode will cause the texture to repeat but in a mirror direction (see Figure 3.19), while CLAMP will simply clamp the values in the 0.0 to 1.0 range. MIRROR_ONCE will mirror the texture one time, while MIRROR will continue it as specified. The BORDER address mode will set any pixels outside of the 0.0 to 1.0 range to a specified border color. The border color is specified by another member of the D3D11_SAMPLER_DESC called BorderColor, which is an array of four floating-point values.

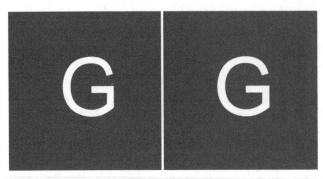

Figure 3.18
Wrapping texture coordinates.

Figure 3.19
Mirror texture address mode.

The next member in the D3D11_SAMPLER_DESC structure is the level-of-detail (LOD) bias for the MIP. This value is an offset of the MIP level to use by Direct3D. For example, if Direct3D specifies that the MIP level to use is 2 and the offset is set to 3, then the MIP ultimately used will be level 5.

Following the LOD bias is the max anisotropic value to use during anisotropic filtering and the comparison function. The max anisotropic value can be between 1 and 16 and is not used for point or bilinear filtering. The COMPARISON function is a value used for the comparison versions of the texture filtering flags. The comparison flags are specified in D3D11_COMPARISON_FUNC and are essentially flags stating the comparison should pass if one value is less than equal to, greater than, etc. another value.

The last two members of the D3D11_SAMPLER_DESC structure are used to clamp the min and max MIP levels that can be used. For example, if the max is set to 1, then level 0 will not be accessed (note that level 0 is the highest resolution).

The last piece of the puzzle besides the shaders is the rendering function. To render our textured geometry, we must add the texture resource and set the sampler state. This is done by calling PSSetShaderResources and PSSetSamplers, which are used to set these items to the pixel shader. The PSSetShaderResources has the following prototype and takes as parameters the start slot to begin inserting resources, the number of resources being inserted, and an array of resources to insert:

```
void PSSetShaderResources(
   UINT StartSlot,
   UINT NumViews,
   ID3D11ShaderResourceView* const* ppShaderResourceViews
);
```

The PSSetSamplers function also takes the start slot and number of samplers being set along with the array of samplers you are providing. With the addition of those two functions to our rendering code from the previous demo, we are ready to see the effect in action. All that is missing is to modify the shaders to perform the actual effect. The rendering function used by the Texture Mapping demo can be seen in Listing 3.11.

Listing 3.11 The Texture Mapping demo's rendering function.

```
void TextureDemo::Render( )
{
    if( d3dContext_ == 0 )
        return;

    float clearColor[4] = { 0.0f, 0.0f, 0.25f, 1.0f };
    d3dContext_->ClearRenderTargetView( backBufferTarget_, clearColor );

    unsigned int stride = sizeof( VertexPos );
    unsigned int offset = 0;

    d3dContext_->IASetInputLayout( inputLayout_ );
    d3dContext_->IASetVertexBuffers( 0, 1, &vertexBuffer_, &stride, &offset );
```

```
    d3dContext_->IASetPrimitiveTopology( D3D11_PRIMITIVE_TOPOLOGY_
TRIANGLELIST );

    d3dContext_->VSSetShader( colorMapVS_, 0, 0 );
    d3dContext_->PSSetShader( colorMapPS_, 0, 0 );
    d3dContext_->PSSetShaderResources( 0, 1, &colorMap_ );
    d3dContext_->PSSetSamplers( 0, 1, &colorMapSampler_ );
    d3dContext_->Draw( 6, 0 );

    swapChain_->Present( 0, 0 );
}
```

In the shader, which can be seen in Listing 3.12, we have two new global shader objects called colorMap_ and colorSampler_. The colorMap_ object hast the type of Texture2D since it is being used for a 2D texture, while the colorSampler_ has the HLSL type of SamplerState. To bind these objects to the shader inputs we are providing in the rendering function, we must use the register keyword of HLSL. To bind to the first texture input we use t0, where t represents texture and 0 is the index to the first texture unit. The same can be said for the sampler state, where we use s0 for the first sampler. Since our PSSetSamplers and PSSetShaderResources functions can pass along an array of data for our shader to use, we must bind each HLSL variable to the specific index we want it to use. Since we only have one texture and one sampler state, we only need to use t0 and s0.

Another change in the shader is that we must update the vertex shader's input structure to allow for texture coordinates and the pixel shader's input structure to also allow texture coordinates. The vertex shader will take the texture coordinates from the vertex buffer and simply pass them to the pixel shader so that the pixel shader has access to it.

The pixel shader uses this texture coordinate (which, remember, is interpolated between vertices) with the texture object to read a color value. This is done by calling the HLSL Texture2D object's Sample function, which takes as parameters the sampler state object to use for sampling and a pair of texture coordinates. Since we are reading from a 2D texture, the texture coordinates must be of the type float2.

Listing 3.12 The Texture Mapping demo's shaders.

```
Texture2D colorMap_ : register( t0 );
SamplerState colorSampler_ : register( s0 );


struct VS_Input
{
    float4 pos   : POSITION;
    float2 tex0 : TEXCOORD0;
};

struct PS_Input
{
    float4 pos   : SV_POSITION;
    float2 tex0 : TEXCOORD0;
};


PS_Input VS_Main( VS_Input vertex )
{
    PS_Input vsOut = ( PS_Input )0;
    vsOut.pos = vertex.pos;
    vsOut.tex0 = vertex.tex0;

    return vsOut;
}


float4 PS_Main( PS_Input frag ) : SV_TARGET
{
    return colorMap_.Sample( colorSampler_, frag.tex0 );
}
```

At this point you should be able to compile and execute the code. What you see should match Figure 3.20.

SPRITES

2D games just wouldn't be the same without sprites. Before you start thinking soda or fairies, sprites are 2D graphical representations of characters or objects

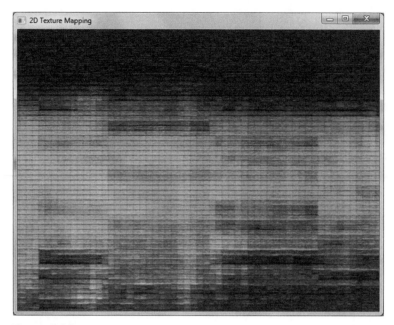

Figure 3.20
Screenshot of the Texture Mapping demo.

within a game. Every tree, treasure chest, or dungeon creature you encounter is presented onscreen using a sprite. Sprites are one of the most widely used and easily understood aspects of 2D game programming. In 2D games, sprites are usually textured rectangles and squares that collectively create a virtual world.

Z-Ordering

In 2D games, some objects act as the background and some as the foreground, while others can be anything between the two, and these objects are known as layers. A layer can be thought of as a piece of transparent paper. For example, the layer that acts as the background layer will only have background sprites rendered to it, while the action layer might have all of the characters, weapons, power-ups, etc. The order in which the layers are rendered will determine which sprites are supposed to appear on top of what other sprites. In addition to having defined layers, there is also Z-ordering, which is the process in which objects are sorted before being drawn. Each sprite you create can be given a different Z-order value designating the depth at which it should be drawn. Sprites with a lower Z-order value are drawn behind those sprites with a higher value, giving the illusion of depth. For example, anything with a Z value of 1 is drawn on top of anything with a Z value of 0, and anything with a Z value of 2 is drawn on top of anything with a value of 0 or 1.

Using layers and/or Z-ordering allows us to define the rendering order in 2D games, but in 3D games we commonly use a concept known as depth testing for ensuring surfaces appear to exist in the correct order, which we'll discuss more in Chapter 6 once we enter 3D graphics.

Hardware depth testing uses a special rendering buffer known as a depth buffer, and it is used to determine if the previous surface's depth at that pixel is farther to the viewer than the current surface's depth. In other words, if the previous surface that was rendered at this location is further away from the camera than the current surface we are rendering, then the current surface is closer to the camera and should be drawn on top of the previous data, else the previous surface is in front of the current surface, and those pixels should not be updated.

Depth testing is one of the ways 3D games are able to correctly render objects without having to pre-sort polygons based on the camera's view (we'll examine this in detail in Chapter 6). Since we are rendering using Direct3D, we could draw our 2D sprites in order of which sprites should appear in front of others without needing to use a depth buffer. By clearing the screen completely and drawing our sprites in layers, we could achieve proper results.

Sprite Image

The most important aspect of a sprite is its image. Traditionally, each sprite needs an image to be associated with it both from a gameplay perspective and a technical one. The image is what the sprite uses to convey its purpose to the player. For instance, your main character's sprite in an RPG game may be the image of a knight or even a spaceship in a space battle. You can choose any image you'd like, but your sprite can't be displayed without an image.

This is because in the early days of 2D games sprite images were drawn directly to the rendering destination and not to actual geometry. This is known as texture blitting. In Direct3D we can opt to draw 2D geometry and texture map that geometry rather than resorting to the old-fashioned methods of 2D game graphics. Texture blitting is essentially copying color values from the sprite image to the rendering destination over a specific location of the destination.

You can do this if you are creating a software rendering API for a 2D game, but using Direct3D it is easier for us to use 2D textured rectangle geometry versus trying to create a software rendering API.

Earlier you learned how to load a texture from the disk; now you'll learn how textures can be used with sprites.

Getting Sprites to the Screen

When drawing sprites, the sprite object needs to know a few things about the environment in which it's drawing. Not only does it need to know the position of each and every sprite to avoid collisions on the same layer between solid objects, but it needs to know the specifics about the area in which it's drawing. This means the sprite object must be aware of the boundaries of the area where the sprites will be drawn. Normally, the size of this area is determined by the viewport associated with the Direct3D device.

The area in which the sprites are drawn is defined by its transformation matrices. Matrices are discussed in detail in Chapter 6, but for now we'll briefly cover the basics of the various matrices we use in graphics rendering. A matrix in Direct3D is a 4×4 matrix. Visually it can be thought of as a table with 4 rows and 4 columns for 16 elements in total. These four rows and columns allow us to do a lot in game graphics and simulations.

Usually in graphics programming we start off with three main types of transformation matrices. The first is used for projection transformation, the second is used for view transformations, and the third is used for world transformations.

When you transform vertices by a matrix, you are manipulating those vertices based on the representation of that matrix. For example, a rotation matrix is used to rotate objects, a translation matrix is used to position objects, and a scaling matrix is used to scale matrices. But why do we need to do this?

Objects in 3D space are usually created using a 3D modeling application such as Autodesk's 3D Studio Max. When models and objects are modeled, it is done in what is called model space. This means that the position of the vertices is specific to that model when it was modeled out in an editor. Usually models are created around the origin, just like we've been doing for our simple triangles and squares in previous chapters (where the origin of (0, 0, 0) is the center of the shape).

In a game we can have one or more instances of this model, and these models can move and interact with the scene. But all of the model's data is defined in model space, and as it moves throughout the world, the location of the vertices must be updated to new positions. Also, when we position our models using a level/map editor or as the models are interacting with the game (e.g., physics, artificial intelligence, etc.), we use matrices to position, rotate, and scale the models. This allows us to have one model data loaded into memory for each instance and just render that model out multiple times for each instance that exists. So if we have an asteroid field with 1,000 rocks, we will need only one rock model and 1,000 matrices to represent the position and orientation of each asteroid. We could take it a step further and use Direct3D's instancing feature to perform one draw call and supply in a buffer the per-instance transformation matrices of all 1,000 rocks.

Simply put, a transformation matrix allows us to define the position and orientation of our objects virtually. A model created in an editor such as 3D Studio Max will be in model-space. When we apply the model's geometry with a transformation matrix that represents positional, scaling, and orientation values, then we are transforming that model-space geometry into world-space. World-space is a context that represents the position of an object in relation to other objects in the world around them.

In games, especially 3D games, cameras play a big role. The orientation of the camera also must be applied to the geometry in order to simulate the camera effect. The camera is represented by another matrix called the view matrix. The view matrix allows us to take models in its current space and transform it into view-space. When combined with the world matrix, we can create a single matrix that does both of these transformations in one called the world-view matrix.

In addition to simulating a camera's position and orientation, we also add projection. A projection matrix is used to simulate orthogonal projection or to simulate perspective projection. We could also apply other effects such as the zoom of a sniper scope by manipulating the projection matrix as well as other effects.

We'll discuss projection matrices in more detail in Chapter 6, but we'll briefly go over them in a high-level view now. Orthographic projection is great for 2D elements because the visual depth of the objects being rendered is not applied to the final output. This means that if you have two boxes that are 10 units in size but 100 units away from each other along the Z axis, using orthogonal projection will cause them to appear to be right next to one other depth wise. Orthographic projection is not only good for 2D games but also 2D interface elements of a 3D game, such as health bars, ammo counters, timers, text, etc.

Perspective projection on the other hand adds perspective to our rendered objects. This means that objects get smaller on the screen as they move further away from the camera or larger as they get closer to it. This can be seen in real life if you look into the distance. Objects that are far away look small in the sense that the area of your vision it occupies gets smaller with distance. If you are standing in from of a building, the height of the building is a lot larger than if you were a mile away.

Combining the model, view, and projection matrices into one will create a new matrix known as the model-view projection matrix. This matrix is used by the vertex shader to transform incoming geometry to the final position it will have after applying the model's position and orientation, the camera's view, and the projection effects. Therefore, technically, we are using the vertex shader to generate the model's real position (known as the absolute position) from its local position (known as its relative position). This is also how character animation systems work in bone animation, where matrices are used to define poses of animation for groups of geometry defined by bones.

There are a few functions that are part of the XNA Math library that are used to build projection matrices, and each will be discussed in more detail in Chapter 6. For now we'll look at XMMatrixOrthographicOffCenterLH as an example to get things started off.

The function XMMatrixOrthographicOffCenterLH is used to create an orthographic projection matrix using a left-handed coordinate system (Chapter 6). The return value for this function is a XMMATRIX structure where the resulting projection matrix is placed. This function is used specifically to offset the coordinates of the view to make the top-left corner have a custom value for the X and Y axes (for example 0, 0). The function prototype for the XMMatrixOrthographicOffCenterLH can be seen as follows:

```
XMMATRIX XMMatrixOrthographicOffCenterLH(
    FLOAT ViewLeft,
```

```
    FLOAT ViewRight,
    FLOAT ViewBottom,
    FLOAT ViewTop,
    FLOAT NearZ,
    FLOAT FarZ
)
```

The parameters to the `XMMatrixOrthographicOffCenterLH` define the projection viewport, where the first parameter is the minimum X value, the second is the maximum X value, the third is the minimum Y value, and the fourth is the maximum Y value. The last two parameters are used to set the near and far clipping planes (Chapter 6). The near clipping plane will discard rendering of anything in front of that value, and the far clipping plane will discard rendering anything after that value. This creates something known as a view volume. The clipping planes play a much larger role in 3D graphics, where depth is more prevalent.

The projection matrix lets the system know the size of the grid on which the sprites will be placed. For example, if the viewport is 640 pixels wide and 480 pixels tall, then the projection matrix would restrict visible sprite drawing to that area. Sprites positioned outside of this area would not be visible on the screen. This is handled by Direct3D in hardware.

The projection matrix only needs to be changed if the size of the viewport changes or if we are performing some special camera effects that require us to switch projection matrices. Do not worry if this is new information, because we'll cover it in detail in Chapter 6. To get started with matrices, you don't need to understand the internal details as long as you understand generally what the XNA Math functions are doing for you. Over time it will become more important to understand the internals so that you can leverage that knowledge to do anything you wish virtually.

Positioning and Scaling Sprites

Now that the sprites know the extent of their environment, positioning them within it is possible. The act of moving an object within a space is called translation, where translation is another term for position. Sprites being two dimensional in nature can be translated in two directions, X and Y, although in Direct3D we technically could move in 3D space even for 2D objects.

If you want to position a sprite in the center of a 640 × 480 display area, you would translate the sprite to an X, Y position of (320, 240). This, in effect, moves the sprite 320 pixels horizontally and 240 pixels vertically when using an orthogonal projection that defines the upper left corner of the screen as (0, 0). When sprites are translated, they're moved based on an internal point called the translation point. The translation point on a sprite is by default the location of the sprite's model-space origin. When using sprites for characters within a game, it is common for the translation point to be moved to the top-left corner of the sprite.

When translating a sprite it is necessary to create another matrix called the translation matrix, which was briefly mentioned earlier in this chapter. The translation matrix, once defined, is used by Direct3D to position the sprite (or any geometric object). The translation matrix can be created by using the function XMMatrixTranslation. The prototype to the XMMatrixTranslation can be seen as follows:

```
XMMATRIX XMMatrixTranslation( FLOAT OffsetX, FLOAT OffsetY, FLOAT OffsetZ )
```

The return value for XMMatrixTranslation is the translation matrix, and the parameters it takes are the X, Y, and Z position values to move by. We also could create a rotation and scaling matrix using other XNA Math functions that will be examined in Chapter 6.

This was a bird's-eye view of matrices, but it should be clear as to their purpose. We create a translation matrix to position objects, a rotation matrix to rotate them, and scaling matrices to scale them (i.e., shrink or enlarge). The concatenation of these three matrices together can be used to create the world transformation matrix. Concatenating the world matrix with the view and projection matrices is used to create the model-view projection matrix, which is used primarily by the vertex shader. The purpose of the vertex shader is to manipulate incoming vertices, and matrix transformation is one of the tasks vertex shaders commonly perform. We won't look at cameras and views until Chapters 6, 7, and 8, so we will largely ignore the view matrix until then.

THE GAME SPRITE DEMO

On the companion website in the Chapter3 folder is a demo called Game Sprites (Chapter3/GameSprite folder). The purpose of this demo is to create a game sprite structure that can be used to represent a single instance of a sprite. We will write code that draws sprites to the screen, which can be used as the first steps toward creating a 2D game.

So far we have a good idea of the values we'll need for each sprite. To begin we'll create a simple game sprite class with the following members:

- Position
- Rotation
- Scale
- Sprite image
- Vertex buffer

Since this is a beginner's book, we will create a vertex buffer and texture for each unique sprite and render them for each sprite instance in the scene (i.e., more than one sprite can use the same texture and vertex buffer). In a commercial game where large amounts of draw calls and state changes are causing perform-ance issues, we'd opt to consider batching geometry and using texture atlases. These topics are move advanced and require a more intermediate level of skill with Direct3D to properly implement.

Note

A word of advice when considering premature optimizations is to avoid it. Only optimize when a bottleneck has been identified, and address the problems of any bottlenecks until an acceptable level of performance is obtained. Optimizing for the sake of doing while developing code can lead to wasted effort on code that is not a performance burden or on code that is not a priority. In other words, don't optimize some code when there are "bigger fish" (worse-performing code and bottlenecks) to fry.

The game sprite class is fairly simple, and its purpose is to use the position, rotation, and scale values to build the sprite's world matrix when it is rendered. Once the world matrix is built, it is passed to the vertex shader using a constant buffer. In order to avoid loading the same texture or creating the same vertex buffer over and over again, we'll create them once in this demo and use them for each sprite we are drawing. Since our focus is on rendering multiple sprites and on using matrices to position them, we won't overly complicate things more than necessary.

The game sprite class can be seen in Listing 3.13. The Game Sprite demo's class can also be seen in Listing 3.14. In the demo's class we have an array of sprite resources that we will be drawing, a constant buffer for allowing us to pass data to the vertex shader, a view projection matrix (as a XMMATRIX), and a new blend state object.

Listing 3.13 The `GameSprite` class from GameSprite.h.

```
#include<xnamath.h>


class GameSprite
{
    public:
        GameSprite( );
        virtual ~GameSprite( );

        XMMATRIX GetWorldMatrix( );

        void SetPosition( XMFLOAT2& position );
        void SetRotation( float rotation );
        void SetScale( XMFLOAT2& scale );


    private:
        XMFLOAT2 position_;
        float rotation_;
        XMFLOAT2 scale_;
};
```

Listing 3.14 The Game Sprite demo class definition from GameSpriteDemo.h.

```
#include"Dx11DemoBase.h"
#include"GameSprite.h"


class GameSpriteDemo : public Dx11DemoBase
{
    public:
        GameSpriteDemo( );
```

```
        virtual ~GameSpriteDemo( );

        bool LoadContent( );
        void UnloadContent( );

        void Update( float dt );
        void Render( );

    private:
        ID3D11VertexShader* solidColorVS_;
        ID3D11PixelShader* solidColorPS_;

        ID3D11InputLayout* inputLayout_;
        ID3D11Buffer* vertexBuffer_;

        ID3D11ShaderResourceView* colorMap_;
        ID3D11SamplerState* colorMapSampler_;
        ID3D11BlendState* alphaBlendState_;

        GameSprite sprites_[2];
        ID3D11Buffer* mvpCB_;
        XMMATRIX vpMatrix_;
};
```

The blend state object has the type of ID3D11BlendState. We will use it in order to render our textured sprites using alpha transparency. This means that we must use 32-bit texture images with an alpha channel. The texture we are going to display can be seen in in Figure 3.21 in Photoshop.

The constant buffer will be used to send the model-view projection matrix to the vertex shader so that the shader can transform the incoming geometry. Since there is no camera, and since the projection matrix does not change unless we resize the window, we can calculate the view-projection matrix once and use it within the rendering function when we calculate the full model-view projection matrix, which is why we have a XMMATRIX as a class member.

Creating and Rendering the Game Sprite

The GameSprite.cpp source file implements the GameSprite member functions, which in this demo we simply have set up as a way to store an individual sprite's

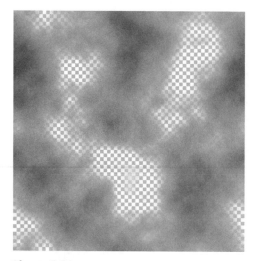

Figure 3.21
Texture with transparent areas.

position, rotation, and scale as well as a way to build the sprite's world (model) matrix. The entire GameSprite.cpp source file can be seen in Listing 3.15. You will notice that the scale is set to 1.0f for each axis, because anything less than 1.0f will shrink the sprite, while anything above 1.0f will make it grow. A value of 1.0f keeps the sprite's size unchanged.

Listing 3.15 The GameSprite.cpp source file.

```
#include<d3d11.h>
#include<d3dx11.h>
#include"GameSprite.h"


GameSprite::GameSprite( ) : rotation_( 0 )
{
    scale_.x = scale_.y = 1.0f;
}


GameSprite::~GameSprite( )
{

}
```

```
XMMATRIX GameSprite::GetWorldMatrix( )
{
    XMMATRIX translation = XMMatrixTranslation( position_.x, position_.y, 0.0f
);
    XMMATRIX rotationZ = XMMatrixRotationZ( rotation_ );
    XMMATRIX scale = XMMatrixScaling( scale_.x, scale_.y, 1.0f );

    return translation * rotationZ * scale;
}


void GameSprite::SetPosition( XMFLOAT2& position )
{
    position_ = position;
}


void GameSprite::SetRotation( float rotation )
{
    rotation_ = rotation;
}


void GameSprite::SetScale( XMFLOAT2& scale )
{
    scale_ = scale;
}
```

To render a game sprite, we draw each game sprite by building the world matrix, applying that world matrix to the vertex shader's constant buffer using VSSetConstantBuffer, we bind the texture and shaders the sprite uses, and we then render the geometry for that sprite resource. If we want to render multiple game sprites, we simply need to do this for each game sprite in the scene, which can be easily accomplished via a loop. The rendering function from the GameSprite demo can be seen in Listing 3.16. Since the only difference between each sprite is its model-view projection matrix, the matrix is the only thing we need to set during each pass of the loop. Each time we call Draw we will draw out the sprite at the position of the last set model-view projection matrix.

Listing 3.16 The rendering function from the Game Sprite demo.

```
void GameSpriteDemo::Render( )
{
    if( d3dContext_ == 0 )
        return;

    float clearColor[4] = { 0.0f, 0.0f, 0.25f, 1.0f };
    d3dContext_->ClearRenderTargetView( backBufferTarget_, clearColor );

    unsigned int stride = sizeof( VertexPos );
    unsigned int offset = 0;

    d3dContext_->IASetInputLayout( inputLayout_ );
    d3dContext_->IASetVertexBuffers( 0, 1, &vertexBuffer_, &stride, &offset );
    d3dContext_->IASetPrimitiveTopology(D3D11_PRIMITIVE_TOPOLOGY_
TRIANGLELIST);

    d3dContext_->VSSetShader( solidColorVS_, 0, 0 );
    d3dContext_->PSSetShader( solidColorPS_, 0, 0 );
    d3dContext_->PSSetShaderResources( 0, 1, &colorMap_ );
    d3dContext_->PSSetSamplers( 0, 1, &colorMapSampler_ );

    for( int i = 0; i < 2; i++ )
    {
        XMMATRIX world = sprites_[i].GetWorldMatrix( );
        XMMATRIX mvp = XMMatrixMultiply( world, vpMatrix_ );
        mvp = XMMatrixTranspose( mvp );

        d3dContext_->UpdateSubresource( mvpCB_, 0, 0, &mvp, 0, 0 );
        d3dContext_->VSSetConstantBuffers( 0, 1, &mvpCB_ );

        d3dContext_->Draw( 6, 0 );
    }

    swapChain_->Present( 0, 0 );
}
```

In the rendering code we set the constant buffer to the vertex shader by calling VSSetConstantBuffers. A constant buffer, like all DirectX 11 buffers, is of the type ID3D11BUFFER and is created in the LoadContent function. As we've mentioned earlier, a constant buffer is created by setting the buffer descriptor's `BindFlags` member to `D3D11_BIND_CONSTANT_BUFFER`.

The game sprite and the various resources it uses are created in the `LoadContent` function of the Game Sprite demo and are released in the `UnloadContent` function, both of which can be seen in Listing 3.17 for the code relevant to game sprites. This demo builds directly off of the Texture Map demo from earlier in this chapter, so we'll leave out the upper portion of the `LoadContent` function that is exactly the same from that demo.

Listing 3.17 The `LoadContent` and `UnloadContent` functions.

```
bool GameSpriteDemo::LoadContent( )
{
    // ... Previous code from the Texture Map demo...

    ID3D11Resource* colorTex;
    colorMap_->GetResource( &colorTex );

    D3D11_TEXTURE2D_DESC colorTexDesc;
    ( ( ID3D11Texture2D* )colorTex )->GetDesc( &colorTexDesc );
    colorTex->Release( );

    float halfWidth = ( float )colorTexDesc.Width / 2.0f;
    float halfHeight = ( float )colorTexDesc.Height / 2.0f;


    VertexPos vertices[] =
    {
        { XMFLOAT3(  halfWidth,  halfHeight, 1.0f ), XMFLOAT2( 1.0f, 0.0f ) },
        { XMFLOAT3(  halfWidth, -halfHeight, 1.0f ), XMFLOAT2( 1.0f, 1.0f ) },
        { XMFLOAT3( -halfWidth, -halfHeight, 1.0f ), XMFLOAT2( 0.0f, 1.0f ) },

        { XMFLOAT3( -halfWidth, -halfHeight, 1.0f ), XMFLOAT2( 0.0f, 1.0f ) },
        { XMFLOAT3( -halfWidth,  halfHeight, 1.0f ), XMFLOAT2( 0.0f, 0.0f ) },
        { XMFLOAT3(  halfWidth,  halfHeight, 1.0f ), XMFLOAT2( 1.0f, 0.0f ) },
    };

    D3D11_BUFFER_DESC vertexDesc;
    ZeroMemory( &vertexDesc, sizeof( vertexDesc ) );
```

```
vertexDesc.Usage = D3D11_USAGE_DEFAULT;
vertexDesc.BindFlags = D3D11_BIND_VERTEX_BUFFER;
vertexDesc.ByteWidth = sizeof( VertexPos ) * 6;

D3D11_SUBRESOURCE_DATA resourceData;
ZeroMemory( &resourceData, sizeof( resourceData ) );
resourceData.pSysMem = vertices;

d3dResult = d3dDevice_->CreateBuffer( &vertexDesc, &resourceData,
    &vertexBuffer_ );

if( FAILED( d3dResult ) )
{
    DXTRACE_MSG( "Failed to create vertex buffer!" );
    return false;
}


D3D11_BUFFER_DESC constDesc;
    ZeroMemory( &constDesc, sizeof( constDesc ) );
    constDesc.BindFlags = D3D11_BIND_CONSTANT_BUFFER;
    constDesc.ByteWidth = sizeof( XMMATRIX );
    constDesc.Usage = D3D11_USAGE_DEFAULT;

    d3dResult = d3dDevice_->CreateBuffer( &constDesc, 0, &mvpCB_ );

    if( FAILED( d3dResult ) )
  {
      return false;
  }


XMFLOAT2 sprite1Pos( 100.0f, 300.0f );
sprites_[0].SetPosition( sprite1Pos );

XMFLOAT2 sprite2Pos( 400.0f, 100.0f );
sprites_[1].SetPosition( sprite2Pos );

XMMATRIX view = XMMatrixIdentity( );
XMMATRIX projection = XMMatrixOrthographicOffCenterLH( 0.0f, 800.0f,
```

```
                0.0f, 600.0f, 0.1f, 100.0f );

        vpMatrix_ = XMMatrixMultiply( view, projection );

        D3D11_BLEND_DESC blendDesc;
        ZeroMemory( &blendDesc, sizeof( blendDesc ) );
        blendDesc.RenderTarget[0].BlendEnable = TRUE;
        blendDesc.RenderTarget[0].BlendOp = D3D11_BLEND_OP_ADD;
        blendDesc.RenderTarget[0].SrcBlend = D3D11_BLEND_SRC_ALPHA;
        blendDesc.RenderTarget[0].DestBlend = D3D11_BLEND_ONE;
        blendDesc.RenderTarget[0].BlendOpAlpha = D3D11_BLEND_OP_ADD;
        blendDesc.RenderTarget[0].SrcBlendAlpha = D3D11_BLEND_ZERO;
        blendDesc.RenderTarget[0].DestBlendAlpha = D3D11_BLEND_ZERO;
        blendDesc.RenderTarget[0].RenderTargetWriteMask = 0x0F;

        float blendFactor[4] = { 0.0f, 0.0f, 0.0f, 0.0f };

        d3dDevice_->CreateBlendState( &blendDesc, &alphaBlendState_ );
        d3dContext_->OMSetBlendState( alphaBlendState_, blendFactor, 0xFFFFFFFF );

        return true;
    }


    void GameSpriteDemo::UnloadContent( )
    {
        if( colorMapSampler_ ) colorMapSampler_->Release( );
        if( colorMap_ ) colorMap_->Release( );
        if( solidColorVS_ ) solidColorVS_->Release( );
        if( solidColorPS_ ) solidColorPS_->Release( );
        if( inputLayout_ ) inputLayout_->Release( );
        if( vertexBuffer_ ) vertexBuffer_->Release( );
        if( mvpCB_ ) mvpCB_->Release( );
        if( alphaBlendState_ ) alphaBlendState_->Release( );

        colorMapSampler_ = 0;
        colorMap_ = 0;
        solidColorVS_ = 0;
        solidColorPS_ = 0;
        inputLayout_ = 0;
```

```
    vertexBuffer_ = 0;
    mvpCB_ = 0;
    alphaBlendState_ = 0;
}
```

The first thing we do in the LoadContent function is to obtain access to the loaded texture. We are doing this so that we can obtain the texture's width and height. This information is used during the creation of the vertex buffer so that the size of the image dictates how large the sprite is on screen.

After we create the vertex buffer using the information (width and height) we've obtained from the texture image, we then create the constant buffer. Since we are setting the constant buffer in each frame, we will hold off until the rendering function before filling in its contents.

The last portion of the LoadContent function sets the positions of our two sprites, creates our orthographic-based view-projection matrix, and creates our blend state. We use the blend state to enable alpha transparency, which is a technique for using the alpha channel of a color to dictate how visible it is. An alpha value of 1.0f is fully visible, 0.0 is invisible, and everything between is semi transparent.

To create the blend state we call the device's CreateBlendState function, and to set the blend state we call the context's OMSetBlendState function. CreateBlend-State takes a blend description and the out address of the blend state object being created. OMSetBlendState takes the blend state that was created by CreateBlendState, a blend factor for each color channel, and a blend mask. The last two parameters are for more advanced blending, but for now we can set them to default values.

The blend description is of the type D3D11_BLEND_DESC. Some of the members of the D3D11_BLEND_DESC are for advanced blending for topics such as multi-sampling, alpha-to-coverage, etc., but the minimum we need to set deals with the render target's source and destination blend. In the code listing you can see that we enable alpha blending on the main rendering target and set up the source of the blend to rely on the source color's alpha value and destination to rely on 1 – alpha (inverse of the alpha). This allows us to take the alpha value of the incoming source color and blend it with the destination based on 1 – alpha. In other words, anything with an alpha value of 0.0f for the source will cause the

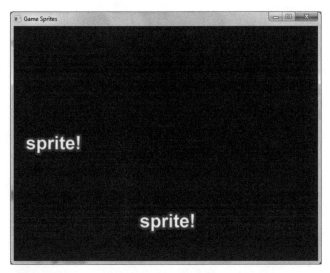

Figure 3.22
Game Sprite demo screenshot.

destination's color to appear, while anything with a 1 will cause the source's color to fully appear. Anything between 0.0f and 1.0f is a blend between the source color (the color of the surface we are rendering) and the destination (the contents of the rendered scene so far).

The last piece of the puzzle, the HLSL shader code, can be seen in Listing 3.18. A screenshot of the running demo can also be seen in Figure 3.22. In the HLSL code we set up the constant buffer using the keyword cbuffer. The cbuffer keyword allows us to create a single constant buffer in HLSL, but the contents within the constant buffer are accessed as if they were normally defined global variables, as you can see in the vertex shader where mvp_ is used directly. The constant buffer we are creating is binding to the input register of b0, whereas textures bind to t0 and higher, and samplers bind to s0 and higher.

The major change in this HLSL set of shaders is the fact that the vertex shader is using the model-view projection matrix to transform the incoming vertex. This is done by simply multiplying the vertex by the matrix. The result is the transformed vertex that is passed down the pipeline to the remaining stages. The pixel shader is unchanged from the Texture Map demo.

Listing 3.18 The Game Sprite demo's HLSL shader code.

```
cbuffer cbChangesPerFrame : register( b0 )
{
    matrix mvp_;
};


Texture2D colorMap_ : register( t0 );
SamplerState colorSampler_ : register( s0 );


struct VS_Input
{
    float4 pos  : POSITION;
    float2 tex0 : TEXCOORD0;
};

struct PS_Input
{
    float4 pos  : SV_POSITION;
    float2 tex0 : TEXCOORD0;
};


PS_Input VS_Main( VS_Input vertex )
{
    PS_Input vsOut = ( PS_Input )0;
    vsOut.pos = mul( vertex.pos, mvp_ );
    vsOut.tex0 = vertex.tex0;

    return vsOut;
}


float4 PS_Main( PS_Input frag ) : SV_TARGET
{
    return colorMap_.Sample( colorSampler_, frag.tex0 );
}
```

Summary

At this point you should have a basic understanding of how sprites and textures work. Using the information presented in this chapter, it's now possible to create a sprite-based demo that you can hopefully build on to create a simple 2D game.

Using Direct3D to draw 2D graphics really came down to using only the X and Y positions of our geometry. We then were able to use the various vector and matrix math code provided by Direct3D to manipulate these 2D objects as we see fit. Technically there is no true 2D mode to Direct3D, and 2D is achieved either using orthographic projection or by placing geometry with only X and Y axes really close to each other in depth. In this chapter we've used orthographic projection, so even if the depth was great between sprites, it wouldn't affect how we view them onscreen. If we used perspective projection, which is commonly used for 3D rendering, then the depth distance plays a greater visual factor and allows us to switch into the realm of 3D.

What You Have Learned

In this chapter you learned the following:

- How textures are loaded.
- What a sprite is and how it's used.

Chapter Questions

Answers to the following chapter review questions can be found in Appendix A on this book's companion website.

1. Define what a texture is.

2. Define what a sprite is. How are sprites different from textures?

3. List at least five different types of textures we've mentioned in this chapter.

4. How many bits are RGB images? How many bits are RGBA images?

5. Define a vertex.

6. Define a triangle.

7. What is the purpose of a vertex buffer? What is the Direct3D 11 object type of buffers?

8. List at least five attributes of a vertex.

9. Define an input layout and what it is used for in Direct3D.

10. What is a vertex shader, and what Direct3D function is used to set (apply) one?

11. What is a pixel shader, and what Direct3D function is used to set (apply) one?

12. List at least three input assembler functions we've used in the rendering functions of our demos.

13. What are MIP levels?

14. What are sampler states, and what is their purpose in Direct3D and HLSL?

15. What are blend states, and for what purpose did we use them in this chapter?

16. Define a matrix.

17. What are the various matrices that make up the model-view projection matrix, and what are their purposes?

18. What are texture address modes? Define each mode of the `D3D11_TEXTURE_ADDRESS_MODE` enumeration.

19. Enabling alpha transparency requires us to create and set what Direct3D 11 object?

20. Why did we decide to use a `XMFLOAT4X4` instead of `XMMATRIX` as the class member in the Game Sprite demo?

On Your Own

Create your own sprite image in the image editor of your choice. Use that newly created image as the texture for the second sprite object.

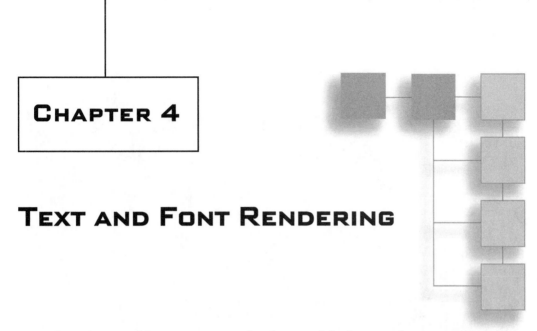

CHAPTER 4

TEXT AND FONT RENDERING

Text doesn't seem like it is going to be that useful when you're writing games; it is a minor feature that doesn't really affect the game. Or is it? Text is used for more than just the title screen or the scrolling credits you see when you've completed a game. Text can be very useful when you have to give the player instructions, designate the goals of the game, or let the user know how many gold coins he has in his inventory. Text can be a valuable tool for user interfaces and feedback as well, such as ammo counters, the player's health or shield amount, energy meters, and so much more.

In this chapter:

- Why fonts and text are useful to game developers.
- How a font system works.
- How to create a simple font system from scratch.
- How to draw text to the screen.

TEXT IN GAMES

From a programmer's standpoint, text can be your best debugging tool. You can add any number of real-time metrics that can be accessible at runtime, such as frame-rate count or text overlays for player names. An example of displaying the frame-rate count and in-game player names in a commercial game can be seen in Figures 4.1 and 4.2.

Figure 4.1
An FPS counter in Epic Games' *Unreal* Development Kit.

In addition, many games implement what is known as a debug console in the game itself, giving them a way to track and manipulate different areas of the game. A debug console is a special screen where users can enter commands using an in-game command prompt to perform different actions. Think about it as a way to type commands into the game to alter values and states, such as displaying the FPS counter in *Unreal Tournament*, entering cheat codes, enabling debugging statistics, spawning objects, changing game properties, etc. An example game console can be seen in Figure 4.2.

Text was also used as a popular way to communicate between players in online matches on the PC. This was often performed by pressing a special chat key button (e.g., the "T" key on the keyboard), either for team chat or global chat,

Figure 4.2
An in-game console in the *Unreal* Development Kit.

and typing in a message that you wished delivered to the screens of other players. Today's home console games for Microsoft's Xbox 360 and Sony's Playstation 3 use microphones and verbal communication for online players, but PC games have historically used text communication as the primary means of communication between players. An example of a text prompt in the Unreal Engine's sample game can be seen in Figure 4.3.

Note

Many home console games indicate that someone is talking by voice chat with a graphical element on the screen such as a speaker or microphone icon next to his in-game nickname/screen name.

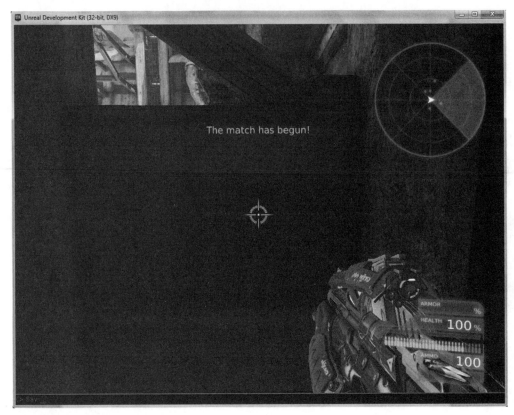

Figure 4.3
A text prompt in the *Unreal* Development Kit.

ADDING TEXT

Over the years, game text has been implemented in multiple ways—textured geometry to the screen, vector drawing, and even just the use of standard message boxes. In modern game development, most game libraries support the concept of text rendering, removing the burden of having to implement this yourself. DirectX does support a method of text rendering prior to Direct3D 11, but Direct3D 11 does not offer the same built-in solutions we once enjoyed. Today we have to manually render our text using a font system based around drawing sprites dynamically, which is also the purpose of this chapter.

The following sections describe how font systems are commonly put together.

Textured Fonts

A font is a series of letters and symbols written in a certain graphical style. For example, the Times New Roman font in Microsoft Word looks different than the Verdana or Arial fonts. In other words, they have different graphical styles. In both 2D and 3D games, text is commonly drawn using textured geometry just as we did with our sprites in Chapter 3. As we've described here, the term *font* is actually applied typography, since the letters and symbols that comprise the font are of a specific artistic style.

Typography is defined as the study, design, and arrangement of type in media. Graphic designers for the web, print, television, etc. look at typography as a very important element in their work. Typography can make or break a design, and there are numerous books dedicated to the subject. Typography is important in games, and its use should never be underestimated. Since our focus is on programming, we will not get caught up in the artistic and graphic design side of things, but be aware that typography is important for designers.

Textured fonts, also known as bitmapped fonts, are based on letters pre drawn into a texture image. The letters are arranged in a grid with a single letter occupying each section of the grid. When it comes time to write out words, the words are built dynamically by drawing the textured letters on the screen. This allows a single series of letters to be used to create any word or phrase you require. Because of the simplistic nature in which the font is used, text rendering can be quite fast. Also, because the fonts are pre drawn on a texture, the look and feel of the text can be changed by altering the applied texture.

Although very useful, textured fonts do have some downsides:

- Textured fonts don't scale well. Because they are pieces of a texture, they can only grow or shrink in size on the screen so much before they become ugly and unreadable due to rendering artifacts.

- The texture must support every possible letter or symbol you might use. This can make texture file sizes quite large.

- Localization. If your game supports multiple languages, you'll need textures with the correct character set (English, Japanese, Chinese, etc.) as well as localized data translating between the languages.

- Because there are different amounts of spacing preceding and following each letter, textured fonts sometimes appear odd when writing certain words because we often use the same amount of space for each character that is not based on that character's actual width. For example, the letter "P" would be wider than the letter "l," but the geometry they are mapped on (the grid space for any single character, as referred to in typography as an em space) would be the same size, leaving more space between some letters than others.

- Creating a robust font system can be quite challenging for the first time.

Textured fonts allow for the buildup of words as they're needed and are managed through some type of font system. Also, textured fonts can be created to match the look and feel of the remainder of the user interface.

A Font System Explained

Occasionally there are instances when it makes sense to hard-code any text in the game into preexisting graphics; a font system is used when the text that you need to draw needs to be drawn dynamically. Examples include when asking for player input, displaying player chat (an example seen in the *Unreal* Development Kit in Figure 4.3), and so forth. If the text is not dynamic, there is little reason to use a font system when a textured square would be sufficient. Of course this might not always be the case.

Imagine that you're playing an RPG and you need to talk to a resident in the village. In a hard-coded text system, what the character says is pre generated into a texture and pulled up at the appropriate time. In other words, we'll need entire textures for every possible conversation exchange in the game. Depending on the amount of text in a single conversation, that could mean a very large number of textures needing to be loaded.

A dynamic text system allows for the buildup of these strings by loading in only a single texture containing all the letters in the font. This method could save load times and large amounts of memory used by textures. In a dynamic system, the text is generated by creating a list of squares side-by-side with texture coordinates matching the region of the desired character.

CREATING A FONT SYSTEM USING SPRITES

Direct3D 11 does not have font and text rendering support as previous versions of Direct3D offered. Therefore we'll take the manual approach to drawing text by looking at a simple example that uses dynamic vertex buffers and texture mapping. On the companion website, the full source code for the text rendering demo, called Direct3D Text, can be found in the Chapter4/Direct3DText folder.

The Direct3D Text demo will build off of the Texture Mapping demo from Chapter 3. In fact, we'll only be adding code to change the vertex buffer from that previous demo into a dynamic buffer, and we'll add a function that fills in that buffer with our textured sprites. Dynamic buffers are optimized for situations where we need to change the contents of a buffer. It is not recommended to ever create and destroy static buffers more than once, especially per-frame. Instead you should always use dynamic buffers for this type of task.

The D3DTextDemo class definition can be seen in Listing 4.1, where the only change from the Texture Mapping demo's class header file is the addition of the function DrawString. DrawString takes as parameters the text we wish to display and the starting X and Y screen positions where the text will begin rendering.

Listing 4.1 The D3DTextDemo class.

```
#ifndef _D3D_TEXT_DEMO_
#define _D3D_TEXT_DEMO_

#include"Dx11DemoBase.h"


class D3DTextDemo : public Dx11DemoBase
{
    public:
        D3DTextDemo( );
        virtual ~D3DTextDemo( );

        bool LoadContent( );
        void UnloadContent( );

        void Update( float dt );
        void Render( );
```

```
   private:
      bool DrawString( char* message, float startX, float startY );

   private:
      ID3D11VertexShader* solidColorVS_;
      ID3D11PixelShader* solidColorPS_;

      ID3D11InputLayout* inputLayout_;
      ID3D11Buffer* vertexBuffer_;

      ID3D11ShaderResourceView* colorMap_;
      ID3D11SamplerState* colorMapSampler_;
};


#endif
```

The demo will work in a straightforward manner. To begin, we'll load a texture image of the letters A through Z. This texture image, shown in Figure 4.4, starts with the A character on the far left and ends with a space on the far right. The space will be used for invalid characters that do not match A through Z. To keep this demo simple we'll only support uppercase letters and no symbols or numbers. Once you've gotten a handle on how this works, you can add support for those items as an additional exercise if you wish to expand upon this text rendering system.

The algorithm for texture rendering using the image seen in Figure 4.4 is simple. For each character in the string we'll create a new sprite. The first sprite starts at the starting X and Y location passed to the DrawString function parameters, and each subsequent sprite (letter) will appear next to the one before it.

In the texture image each letter is 32×32 pixels in size. Since there are 26 letters and one space (empty letter), the image has a resolution of 864×32, since $27 \times 32 = 864$. To keep the code easier to follow, all letters appear one after the other horizontally in the texture image. It also makes it easier to imagine how the texture coordinates and vertex positions are calculated if we don't have to worry about multiple rows and symbols.

To recap, when we create the text's geometry we loop through each character of the string and create a new sprite right next to the last sprite. When we generate the texture coordinates, we use the desired letter to dictate how we set them up. We'll use the empty space at the end of the texture to handle invalid characters.

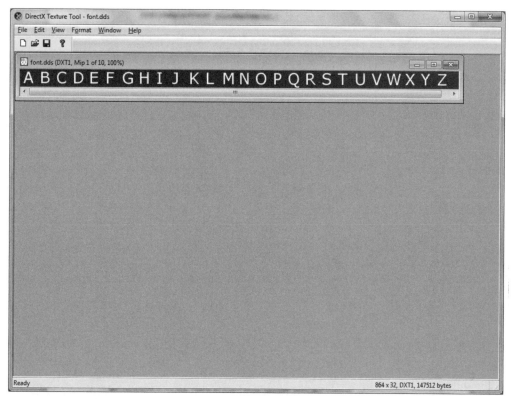

Figure 4.4
The font.dds texture image displayed in the DirectX Texture Tool.

Before we dive into code that generates the text geometry, take a look at the updated Render function in Listing 4.2. The d3dContext_->Draw function from the Texture Mapping demo was replaced with a call to our new DrawString function. DrawString will have the responsibility to both generate the text geometry and render it. The remainder of the function remains the same, with the exception that we are rendering a highly dark blue background for the clear color.

Listing 4.2 Rendering text.

```
void D3DTextDemo::Render( )
{
    if( d3dContext_ == 0 )
```

```
        return;

    float clearColor[4] = { 0.2f, 0.22f, 0.24f, 1.0f };
    d3dContext_->ClearRenderTargetView( backBufferTarget_, clearColor );

    unsigned int stride = sizeof( VertexPos );
    unsigned int offset = 0;

    d3dContext_->IASetInputLayout( inputLayout_ );
    d3dContext_->IASetVertexBuffers( 0, 1, &vertexBuffer_, &stride, &offset );
    d3dContext_->IASetPrimitiveTopology( D3D11_PRIMITIVE_TOPOLOGY_TRIANGLELIST );

    d3dContext_->VSSetShader( solidColorVS_, 0, 0 );
    d3dContext_->PSSetShader( solidColorPS_, 0, 0 );
    d3dContext_->PSSetShaderResources( 0, 1, &colorMap_ );
    d3dContext_->PSSetSamplers( 0, 1, &colorMapSampler_ );

    DrawString( "HELLO WORLD", -0.2f, 0.0f );

    swapChain_->Present( 0, 0 );
}
```

Also let's take a look at the updated LoadContent function. The only changes here are that we are loading a texture image called font.dds (instead of decal.dds from the Texture Mapping demo), and we are creating a dynamic vertex buffer. To create a dynamic vertex buffer we perform the following steps:

1. Set the usage to D3D11_USAGE_DYNAMIC to allow our buffer to be updated dynamically by the CPU. In the previous demos this was set to D3D11_USAGE_DEFAULT for static buffers.

2. Set the CPU access flags to D3D11_CPU_ACCESS_WRITE. This must be done in order to grant the CPU write access for a resource within the GPU. Other access flags include read and read/write access, but we only need to write because the CPU does not need to read anything for this demo.

3. When creating the vertex buffer we can set null for the sub-resource parameter (parameter 2). Since we are dynamically updating the vertex buffer's contents, we don't need to set any data at this point.

With the dynamic buffer created, we are able to update its contents at any time. The changes we've made to the LoadContent function from the Texture Mapping demo can be seen in Listing 4.3. Since the DrawString function will create the geometry, we also deleted the code from the Texture Mapping demo that defined the two triangles and the code that copied that triangle data using the sub-resource Direct3D 11 object. Also notice in Listing 4.3 that we set up the vertex buffer to store up to 24 sprites (i.e., 24 letters). You can change the max character size if you desire.

Listing 4.3 Updating the LoadContent function.

```
bool D3DTextDemo::LoadContent( )
{
    ...

    d3dResult = D3DX11CreateShaderResourceViewFromFile( d3dDevice_,
        "font.dds", 0, 0, &colorMap_, 0 );

    ...

    D3D11_BUFFER_DESC vertexDesc;
    ZeroMemory( &vertexDesc, sizeof( vertexDesc ) );
    vertexDesc.Usage = D3D11_USAGE_DYNAMIC;
    vertexDesc.CPUAccessFlags = D3D11_CPU_ACCESS_WRITE;
    vertexDesc.BindFlags = D3D11_BIND_VERTEX_BUFFER;

    const int sizeOfSprite = sizeof( VertexPos ) * 6;
    const int maxLetters = 24;

    vertexDesc.ByteWidth = sizeOfSprite * maxLetters;

    d3dResult = d3dDevice_->CreateBuffer( &vertexDesc, 0, &vertexBuffer_ );

    if( FAILED( d3dResult ) )
    {
        DXTRACE_MSG( "Failed to create vertex buffer!" );
        return false;
    }
    return true;
}
```

The final function in this demo is the `DrawString` function, which is also the function that performs all the work. This function is a bit long, so we'll look at it in sections. In the first section we set up for values that we'll need for the algorithm. These values are broken down as follows:

- **`sizeOfSprite`**—The size of a single sprite in bytes. A sprite is two triangles made up of six vertices. This constant is here to aid in readability.

- **`maxLetters`**—We are coding this demo to be able to render up to 24 characters at a time for simplicity, but you can always make this more robust in the future once you have a handle on this topic.

- **`length`**—The length of the string we are attempting to render.

- **`charWidth`**—The width of an individual letter in screen coordinates.

- **`charHeight`**—The height of an individual letter in screen coordinates.

- **`texelWidth`**—The width of an individual letter in the texture image.

- **`verticesPerLetter`**—A constant storing the total vertices in each sprite (two triangles at six vertices).

For strings longer than 24 characters, we'll clamp the total letters drawn to 24, else we'll draw only the total number of letters in the string's size. The first section of the `DrawString` function with the values we'll be using for the algorithm can be seen in Listing 4.4.

Listing 4.4 The `DrawString` function.

```
bool D3DTextDemo::DrawString( char* message, float startX, float startY )
{
    // Size in bytes for a single sprite.
    const int sizeOfSprite = sizeof( VertexPos ) * 6;

    // Demo's dynamic buffer set up for max of 24 letters.
    const int maxLetters = 24;

    int length = strlen( message );

    // Clamp for strings too long.
    if( length > maxLetters )
```

```
        length = maxLetters;

    // Char's width on screen.
    float charWidth = 32.0f / 800.0f;

    // Char's height on screen.
    float charHeight = 32.0f / 640.0f;

    // Char's texel width.
    float texelWidth = 32.0f / 864.0f;

    // verts per-triangle (3) * total triangles (2) = 6.
    const int verticesPerLetter = 6;

    ...
}
```

To update the contents of a dynamic buffer we need to call the Direct3D context's Map function. The Map function takes as parameters the buffer we are mapping, the sub-resource index (set to 0 since there are not multiple sub-resources), the mapping type, the map flags, and the mapped sub-resource that will hold the obtained data. The mapping type in this demo is D3D11_MAP_WRITE_DISCARD, which tells Direct3D that the previous values in the buffer should be considered undefined. For other map types, the map flags can be D3D11_MAP_FLAG_DO_NOT_WAIT, but while using D3D11_MAP_WRITE_DISCARD we must use 0 for the map flags since D3D11_MAP_FLAG_ DO_NOT_WAIT cannot be used with this mapping type.

Once Map has succeeded we will then have access to the buffer's contents via the D3D11_MAPPED_SUBRESOURCE object we passed to the final parameter. To update the buffer we can simply copy whatever data we want to the D3D11_MAPPED_SU-BRESOURCE's pData member. The mapping section (second section) of the Draw-String function can be seen in Listing 4.5. We also set up values that tell us the ASCII values of the letters A and Z, which will be used in Listing 4.6 when we loop through and generate the string geometry.

Listing 4.5 Mapping of our vertex buffer.

```
bool D3DTextDemo::DrawString( char* message, float startX, float startY )
{
    ...
```

```
D3D11_MAPPED_SUBRESOURCE mapResource;
HRESULT d3dResult = d3dContext_->Map( vertexBuffer_, 0,
    D3D11_MAP_WRITE_DISCARD, 0, &mapResource );

if( FAILED( d3dResult ) )
{
    DXTRACE_MSG( "Failed to map resource!" );
    return false;
}

// Point to our vertex buffer's internal data.
VertexPos *spritePtr = ( VertexPos* )mapResource.pData;

const int indexA = static_cast<char>( 'A' );
const int indexZ = static_cast<char>( 'Z' );


    ...
}
```

In Listing 4.5 we obtain a pointer to the pData of the sub-resource so that we can loop through and set the geometry that will make up the string. To do this we use a for-loop that iterates over the entire string. For each character, we set the starting X and Y positions for the character. For the first character, the starting X will be the startX parameter of the DrawString function. As we loop through the characters, we essentially want to add the width of a character to this starting position to get the next. By using the loop index we can multiply that by the size of a character's width and add that to the starting position to get the current letter's position, which also allows us to not have to keep track of the previous X position, since this formula easily calculates the value we are looking for.

The starting X position is the left side of the sprite, and the ending X position is the right side of the character, which is simply the start X position plus the size of an individual character.

Once we have set the vertex positions, we must do the same with the texture coordinates. The texture coordinates are set in the same fashion, with one minor difference. Instead of using the loop index as the positions did, for texture coordinates generation we use the letter itself. This can be easily done by calculating the ASCII value of the letter, which is equivalent to casting it to an integer. Since the first letter in our font.dds image is the letter A, if we subtract the

ASCII value of the current letter by the ASCII value of A, we can get a value of 0 if the current letter is A, 1 if it is B, and so forth. We can use this value, called texLookup in the DrawString function in the exact same manner as we used the loop index for the creation of the geometry positions. Just as the loop index i starts at 0 and increments upward, the texLookup variable starts at 0 for the first letter (A) and increments upward.

The texture coordinates usually range from 0.0 to 1.0. Our starting TU texture coordinate will always be 0.0 for the first letter. In the DrawString function this is written mostly for consistency rather than necessity.

The texture coordinate formula matches the geometry formula exactly upon closer inspection. For any invalid character, we set it to the last character in the font.dds image, which is just an empty 32×32 space at the end of the image. We access this space by assuming that the current letter is 1 + Z because our font texture is set up to have the space appear after the Z graphic. The geometry generation of the DrawString function can be seen in Listing 4.6.

Listing 4.6 The loop in the DrawString function that creates the text.

```
bool D3DTextDemo::DrawString( char* message, float startX, float startY )
{
    ...

    for( int i = 0; i < length; ++i )
    {
        float thisStartX = startX + ( charWidth * static_cast<float>( i ) );
        float thisEndX = thisStartX + charWidth;
        float thisEndY = startY + charHeight;

        spritePtr[0].pos = XMFLOAT3( thisEndX,   thisEndY, 1.0f );
        spritePtr[1].pos = XMFLOAT3( thisEndX,   startY,   1.0f );
        spritePtr[2].pos = XMFLOAT3( thisStartX, startY,   1.0f );
        spritePtr[3].pos = XMFLOAT3( thisStartX, startY,   1.0f );
        spritePtr[4].pos = XMFLOAT3( thisStartX, thisEndY, 1.0f );
        spritePtr[5].pos = XMFLOAT3( thisEndX,   thisEndY, 1.0f );

        int texLookup = 0;
        int letter = static_cast<char>( message[i] );
```

```
if( letter < indexA || letter > indexZ )
{
    // Grab one index past Z, which is a blank space in the texture.
    texLookup = ( indexZ - indexA ) + 1;
}
else
{
    // A = 0, B = 1, Z = 25, etc.
    texLookup = ( letter - indexA );
}

float tuStart = 0.0f + ( texelWidth * static_cast<float>( texLookup ) );
float tuEnd = tuStart + texelWidth;

spritePtr[0].tex0 = XMFLOAT2( tuEnd, 0.0f );
spritePtr[1].tex0 = XMFLOAT2( tuEnd, 1.0f );
spritePtr[2].tex0 = XMFLOAT2( tuStart, 1.0f );
spritePtr[3].tex0 = XMFLOAT2( tuStart, 1.0f );
spritePtr[4].tex0 = XMFLOAT2( tuStart, 0.0f );
spritePtr[5].tex0 = XMFLOAT2( tuEnd, 0.0f );

spritePtr += 6;
}


...
}
```

The final step in the DrawString function is to unmap the vertex buffer. Unmapping must be done for any resource that was mapped by calling the device context's Unmap function, which takes the buffer to unmap and the sub-resource index. With the vertex buffer updated with the necessary sprites to draw our text, we can call the Draw function to display our results. The Draw function takes six times the length of the string for the vertex count because we have six vertices for each sprite, and the length of the string represents the total sprites we are drawing.

The final section of the DrawString function can be seen in Listing 4.7. A screenshot of the Direct3D Text demo can be seen in Figure 4.5.

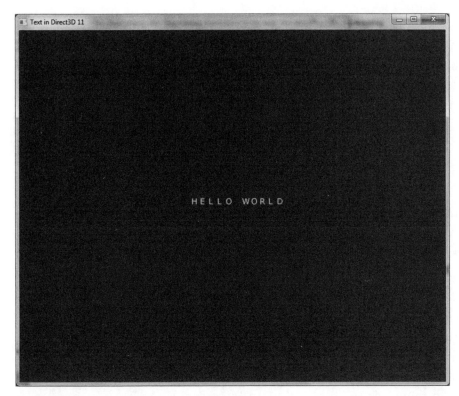

Figure 4.5
A screenshot of the Direct3D Text demo.

Listing 4.7 The unmapping and drawing of our text.

```
bool D3DTextDemo::DrawString( char* message, float startX, float startY )
{
    ...

    d3dContext_->Unmap( vertexBuffer_, 0 );
    d3dContext_->Draw( 6 * length, 0 );

    return true;
}
```

ADVANCED TOPICS

There are many uses for text in video games. Some of these uses we've seen in this chapter, and others you no doubt have seen in commercial games. Although additional uses for text beyond what was covered in this chapter are beyond the scope of this book, at www.UltimateGameProgramming.com there are several tutorials aimed at making more advanced use of text. If you're interested, these tutorials can be very useful when expanding your knowledge past the beginner level. These tutorials include the following:

- Implementing text boxes (and other interface elements)
- In-game debug console
- Game screens
- In-game heads-up display (HUD)

In-Game Text Boxes

Text boxes sound like a simple concept, but their implementation takes some thought. A text box is not only its graphical element for where text is entered, but it also must display text on top of it. This would be simple, but we would also have to add to it the ability for the text box to scroll the text for strings larger than the text box's area. We would need to consider a visual cue to indicate that the text box is ready to accept input, such as a flickering vertical line as seen in many text editors including Microsoft Word.

In-Game Console Window

An in-game console is another tricky-to-implement concept. For starters, the console window itself must store multiple lines of text for the past commands and system text that were submitted. This can be done by displaying multiple lines of text on top of a full-screen textured background (or even no background and display on top of the game screen itself). The text itself would most likely be stored in an array that stores the most recent text from oldest to newest.

The second part of the in-game console will be to provide a text box area for user input, which was described in the previous section, "In-Game Text Boxes." The combination of the string array display and the text box will allow us to create a good in-game console display.

But wait—there is one more thing. For any commands entered into the in-game console, the game and/or game engine will have to process those commands and perform the actions they require. This can be done using what is known as command scripting, a topic that is covered on www.UltimateGameProgramming. com. With a command script processor in place, the commands entered into the in-game console can be executed by the game.

Game Menus

A game's menu system is far more complex than one would originally assume without having had any experience implementing them. Game menus are part of a bigger concept known as game screens. There can be title screens, which are screens that appear usually with developer and publisher names in text or video before the main menu appears, the main menu itself, a start game menu screen, a load game screen, an options screen, a high score screen, and many more. In commercial games these screens can look and act in very complex ways, such as in the UDK seen in Figure 4.6.

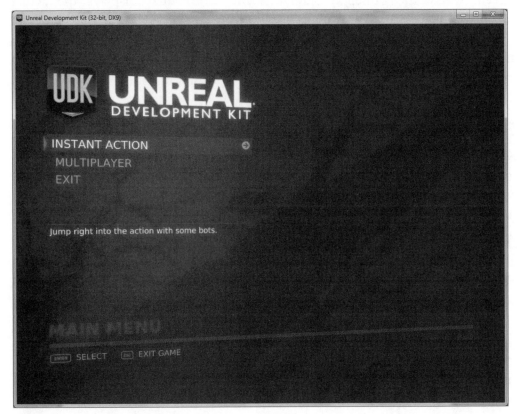

Figure 4.6
Game menu screens in the *Unreal* Development Kit.

Other screens include the game screen (the screen responsible for playing the actual game), a pause menu screen, a multiplayer lobby screen, a control setup screen, and many more. The next time you are playing a commercial game, notice how many different views and screens often appear. Usually there are many.

Note

Microsoft has released a game screen demo and its source for their XNA Game Studio Express, which is available at http://creators.xna.com.

Heads-Up Display

Heads-up display is a special type of screen displayed over the primary gameplay screen, where the gameplay screen is the screen that displays the actual gameplay. The heads-up display, also known as the HUD, is the graphical element that appear on top of the action. This can include timers, ammo amounts, health indicators, enemy radar, and so forth. An example of a HUD can be seen in Figure 4.7.

Summary

Knowing how to draw text to the screen can be a useful skill. You should be able to easily implement font rendering using the Direct3D font object, or you can roll out your own text rendering system if desired. By manipulating where the text is placed, the text can be used for real-time debugging information or as part of your user interface.

Taking the concepts you've learned up to this point, you can create your own heads-up displays and game menus. This is more advanced and is definitely a subject to explore once you've mastered this book.

Chapter Questions

Answers to the following chapter review questions can be found in Appendix A on this book's companion website.

Figure 4.7
Heads-up display.

1. What is another term for textured fonts?

   A. Sprite

   B. Textured sprite

   C. Bitmap font

   D. None of the above

2. What is a font?

   A. A style of characters.

   B. A string of text.

   C. A type of sprite.

   D. None of the above.

3. True or False: Static text is best displayed using texture-mapped surfaces, not dynamically created sprites.

   A. True

   B. False

4. True or False: Write/discard map types must use the `D3D11_MAP_FLAG_DO_NOT_WAIT` flag.

   A. True

   B. False

5. True or False: Direct3D has built-in text rendering.

   A. True

   B. False

On Your Own

1. Add alpha blending to the sprite-based font system.

2. Write a `Render` function that is capable of drawing multiple lines of text.

3. Add lowercase letters and numbers to the system.

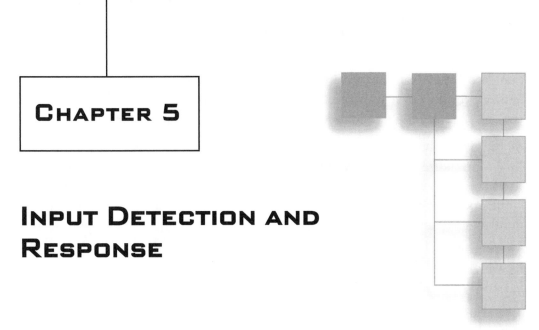

CHAPTER 5

INPUT DETECTION AND RESPONSE

Being able to interact with your virtual world is critical in any game—be it through the keyboard, mouse, or any number of other devices. In this chapter we'll explain the benefits of the various options for performing input detection and how to use them.

In this chapter:

- Examine the various methods of input detection
- How DirectInput can make your life easier
- How to detect the input devices currently installed
- How to use keyboards, mice, and joysticks
- How to use Xbox 360 controllers

I NEED INPUT

Every game needs the ability to interact with its user. Whether through a keyboard, mouse, dance pad, or other device, your game needs a way of getting direction from the person playing. The input device can be used to drive a car around a track, move your character around in its world, or anything else that you can imagine.

Back in the days of DOS, game developers had very little choice but to poll hardware interrupts if they wanted to get keystrokes from the keyboard.

Standard C functions of the time, such as getchar, were too slow to be useful for games. Developers needed a better way; enter the Basic Input Output System (BIOS). The BIOS is the lowest level of software in a computer.

Stored normally in a flash ROM on the motherboard, the BIOS tells the system how to initialize and prepares the hardware for the operating system. The BIOS itself used to be directly accessible to programmers through assembly language while under DOS. Since the BIOS knew everything that the hardware was doing, developers were able to ask it for certain information. One of the important bits of the system that the BIOS was always watching was the keyboard. Every stroke of a key triggered a hardware interrupt, informing the system that a key had been pressed. Since this happened almost instantaneously, a very quick and efficient method for getting keystrokes from the keyboard was available.

When Windows NT came along, the ability to read the keyboard directly from the hardware was eliminated. Windows became an absolute boundary between applications and the hardware. Any information needed about the system had to be gained from the operating system because applications were no longer allowed direct access to the hardware. Windows had its own way of getting user input, and that was through the message queue. An example message queue is as follows:

```
MSG msg = {0};

while (WM_QUIT != msg.message)
{
    while( PeekMessage( &msg, NULL, 0U, 0U, PM_REMOVE ) == TRUE )
    {
        TranslateMessage( &msg );
        DispatchMessage( &msg );
    }
}
```

The message queue collects events, such as mouse movement and keyboard input, from the system. While this method is normally sufficient for Windows applications, it isn't fast enough for games. Most developers at this point turned to another Windows function, GetAsyncKeyState, to get the information they needed. GetAsyncKeyState's function prototype is as follows, where its only parameter is a virtual key code:

```
SHORT WINAPI GetAsyncKeyState( int vKey );
```

There are virtual key codes for every key on the keyboard; each is listed in the MSDN documentation. The GetAsyncKeyState function allowed for very quick checking of the keys on the keyboard and even allowed for checking of multiple keys and the state of the mouse buttons. This method of collecting user input became common among game developers, but it had one major issue: It didn't allow for input to be collected from other devices such as game pads and joysticks. Game makers were stuck specifically supporting only certain devices because each device had a different way of collecting and transmitting the input data to the system.

A standard way of getting fast input from the user was needed regardless of the method or device used. The DirectX SDK offered DirectInput, which provided the common layer needed to solve this problem.

Input Options

In this chapter we will look at obtaining input using various Win32 functions such as GetAsyncKeyState, DirectInput, and XInput. DirectInput allows your game to support a myriad of input devices without forcing you to know the exact details of each device. A small sample of the devices supported by DirectInput is shown here.

- Keyboards
- Mice
- Game pads
- Joysticks
- Steering wheels

DirectInput was last updated in DirectX 8 and is generally considered deprecated. But Microsoft's new API XInput only supports Xbox 360 controllers, which means that XInput does not support keyboards and mice devices. We can still use DirectInput for keyboards and mice, but we could easily obtain the states of these devices using various Win32 functions, which we'll see throughout this chapter. For game pads and other next-generation controllers for the Windows OS it is recommended to use XInput.

Unfortunately this alienates non-Xbox 360 controllers, and if the need to support these devices exists, developers can still fall back to DirectInput since there are no Win32 functions for game controllers in the same way there are for mice and keyboards. Because a need to support these devices still exists, and since XInput does not support them, DirectInput is still a viable solution that is worth learning.

XInput is a relatively new API that first hit the scene in the later versions of DirectX 9 and is available for detecting input from Xbox 360 game controllers. Game controllers include not only the standard Xbox 360 game pad but also these various devices:

- Arcade sticks
- *Guitar Hero/Rock Band* musical instruments
- Big button controllers
- Dance pads
- And more

In this chapter we will look at detecting keyboard and mouse input by obtaining the device states using Win32 functions as well as through DirectInput. We'll also look at how to detect input from Xbox 360 controllers through XInput.

KEYBOARD INPUT

The keyboard is one of two devices that we can assume a PC user has. Keyboards and mice will likely always be highly important for PC games and the gamers who support the platform.

In this section we will briefly discuss three options of obtaining input via the keyboard in Windows. The first is to use the message queue, the second is to obtain the key states via Win32 functions such as GetAsyncKeyState, and the third is to use DirectInput.

Win32 Keyboard Input

Win32 applications that we've been developing throughout this book have generally used the following windows procedure callback function for events:

```
LRESULT CALLBACK WndProc( HWND hwnd, UINT message, WPARAM wParam, LPARAM lParam )
{
    PAINTSTRUCT paintStruct;
    HDC hDC;

    switch( message )
    {
        case WM_PAINT:
            hDC = BeginPaint( hwnd, &paintStruct );
            EndPaint( hwnd, &paintStruct );
            break;

        case WM_DESTROY:
            PostQuitMessage( 0 );
            break;

        default:
            return DefWindowProc( hwnd, message, wParam, lParam );
    }

    return 0;
}
```

There are a ton of events that we could support, one of which is the WM_KEY DOWN and WM_KEYUP events for keyboard actions. As an example, responding to the Escape key being pressed, and exiting the application as a result, would look like this:

```
LRESULT CALLBACK WndProc(HWND hwnd, UINT message, WPARAM wParam, LPARAM lParam)
{
    PAINTSTRUCT paintStruct;
    HDC hDC;

    switch( message )
    {
        case WM_PAINT:
            hDC = BeginPaint( hwnd, &paintStruct );
            EndPaint( hwnd, &paintStruct );
            break;

        case WM_DESTROY:
```

```
                PostQuitMessage( 0 );
                break;

        case WM_KEYDOWN:
            switch(wParam)
            {
                case VK_ESCAPE:
                    PostQuitMessage(0);
                    break;
            }
            break;


        default:
            return DefWindowProc( hwnd, message, wParam, lParam );
    }

    return 0;
}
```

The main problem with the message queue is that this method is far too slow. This method relies on the operating system sending the message to the application that a key was pressed. This is not instant, and there is often a delay between messages. For video games it is highly recommended that you avoid the message queue.

A better option is to obtain the state of the device the moment we want it (e.g., every frame). This can easily be done in our demos by adding the following code to the Update function:

```
void KeyboardDemo::Update( float dt )
{
    if( GetAsyncKeyState( VK_ESCAPE ) )
    {
        PostQuitMessage( 0 );
    }
}
```

We can use GetAsyncKeyState to essentially tell us if a button is being pressed. The only parameter to this function is the virtual key code for the keyboard button we want to test for, and this provides an easy method to detect keyboard input. There is also the option to use the Win32 functions `GetKeyState` and `GetKeyboardState`, whose prototypes can be seen as follows:

```
SHORT WINAPI GetKeyState( int nVirtKey );

BOOL WINAPI GetKeyboardState( PBYTE lpKeyState );
```

DirectInput Keyboard Input

DirectInput is initialized in a very similar manner to other DirectX components, requiring the creation of both a DirectInput object as well as an input device.

The DirectInput object provides the interface needed to access DirectInput devices. Through this interface, you are able to create an instance of a device, enumerate the devices on a system, or check the status of a particular device.

Once you have the DirectInput object created, you have to create the device. The DirectInput device that you create will enable you to gain specific access to an input device, be it a keyboard, joystick, or other gaming device.

After creating the device, you need to gain access to its input. This is done through a process called acquiring a device. When you acquire a device, you are provided with access to initialize the device, get a list of its capabilities, or read its input.

It may seem like a lot of trouble to go through just to get a couple of keystrokes from a keyboard or game pad, but having direct access to your input device will make your life simpler later on.

Now that you have access to the device, you're able to read input from it each frame. For example, if you are using a game pad as your input device, you can check to see if the user has pressed the direction buttons or if one of the predefined action buttons has been pressed. If so, you can then act on this information.

At this point, you should have a clear understanding of the process needed to get DirectInput up and running and getting data from an input device. We'll now walk you through the code needed to do just that.

Creating the DirectInput Object

As mentioned, the first step to using DirectInput is the creation of the DirectInput object. The function `DirectInput8Create` is used to create the DirectInput object.

The `DirectInput8Create` function is defined as:

```
HRESULT WINAPI DirectInput8Create(
HINSTANCE hinst,
DWORD dwVersion,
REFIID riidltf,
LPVOID *ppvOut,
LPUNKNOWN punkOuter );
```

Five parameters need to be passed to the `DirectInput8Create` function.

- `hInst`. An instance to the application that is creating the DirectInput object.

- `dwVersion`. This is the version number of DirectInput that this application requires. The standard value for this parameter is `DIRECTINPUT_ VERSION`.

- `riidltf`. The identifier of the required interface. Using the default value of `IID_IDirectInput8` is acceptable for this parameter.

- `ppvOut`. The pointer to the variable that will hold the created `DirectInput` object.

- `punkOuter`. This parameter is normally set to null.

Below is a small snippet of code that will create a DirectInput object.

```
LPDIRECTINPUT8 directInputObject;

HRESULT hr = DirectInput8Create( hInst, DIRECTINPUT_VERSION,
    IID_IDirectInput8, ( void** )&directInputObject, 0 );

if FAILED( hr )
{
    return false;
}
```

Note

As a reminder, make sure to check the return value when creating DirectX objects. This will let you know when an object creation has failed as well as help you track down bugs in your code. A failure with a call to `DirectInput8Create` could possibly indicate a problem with the DirectX runtime, which can occur if the runtime was not installed properly.

The preceding code first creates two variables: hr and directInputObject. The first variable, hr, is defined as a standard HRESULT. This variable is used to check the return code of a function call. The second variable, directInputObject, is used to hold the soon-to-be-created DirectInput object.

The code then continues by making the call to DirectInput8Create. A quick check of the return code in the variable hr is done to make sure that the function returned successfully.

Creating the DirectInput Device

Now that you have a valid DirectInput object, you are free to create the device. The device is created using the function CreateDevice.

```
HRESULT CreateDevice( REFGUID rguid, LPDIRECTINPUTDEVICE *lplpDirectInputDe
vice, LPUNKNOWN pUnkOuter  );
```

The CreateDevice function requires three parameters. The first parameter will be either GUID_SysKeyboard or GUID_SysMouse for keyboards and mice devices, respectively, the second will be an out address for the DirectInput device object being created, and a final parameter will deal with COM interfaces. Most applications will set the third parameter to null.

The following code assumes that you want to create a DirectInput device for an installed system keyboard.

```
LPDIRECTINPUTDEVICE8 keyboardDevice;

HRESULT hr = directInputObject ->CreateDevice( GUID_SysKeyboard,
    &keyboardDevice, 0 );

if FAILED(hr)
{
    return false;
}
```

The preceding code first creates the object keyboardDevice. This type LPDIR ECTINPUTDEVICE8 is used to hold the created DirectInput device.

The call to CreateDevice, which is a method available to you through the DirectInput object, is made by passing in the value GUID_SysKeyboard as the first parameter. This tells CreateDevice that you want a device object created based on the system keyboard. The second parameter is the device object that will be created as a result of this function call, and the third parameter dealing with COM interfaces is null.

After this function call is complete, the keyboard device will hold a valid DirectInput device. Be sure that the return code for this function is checked to confirm that the device is valid.

Setting the Data Format

After a valid DirectInput device has been created, you need to set up the data format that DirectInput will use to read input from the device. The SetData Format function defined next requires a DIDATAFORMAT structure as its only parameter.

```
HRESULT SetDataFormat( LPCDIDATAFORMAT lpdf )
```

The DIDATAFORMAT structure describes various elements of the device for DirectInput. The DIDATAFORMAT structure is defined here:

```
typedef struct DIDATAFORMAT
{
    DWORD dwSize;
    DWORD dwObjSize;
    DWORD dwFlags;
    DWORD dwDataSize;
    DWORD dwNumObjs;
    LPDIOBJECTDATAFORMAT rgodf;
} DIDATAFORMAT, *LPDIDATAFORMAT;
```

It is necessary to create and use your own DIDATAFORMAT structure if the input device you want to use is not a standard device. There are a number of predefined DIDATAFORMAT structures for common input devices.

- c_dfDIKeyboard

- c_dfDIMouse

- c_dfDIMouse2

- c_dfDIJoystick

- c_dfDIJoystick2

If the input device you want to use is not included as one of the predefined types, you will need to specifically create a DIDATAFORMAT object. Most of the common input devices will not require this since it is rare to need the ability to create a custom data format.

The following code sample calls the SetDataFormat function using the predefined DIDATAFORMAT structure for a keyboard device.

```
HRESULT hr = keyboardDevice ->SetDataFormat( &c_dfDIKeyboard );

if FAILED(hr)
{
    return false;
}
```

Setting the Cooperation Level

The cooperative level is needed to tell the system how the input device that you are creating will work with the system. Input devices can be set to use either exclusive or non-exclusive access. Exclusive access means that only your application has the ability to use a particular device and does not need to share it with other applications that Windows may be running. This is most useful when your game is a full-screen application. When a device, such as the mouse or keyboard, is being used exclusively by a game, any attempt for another application to use this device will fail.

If your game doesn't mind sharing the device, then this is called non-exclusive access. When a game creates the device with non-exclusive access, other applications running will be able to use that same device. This is most useful when your game is running in windowed mode on the Windows desktop. Using the mouse as a non-exclusive input device will not restrict the use of the mouse in other application windows.

Each game that uses a DirectInput device must set the cooperative level for its use. This is done through the function SetCooperativeLevel, defined here:

```
HRESULT SetCooperativeLevel( HWND hwnd, DWORD dwFlags );
```

The SetCooperativeLevel function requires only two parameters, where the first parameter is a handle to the window that is requesting access to the device and the second is a series of flags that describe the type of access you are requesting. The available flags are these:

- DISCL_BACKGROUND. The application is requiring background access to the device, which means that the input device can be used even when the game window is not the window currently active.

- DISCL_EXCLUSIVE. The game is requesting complete and exclusive control over the device.

- DISCL_FOREGROUND. The game only requires input when the window is the current active window on the desktop. If the game window loses focus, input to this window is halted.

- DISCL_NONEXCLUSIVE. Exclusive access is not needed, and the device can be shared with other applications.

- DISCL_NOWINKEY. This tells DirectInput to disable the Windows key on the keyboard.

Note

Each application must specify whether it needs foreground or background access to the device by setting either the DISCL_BACKGROUND or DISCL_FOREGROUND flag. The application is also required to set either the DISCL_EXCLUSIVE or DISCL_NONEXCLUSIVE flag. The DISCL_NOWINKEY flag is completely optional.

The following code sample sets the device to use non-exclusive access and only be active when the application window has focus.

```
hr = keyboardDevice->SetCooperativeLevel( hwnd,
    DISCL_FOREGROUND | DISCL_NONEXCLUSIVE );

if FAILED(hr)
{
    return false;
}
```

You'll notice that the SetCooperativeLevel function is a method callable through the DirectInput device interface. The keyboardDevice object above represents the current DirectInput device created by the call to CreateDevice.

The parameters being passed in the example `SetCooperativeLevel` function above consist of `hwnd`, which represents the handle to the window requesting access to the input device, and the flags `DISCL_FOREGROUND` and `DISCL_NONEX CLUSIVE`, telling DirectInput the access you are requesting for the device.

Acquiring the Device

The final step required before you are able to read input from a particular device is called "acquiring the device." When you acquire access to an input device, you are telling the system that you are ready to use and read from this device. The function `Acquire`, another method of the DirectInput device, performs this action. The `Acquire` function, defined next, takes no parameters and returns only whether or not it was successful.

```
HRESULT Acquire( VOID );
```

The following small code example shows how the `Acquire` function is called:

```
HRESULT hr = keyboardDevice->Acquire( );

If( FAILED( hr ) )
{
    return false;
}
```

You'll notice again that the return code for this function is checked to make sure it was completed successfully. Since this is the last step needed before reading input from a device, it's best to check the return code to make sure the device is ready and available.

Getting Input

Now that we've completed the required steps to initialize an input device through DirectInput, it's time to actually use it. All devices use the function `GetDeviceState` when reading input. Whether the input device is a keyboard, mouse, or game pad, the `GetDeviceState` function is used.

```
HRESULT GetDeviceState( DWORD cbData, LPVOID lpvData );
```

The first parameter required is a `DWORD` value that holds the size of the buffer being passed as the second parameter. The second parameter is a pointer to the buffer that will hold the data read from the device. As a reminder, the format of the data from the input device was defined earlier using the `SetDataFormat` function.

The next few sections will show how to enumerate the input devices available to your application through DirectInput.

Enumerating Input Devices

Most games available for the PC allow for use of input devices other than a keyboard or a mouse, such as a game pad or joystick. Many computers do not have these non-standard devices by default, so DirectInput cannot just assume their presence. Also, since Windows allows for multiple game pads or joysticks to be installed simultaneously, DirectInput needs a way of determining how many and what type these devices are. The method DirectInput uses to get the needed information on the input devices is called enumeration.

Just as Direct3D can enumerate through the video adapters installed in a system and get the capabilities of each, DirectInput can do the same for input devices.

Using functions available through the DirectInput object, DirectInput is able to retrieve the number of input devices available in a system as well as each one's type and functionality. For instance, if your game requires the use of a game pad with an analog control stick, you can enumerate the installed devices and see if any of them meet your criteria.

The process of enumerating the installed devices on a system requires first gathering a list of the devices that meet your input need, and secondly gathering the specific capabilities of these devices.

DirectInput uses the function EnumDevices to gather the list of installed input devices. Since there are different types of devices possibly installed on a machine, and you probably wouldn't be interested in getting a list of them all, EnumDevices allows you to specify the type of devices you are searching for. For instance, if you're not interested in the mouse and keyboard devices and are searching specifically for joystick devices, EnumDevices provides a way of eliminating the unwanted devices from the list.

First we'll explain how EnumDevices is used. The function EnumDevices is defined as:

```
HRESULT EnumDevices( DWORD dwDevType, LPDIENUMDEVICESCALLBACK lpCallback,
    LPVOID pvRef, DWORD dwFlags );
```

This function requires four parameters.

- `dwDevType`. This parameter sets the filter for the device search. As mentioned above, you can tell `EnumDevices` to only search the system for a particular type of device.

- `lpCallback`. `EnumDevices` utilizes a callback mechanism when searching the system for input devices. This parameter is the address of the function you define to work as the callback.

- `pvRef`. This parameter is used to pass data to the callback function defined in the `lpCallback` parameter. Any 32-bit value can be used here. If no information is needed to be sent to the callback function, then you can pass `NULL`.

- `dwFlags`. The final parameter is a `DWORD` value consisting of a set of flags letting `EnumDevices` know the scope of the enumeration.

The `dwDevType` can have one of the following values:

- `DI8DEVCLASS_ALL`. This value will cause `EnumDevices` to return a list of all input devices installed in a system.

- `DI8DEVCLASS_DEVICE`. This value will cause a search for devices that do not fall into another class of device, such as keyboard, mice, or game controllers.

- `DI8DEVCLASS_GAMECTRL`. This causes `EnumDevices` to search for all game controller types of devices, such as game pads or joysticks.

- `DI8DEVCLASS_KEYBOARD`. `EnumDevices` will search the system for all keyboard devices.

- `DI8DEVCLASS_POINTER`. This value tells `EnumDevices` to search for pointer devices, such as mice.

The value of `dwFlags` can be one of the following:

- `DIEDFL_ALLDEVICES`. This is the default value. All devices in the system will be enumerated.

- `DIEDFL_ATTACHEDONLY`. Only devices currently attached to the system are returned.

- `DIEDFL_FORCEFEEDBACK`. Only the devices supporting force feedback will be returned.

- DIEDFL_INCLUDEALIASES. Windows allows aliases to be created for devices. These aliases appear to the system as input devices, but they represent another device in the system.

- DIEDFL_INCLUDEHIDDEN. This causes EnumDevices to only return hidden devices.

- DIEDFL_INCLUDEPHANTOMS. Phantom devices are placeholder devices.

The following code sample utilizes the EnumDevices function call to gather a list of game controllers that are currently attached to the system.

```
HRESULT hr;

hr = directInputObject->EnumDevices( DI8DEVCLASS_GAMECTRL,
    EnumDevicesCallback, NULL, DIEDFL_ATTACHEDONLY ) ;

If( FAILED( hr ) )
    return false;
```

The call to EnumDevices used the values DI8DEVCLASS_GAMECTRL to search for game controllers. The value DIEDFL_ATTACHEDONLY was used to look for only those devices attached to the system.

The second parameter value of EnumDevicesCallback represents the name of the callback function that will receive the devices found.

The third parameter is null because no additional information needs to be sent to the callback function.

The callback function provided to EnumDevices is called every time a device matching the search criteria is found. For instance, if you are searching the system for game pads, and there are currently four plugged in, the callback function will be called a total of four times.

The purpose of the callback function is to give your application the chance to create a DirectInput device for each piece of hardware, allowing you to then scan the device for its capabilities.

The callback function must be defined in your code utilizing a specific format, DIEnumDevicesCallback.

```
BOOL CALLBACK DIEnumDevicesCallback( LPCDIDEVICEINSTANCE lpddi, LPVOID pvRef );
```

The `DIEnumDevicesCallback` function requires two parameters, the first being a pointer to a `DIDEVICEINSTANCE` structure, and the second being the value passed to the `pvRef` parameter of `EnumDevices`.

The `DIDEVICEINSTANCE` structure holds the details concerning an input device, such as its GUID and its product name. The information within this structure is useful when displaying a choice of devices to the user because it enables them to recognize a device based on its name. The `DIDEVICEINSTANCE` structure has the following definition:

```
typedef struct DIDEVICEINSTANCE {
    DWORD dwSize;
    GUID guidInstance;
    GUID guidProduct;
    DWORD dwDevType;
    TCHAR tszInstanceName[MAX_PATH];
    TCHAR tszProductName[MAX_PATH];
    GUID guidFFDriver;
    WORD wUsagePage;
    WORD wUsage;
} DIDEVICEINSTANCE, *LPDIDEVICEINSTANCE;
```

- `dwSize`—Size of this structure, in bytes.

- `guidInstance`—Unique identifier for the instance of the device.

- `guidProduct`—Unique identifier for the product, which is established by the manufacturer of the device.

- `dwDevType`—Device type specifier.

- `tszInstanceName[MAX_PATH]`—Friendly name for the instance (e.g., "Joystick 1").

- `tszProductName`—Friendly name for the product.

- `guidFFDriver`—Unique identifier for the driver.

- `wUsagePage`—Usage page codes for human interface devices.

- `wUsage`—Usage codes for human interface devices.

The `DIEnumDevicesCallback` function requires a Boolean value to be returned. DirectInput has defined two values that should be used instead of the standard true or false. This value should be `DIENUM_CONTINUE` or `DIENUM_STOP`.

These values are used to control the device enumeration process. If you are searching the system for only one joystick device, it's useless to enumerate through all the installed joysticks. Returning DIENUM_STOP after finding the first suitable device would be all that was needed.

Commonly, you will want to collect a list of all the suitable devices so the user can select which specific device he wants to use. Using the callback mechanism, you can create DirectInput devices for each piece of hardware and place them in a list. The user would then be able to select the device he wants to use.

The following code example shows the callback function that will return upon finding the first joystick device that meets the EnumDevices criteria.

```
BOOL CALLBACK EnumDevicesCallback ( const DIDEVICEINSTANCE* pdidInstance,
    VOID* pContext )
{
    HRESULT hr;

    hr = directInputObject ->CreateDevice( pdidInstance->guidInstance,
        &keyboardDevice, 0 );

    if( FAILED( hr ) )
    {
        return DIENUM_CONTINUE;
    }

    return DIENUM_STOP;
}
```

The code first attempts to use the CreateDevice function to gain access to the device passed into the callback function. If the call to CreateDevice fails, the callback function returns DIENUM_CONTINUE, telling the enumeration of input devices to continue. Otherwise, if the call to CreateDevice is successful, the callback returns the value DIENUM_STOP.

Getting the Device Capabilities

After you have a valid device returned from EnumDevices, you may need to check for specific functionality. For instance, you may need to find the type of force feedback the device can support.

Enumerating the capabilities of a device is very similar to enumerating for the devices themselves. To get the specific details for a device, you call a function called EnumObjects. Like the call to EnumDevices, this function works along with a callback method.

```
HRESULT EnumObjects( LPDIENUMDEVICEOBJECTSCALLBACK lpCallback,
    LPVOID pvRef, DWORD dwFlags );
```

The EnumObjects function requires three parameters. The first parameter is the address of the callback function, and the second parameter is reference data for callback (data we are sending to the callback and flags that specify the types of devices to enumerate).

The purpose of the EnumObjects callback function is to gather information regarding a particular input device. The information collected for each device is passed to the callback as a DIDEVICEOBJECTINSTANCE structure. The flags that can be used for the EnumObjects function include:

- DIDFT_ABSAXIS—An absolute axis.

- DIDFT_ALIAS—Controls identified as human interface devices.

- DIDFT_ALL—All objects.

- DIDFT_AXIS—An absolute or relative axis.

- DIDFT_BUTTON—A push or toggle button.

- DIDFT_COLLECTION—Human interface device link collections.

- DIDFT_ENUMCOLLECTION(n)—An object that belongs to a link collection.

- DIDFT_FFACTUATOR—An object that contains a force feedback actuator.

- DIDFT_FFEFFECTTRIGGER—An object used to trigger force feedback effects.

- DIDFT_NOCOLLECTION—An object not belonging to a human interface device collection.

- DIDFT_NODATA—An object generates no data.

- DIDFT_OUTPUT—An object supports some type of output.

- DIDFT_POV—An object is a point-of-view controller.

- `DIDFT_PSHBUTTON`—An object has a push button.

- `DIDFT_RELAXIS`—An object has a relative axis.

- `DIDFT_TGLBUTTON`—An object has a toggle button.

- `DIDFT_VENDORDEFINED`—An object has vendor-specific capabilities.

The callback function defined in the call to `EnumObjects` must follow the function signature of `DIEnumDeviceObjectsCallback`.

```
BOOL CALLBACK DIEnumDeviceObjectsCallback (
    LPCDIDEVICEOBJECTINSTANCE lpddoi, LPVOID pvRef );
```

The `DIEnumDeviceObjectsCallback` function takes two parameters. The first parameter is the structure of type `DIDEVICEOBJECTINSTANCE`, which holds the returned information regarding the device. The second parameter is any value that was passed into the `EnumObjects` function in its `pvRef` parameter.

The `DIDEVICEOBJECTINSTANCE` structure contains a wealth of valuable information about the device. It's useful for setting the limits for force feedback as well as helping to determine the specific types and number of controls on the device.

A full explanation of the `DIDEVICEOBJECTINSTANCE` structure can be found in the DirectInput documentation.

Reacquiring a Device

Sometimes during the course of a game the input device may be lost. If your game set the cooperative level for the device to nonexclusive, the possibility exists for another application to start and restrict your access to the device. In this case, you need to attempt to reacquire the device before you can continue to read from it and use its input.

When access to a device is lost, the return code from the `GetDeviceState` function is `DIERR_INPUTLOST`. When this happens, you need to call the `Acquire` function in a loop until access to the device is restored.

The following code demonstrates how to reacquire a device once access to it has been lost:

```
while( 1 )
{
```

```
HRESULT hr = keyboardDevice->GetDeviceState( sizeof( buffer ),
    ( LPVOID )&buffer );

if( FAILED( hr ) )
{
    hr = keyboardDevice->Acquire( );

    while( hr == DIERR_INPUTLOST )
    {
        hr = mouseDevice->Acquire( );
    }
}
```

Note

Most games require more than one input device for multiple people to play. By creating multiple DirectInput devices, you can support a number of separate devices.

Cleaning Up DirectInput

DirectInput, like Direct3D, requires that you release the objects that you've defined upon completion of your application. In addition to the DirectInput objects, you must also unacquire any devices that you have gained control over. If you forget to unacquire the input devices you've been using, when your game ends those devices may still be locked by the system and may be unable to be used.

The function Unacquire is used to release a device that had been previously acquired through DirectInput.

```
HRESULT Unacquire( VOID );
```

Unacquire is a method provided by the DirectInput device interface.

The following example code will correctly unacquire the input devices and release both the DirectInput device and object:

```
if( directInputObject )
{
    if( keyboardDevice )
    {
        keyboardDevice->Unacquire( );
```

```
            keyboardDevice->Release( );
            keyboardDevice = 0;
    }

    directInputObject->Release( );
    directInputObject = 0;
}
```

DirectInput Keyboard Demo

Getting input from the keyboard is rather simple because it is a default device. The keyboard requires a buffer consisting of a 256-element character array.

The character array holds the state of each key on the keyboard. The state of one or multiple keys can be held in this array each time the keyboard device is read from. Most games will require that the input device be read from each frame from within the main game loop.

Before you can read from the keyboard though, you need an easy way of determining which key on the keyboard was pressed. The macro KEYDOWN, provided next, simply returns TRUE or FALSE based on whether the key you are checking for is pressed.

```
#define KEYDOWN( name, key ) ( name[key] & 0x80 )
```

An example of reading from the keyboard is found here:

```
#define KEYDOWN( name, key ) ( name[key] & 0x80 )

char buffer[256];

while ( 1 )
{
    keyboardDevice->GetDeviceState( sizeof( buffer ), ( LPVOID )&buffer );

    if( KEYDOWN( buffer, DIK_LEFT ) )
    {
        // Do something with the left arrow
    }

    if( KEYDOWN( buffer, DIK_UP ) )
    {
```

```
        // Do something with the up arrow
    }
}
```

As you can see, the main game loop calls `GetDeviceState` each frame and places the current state of the keyboard into the input buffer. The `KEYDOWN` macro is then used to check for the state of certain keys.

On the companion website in the Chapter5/Keyboard folder is a demo application that demonstrates keyboard input using DirectInput and `GetA syncKeyState`. The `GetAsyncKeyState` function is used to test whether the Escape key was pressed, which will cause the demo to quit. This is done for demonstration purposes and did not require its own demo for such a simple line of code.

The Keyboard demo builds off of the Triangle demo from Chapter 2. In this demo we will change the color of the triangle being displayed as the user presses the up and down arrow keys. To accomplish this we will have a variable that keeps track of the currently selected color, and we'll cycle through the colors using this value. The KeyboardDemo.h header file can be seen in Listing 5.1.

Listing 5.1 The KeyboardDemo.h header file.

```
#include"Dx11DemoBase.h"

class KeyboardDemo : public Dx11DemoBase
{
    public:
        KeyboardDemo( );
        virtual ~KeyboardDemo( );

        bool LoadContent( );
        void UnloadContent( );
        void Update( float dt );
        void Render( );
    private:
        ID3D11VertexShader* customColorVS_;
        ID3D11PixelShader* customColorPS_;
```

```
        ID3D11InputLayout* inputLayout_;
        ID3D11Buffer* vertexBuffer_;

        ID3D11Buffer* colorCB_;
        int selectedColor_;
};
```

We will use a constant buffer in the HLSL shader code to store the color value with which we want to shade the surface. A constant buffer, like all DirectX 11 buffers, is of the type ID3D11BUFFER, and it is created in the LoadContent function. The only new code in the LoadContent function is the creation of the constant buffer, which can be seen in Listing 5.2.

Listing 5.2 The new code added to the end of the LoadContent function.

```
bool KeyboardDemo::LoadContent( )
{
    // ...Code from the Triangle demo...

    d3dResult = d3dDevice_->CreateBuffer( &vertexDesc,
        &resourceData, &vertexBuffer_ );

    if( FAILED( d3dResult ) )
    {
        return false;
    }

        D3D11_BUFFER_DESC constDesc;
        ZeroMemory( &constDesc, sizeof( constDesc ) );
        constDesc.BindFlags = D3D11_BIND_CONSTANT_BUFFER;
        constDesc.ByteWidth = sizeof( XMFLOAT4 );
        constDesc.Usage = D3D11_USAGE_DEFAULT;

        d3dResult = d3dDevice_->CreateBuffer( &constDesc, 0, &colorCB_ );
        if( FAILED( d3dResult ) )
    {
        return false;
    }

    return true;
}
```

As mentioned in Chapter 3, a constant buffer is created by setting the buffer descriptor's BindFlags member to D3D11_BIND_CONSTANT_BUFFER. Although we could initially set the data of the constant buffer, we pass null to CreateBuffer because we'll fill it in during the Render function. Also, we need to release the data held by the constant buffer when the application exits, which is done in the Unload function seen in Listing 5.3.

Listing 5.3 The Keyboard demo's Unload function.

```
void KeyboardDemo::UnloadContent( )
{
    if( customColorVS_ ) customColorVS_->Release( );
    if( customColorPS_ ) customColorPS_->Release( );
    if( inputLayout_ ) inputLayout_->Release( );
    if( vertexBuffer_ ) vertexBuffer_->Release( );
    if( colorCB_ ) colorCB_->Release( );

    customColorVS_ = 0;
    customColorPS_ = 0;
    inputLayout_ = 0;
    vertexBuffer_ = 0;
    colorCB_ = 0;
}
```

The colors we are using are red, green, and blue for the shape. The Update function is responsible for determining whether the up or down arrow key was pressed and for setting the selectedColor_ class variable to either 0 (red), 1 (green), or 2 (blue). There are also conditional statements in place to ensure that the selectedColor_ class variable stays within the 0–2 range. The Update function can be seen in Listing 5.4.

Listing 5.4 The Keyboard demo's Update function.

```
void KeyboardDemo::Update( float dt )
{
    keyboardDevice_->GetDeviceState( sizeof( keyboardKeys_ ),
        ( LPVOID )&keyboardKeys_ );

    // Button press event.
```

```
if( GetAsyncKeyState( VK_ESCAPE ) )
{
    PostQuitMessage( 0 );
}

// Button up event.
 if(KEYDOWN( prevKeyboardKeys_, DIK_DOWN ) &&
   !KEYDOWN( keyboardKeys_, DIK_DOWN ) )
{
    selectedColor_-;
}

// Button up event.
 if(KEYDOWN( prevKeyboardKeys_, DIK_UP ) &&
   !KEYDOWN( keyboardKeys_, DIK_UP ) )
{
    selectedColor_++;
}

memcpy( prevKeyboardKeys_, keyboardKeys_, sizeof( keyboardKeys_ ) );

if( selectedColor_ < 0 ) selectedColor_ = 2;
if( selectedColor_ > 2 ) selectedColor_ = 0;
}
```

A key can be either up, pressed, pushed, or released. Although they seem similar, they are not. When a button is up, that means it is not being pressed. When a button is being pressed, that means it is being held down. When a button is pushed, that means it was pressed once but is not being held down. And when a button is released, that means it was down (pushed or being pressed) but now is up.

This is important when detecting button input from any device. In a game, if the player needs to hold down a button to perform some action, such as the acceleration button in a racing game, then we need to know whether the button is pressed or not. If the player has to press the button each time the action needs to occur, such as shooting the DMR weapon in Bungie's *Halo Reach*, then we don't want it to respond to the button being pressed, but instead we only want it to respond when it was pushed once.

Testing whether a button is up is simply a matter of "if it is not down, then it is up." To test whether a button is in a pressed state, we have to look at the current state of the button and the previous state. If the previous state of the button was down, and if the current state of the button is down (or you can say still down), then the button is being pressed.

To test if the button was pressed once, we look to see if the previous state of the button was up and the current state of the button is down. If so, then we have a single pushed event. During the next frame, if the button is still down, the state switches from pushed to pressed. This means that pushed would only count once until the player releases the button and pushes it again.

And finally, to test if the button was released, we need to see if the previous state of the button was down and the current state of the button is up. If so, we know that button was down, and now it is up. This will only occur once because in the next frame the previous and current states will both equal up.

In the Update function in Listing 5.4 we only want to change colors when the user has released one of the arrow keys. If we simply checked if the button was down, then the color will rapidly change each frame faster than we can keep up with.

The last demo class level function is the Render function. In this function we simply fill the constant buffer with the color of red if selectedColor_ is 0, green if it is 1, and blue if it is 2. The Render function can be seen in Listing 5.5. The content of the constant buffer is updated with a call to the Direct3D context's UpdateSubresource function.

Listing 5.5 The Render function.

```
void KeyboardDemo::Render( )
{
    if( d3dContext_ == 0 )
        return;

    float clearColor[4] = { 0.0f, 0.0f, 0.25f, 1.0f };
    d3dContext_->ClearRenderTargetView( backBufferTarget_, clearColor );
    unsigned int stride = sizeof( VertexPos );
    unsigned int offset = 0;

    d3dContext_->IASetInputLayout( inputLayout_ );
```

```
    d3dContext_->IASetVertexBuffers( 0, 1, &vertexBuffer_, &stride, &offset );
    d3dContext_->IASetPrimitiveTopology(D3D11_PRIMITIVE_TOPOLOGY_
TRIANGLELIST);

    XMFLOAT4 redColor( 1.0f, 0.0f, 0.0f, 1.0f );
    XMFLOAT4 greenColor( 0.0f, 1.0f, 0.0f, 1.0f );
    XMFLOAT4 blueColor( 0.0f, 0.0f, 1.0f, 1.0f );

    if( selectedColor_ == 0 )
    {
        d3dContext_->UpdateSubresource( colorCB_, 0, 0, &redColor, 0, 0 );
    }
    else if( selectedColor_ == 1 )
    {
        d3dContext_->UpdateSubresource( colorCB_, 0, 0, &greenColor, 0, 0 );
    }
    else
    {
        d3dContext_->UpdateSubresource( colorCB_, 0, 0, &blueColor, 0, 0 );
    }

    d3dContext_->VSSetShader( customColorVS_, 0, 0 );
    d3dContext_->PSSetShader( customColorPS_, 0, 0 );
    d3dContext_->PSSetConstantBuffers( 0, 1, &colorCB_ );
    d3dContext_->Draw( 3, 0 );

    swapChain_->Present( 0, 0 );
}
```

The shader for this demo can be found in a file called CustomColor.hlsl. Constant buffers in HLSL are defined in a special structure denoted by the keyword cbuffer, and it is registered to inputs starting at b0 (remember that textures were registered using t0 and shader resource views with s0).

All variables and objects within a constant buffer can be used as if they are regular global variables. In the Keyboard demo's shader we create a variable named col that is defined within the constant buffer and that will hold the incoming color value. In the pixel shader we simply return this variable, and the custom color we set on the application side is applied to the rendering. The shader can be seen in Listing 5.6.

Listing 5.6 The Keyboard demo's CustomColor.hlsl file.

```
cbuffer cbChangesPerFrame : register( b0 )
{
    float4 col;
};


float4 VS_Main( float4 pos : POSITION ) : SV_POSITION
{
    return pos;
}


float4 PS_Main( float4 pos : SV_POSITION ) : SV_TARGET
{
    return col;
}
```

The last new code to examine is the code related to setting up and releasing DirectInput, which is done in the DX11DemoBase header and source files with the Direct3D code. In the DX11DemoBase.h header file, we create new objects for DirectInput and the DirectInput keyboard as seen in Listing 5.7. We also create two 256-size arrays, with one being used for the current keyboard state and the other being used for the previous state.

Listing 5.7 The updated DX11DemoBase.h header file.

```
#define KEYDOWN(name, key) ( name[key] & 0x80 )


class Dx11DemoBase
{
    public:
        Dx11DemoBase();
        virtual ~Dx11DemoBase();
        bool Initialize( HINSTANCE hInstance, HWND hwnd );
        void Shutdown( );

        bool CompileD3DShader( char* filePath, char* entry,
                             char* shaderModel, ID3DBlob** buffer );
```

```
        virtual bool LoadContent( );
        virtual void UnloadContent( );

        virtual void Update( float dt ) = 0;
        virtual void Render( ) = 0;

    protected:
        HINSTANCE hInstance_;
        HWND hwnd_;

        D3D_DRIVER_TYPE driverType_;
        D3D_FEATURE_LEVEL featureLevel_;

        ID3D11Device* d3dDevice_;
        ID3D11DeviceContext* d3dContext_;
        IDXGISwapChain* swapChain_;
        ID3D11RenderTargetView* backBufferTarget_;

        LPDIRECTINPUT8 directInput_;
        LPDIRECTINPUTDEVICE8 keyboardDevice_;
        char keyboardKeys_[256];
        char prevKeyboardKeys_[256];
};
```

The code to initialize DirectInput is done in the Initialize function of the
demo's base class. This new code was added to the end of the function after the
creation of the viewport, which can be seen in Listing 5.8.

Listing 5.8 The code added to the base class Initialize function.

```
bool Dx11DemoBase::Initialize( HINSTANCE hInstance, HWND hwnd )
{
    // ... Previous code ...

    ZeroMemory( keyboardKeys_, sizeof( keyboardKeys_ ) );
    ZeroMemory( prevKeyboardKeys_, sizeof( prevKeyboardKeys_ ) );

    result = DirectInput8Create( hInstance_, DIRECTINPUT_VERSION,
        IID_IDirectInput8, ( void** )&directInput_, 0 );

    if( FAILED( result ) )
```

```
    {
        return false;
    }

    result = directInput_->CreateDevice(GUID_SysKeyboard, &keyboard
Device_, 0);

    if( FAILED( result ) )
    {
        return false;
    }

    result = keyboardDevice_->SetDataFormat( &c_dfDIKeyboard );

    if( FAILED( result ) )
    {
        return false;
    }

    result = keyboardDevice_->SetCooperativeLevel( hwnd_, DISCL_FOREGROUND |
        DISCL_NONEXCLUSIVE );

    if( FAILED( result ) )
    {
        return false;
    }

    result = keyboardDevice_->Acquire( );

    if( FAILED( result ) )
    {
        return false;
    }

    return LoadContent( );
}
```

And last but not least we must release DirectInput and the keyboard device, which is done in the base class' Shutdown function in Listing 5.9.

Listing 5.9 The base class Shutdown function.

```
void Dx11DemoBase::Shutdown( )
{
    UnloadContent( );

    if( backBufferTarget_ ) backBufferTarget_->Release( );
    if( swapChain_ ) swapChain_->Release( );
    if( d3dContext_ ) d3dContext_->Release( );
    if( d3dDevice_ ) d3dDevice_->Release( );

    if( keyboardDevice_ )
    {
        keyboardDevice_->Unacquire( );
        keyboardDevice_->Release( );
    }

    if( directInput_ ) directInput_->Release( );

    backBufferTarget_ = 0;
    swapChain_ = 0;
    d3dContext_ = 0;
    d3dDevice_ = 0;
    keyboardDevice_ = 0;
    directInput_ = 0;
}
```

MOUSE INPUT

For the mouse buttons, we also could use the message queue or the various key state functions while using the virtual codes for the mouse buttons. But as mentioned previously, the message queue is ineffective for video games, so that is not an option. Along with obtaining the button states of the mouse, we could also call the Win32 function GetCursorPos to obtain the mouse's position. The GetCursorPos function has the following prototype:

```
BOOL WINAPI GetCursorPos( LPPOINT lpPoint );
```

In this section we'll focus largely on using DirectInput for mouse input.

DirectInput Mouse Input

Reading input from the mouse is very similar to reading it from the keyboard. The main difference is the GUID passed to the CreateDevice function and the DIDATAFORMAT structure used to hold the input for this device.

In the previous example, the call to CreateDevice used GUID_SysKeyboard as the first parameter. When using the mouse, the GUID for CreateDevice must be set to GUID_SysMouse.

Note

Setting the cooperative level to exclusive mode for mouse input keeps the Windows cursor from being displayed. In exclusive mode, you are responsible for drawing the mouse cursor yourself.

```
hr = directInputObject->CreateDevice( GUID_SysMouse, &mouseDevice, 0 );

if( FAILED( hr ) )
{
    return FALSE;
}
```

Also, the call to SetDataFormat used the predefined data format c_dfDIKeyboard. This value must be changed to c_dfDIMouse when using the mouse as the input device.

```
hr = mouseDevice->SetDataFormat( &c_dfDIMouse );

if( FAILED( hr ) )
{
    return FALSE;
}
```

The final change that needs to be made before you can read from the mouse is the addition of the DIDATAFORMAT buffer. The keyboard needs a character buffer consisting of 256 elements, whereas the mouse needs a buffer of type DIMOUSESTATE.

The DIMOUSESTATE structure consists of three variables holding the X, Y, and Z positions of the mouse as well as a BYTE array of four elements for holding the state of the mouse buttons. The DIMOUSESTATE structure is defined as:

```
typedef struct DIMOUSESTATE {
```

```
    LONG lX;
    LONG lY;
    LONG lZ;
    BYTE rgbButtons[4];
} DIMOUSESTATE, *LPDIMOUSESTATE;
```

Previously, a macro was used to help determine if specific keys on the keyboard had been pressed. A similar macro can be used to check the state of the mouse buttons.

The X, Y, and Z values in the DIMOUSESTATE structure do not hold the current position of the mouse but rather the relative position to where the mouse previously was. For example, if you moved the mouse slightly to the left about 5 pixels, the X value would be −5. If you moved the mouse down 10 pixels, the Y value would be 10.

When reading from a mouse, you must keep track of the values read from the mouse on the previous frame to be able to correctly interpret the mouse movement.

The following code fragment demonstrates the code needed to read from the mouse device. This code handles checking both the movement of the mouse as well as the state of the mouse buttons. In the code fragment we use a custom macro called BUTTONDOWN to test the DIMOUSESTATE to determine if it is pressed. Alternatively, if support for a four-button mouse is needed, then the DIMOUSESTATE2 structure can provide the necessary data.

```
#define BUTTONDOWN(name, key) ( name.rgbButtons[key] & 0x80 )

curX = 320;
curY = 240;

while ( 1 )
{
    mouseDevice->GetDeviceState( sizeof ( mouseState ), (LPVOID) &mouseState );

    if( BUTTONDOWN( mouseState, 0 ) )
    {
        // Do something with the first mouse button
    }
```

```
if( BUTTONDOWN( mouseState, 1 ) )
{
    // Do something with the up arrow
}

curX += mouseState.lX;
curY += mouseState.lY;
}
```

The Mouse demo can be found on the companion website in the Chapter5/ Mouse folder. The demo builds off of the Keyboard demo but adds a mouse device. This code is essentially the keyboard device code copied and pasted underneath. The only change is to change the keyboard-specific flags to mouse-specific flags, such as changing c_dfDIKeyboard to c_dfDIMouse.

Listing 5.10 has the Update function from the Mouse demo. The lZ member of the mouse state holds the mouse wheel value. If the mouse does not have a mouse wheel, this value will remain 0. You can increase or decrease this value to indicate which direction the mouse wheel has moved, whereas the lX and lY represent the X and Y mouse position changes.

Listing 5.10 The Update function from the Mouse demo.

```
void MouseDemo::Update( float dt )
{
    keyboardDevice_->GetDeviceState( sizeof( keyboardKeys_ ),
        ( LPVOID )&keyboardKeys_ );

    mouseDevice_->GetDeviceState( sizeof ( mouseState_ ),
        ( LPVOID ) &mouseState_ );

    // Button press event.
    if( GetAsyncKeyState( VK_ESCAPE ) )
    {
        PostQuitMessage( 0 );
    }

    // Button up event.
    if( KEYDOWN( prevKeyboardKeys_, DIK_DOWN ) &&
        !KEYDOWN( keyboardKeys_, DIK_DOWN ) )
```

```
    {
        selectedColor_--;
    }

    // Button up event.
    if( KEYDOWN( prevKeyboardKeys_, DIK_UP ) &&
      ;!KEYDOWN( keyboardKeys_, DIK_UP ) )
    {
        selectedColor_++;
    }

    if( BUTTONDOWN( mouseState_, 0 ) && !BUTTONDOWN( prevMouseState_, 0 ) )
    {
        selectedColor_++;
    }

    if( BUTTONDOWN( mouseState_, 1 ) && !BUTTONDOWN( prevMouseState_, 1 ) )
    {
        selectedColor_--;
    }

    mousePosX_ += mouseState_.lX;
    mousePosY_ += mouseState_.lY;
    mouseWheel_ += mouseState_.lZ;


    memcpy( prevKeyboardKeys_, keyboardKeys_, sizeof( keyboardKeys_ ) );
    memcpy( &prevMouseState_, &mouseState_, sizeof( mouseState_ ) );

    if( selectedColor_ < 0 ) selectedColor_ = 2;
    if( selectedColor_ > 2 ) selectedColor_ = 0;
}
```

The code that creates the keyboard and mouse device, and the code that includes the release of the mouse device, can be seen in Listing 5.11. The code to set up the mouse, as you can see, is nearly identical to that of the keyboard.

Listing 5.11 Mouse-related setup and release.

```
bool Dx11DemoBase::Initialize( HINSTANCE hInstance, HWND hwnd )
{
```

```
// ...Previous code...

ZeroMemory( keyboardKeys_, sizeof( keyboardKeys_ ) );
ZeroMemory( prevKeyboardKeys_, sizeof( prevKeyboardKeys_ ) );

result = DirectInput8Create( hInstance_, DIRECTINPUT_VERSION,
    IID_IDirectInput8, ( void** )&directInput_, 0 );

if( FAILED( result ) )
{
    return false;
}

result = directInput_->CreateDevice(GUID_SysKeyboard, &keyboardDevice_,
0);

if( FAILED( result ) )
{
    return false;
}

result = keyboardDevice_->SetDataFormat( &c_dfDIKeyboard );

if( FAILED( result ) )
{
    return false;
}

result = keyboardDevice_->SetCooperativeLevel( hwnd_,
    DISCL_FOREGROUND | DISCL_NONEXCLUSIVE );

if( FAILED( result ) )
{
    return false;
}

result = keyboardDevice_->Acquire( );
if( FAILED( result ) )
{
    return false;
```

```
    }

    mousePosX_ = mousePosY_ = mouseWheel_ = 0;

    result = directInput_->CreateDevice( GUID_SysMouse, &mouseDevice_, 0 );

    if( FAILED( result ) )
    {
        return false;
    }

    result = mouseDevice_->SetDataFormat( &c_dfDIMouse );

    if( FAILED( result ) )
    {
        return false;
    }

    result = mouseDevice_->SetCooperativeLevel( hwnd_,
        DISCL_FOREGROUND | DISCL_NONEXCLUSIVE );

    if( FAILED( result ) )
    {
        return false;
    }

    result = mouseDevice_->Acquire( );

    if( FAILED( result ) )
    {
        return false;
    }
    return LoadContent( );
}

void Dx11DemoBase::Shutdown( )
{
    UnloadContent( );

    if( backBufferTarget_ ) backBufferTarget_->Release( );
```

```
if( swapChain_ ) swapChain_->Release( );
if( d3dContext_ ) d3dContext_->Release( );
if( d3dDevice_ ) d3dDevice_->Release( );

if( keyboardDevice_ )
{
    keyboardDevice_->Unacquire( );
    keyboardDevice_->Release( );
}

if( mouseDevice_ )
{
    mouseDevice_->Unacquire( );
    mouseDevice_->Release( );
}

if( directInput_ ) directInput_->Release( );

backBufferTarget_ = 0;
swapChain_ = 0;
d3dContext_ = 0;
d3dDevice_ = 0;
keyboardDevice_ = 0;
mouseDevice_ = 0;
directInput_ = 0;
}
```

XINPUT—GAME CONTROLLERS

XInput is an input API that is part of the DirectX SDK, XNA Game Studio, and the XDK (Xbox Developer Kit). XNA Game Studio is a game development tool built on top of DirectX 9 for video game development on Windows PC (Windows XP with Service Pack 1 and higher) and the Xbox 360 video game console. XNA Game Studio is available as a free download from Microsoft and works with retail Xbox 360 game consoles.

XInput supports a wide range of Xbox game controllers. It also supports voice input via the Xbox 360 headset as well as force feedback vibrations. Xbox 360 controllers that are compatible with Windows can be used for both the Xbox game console and Windows PC video games. In addition to supporting wired controllers via the USB port, wireless controllers are also supported using an Xbox 360 wireless controller wireless adapter that is usually found in the computer department of most major retailers such as Best Buy. The only limitation is that only four controllers can be used at a single time, which is more a limitation carried over from those controllers being meant for the Xbox 360 game console.

The first step is to plug an Xbox 360 controller into your PC. The Windows operating system should automatically install the necessary drivers for the device immediately. If it does not, you can always download the drivers from Microsoft's website or use the driver CD that came with the controller. You can buy Xbox 360 controllers with this driver CD from the computer department of most major retailers. If you already have a wired controller that you've originally used for your Xbox 360, you can always opt to download the drivers over the Internet. You can download these drivers from www.windowsgaming.com.

Also, when writing applications with XInput using the DirectX SDK, we must include the xinput.lib library.

Setting Up XInput

DirectInput had a lot of setup code for the simple tasks it performed. In XInput we technically don't have any special initialization code. We can check whether or not an Xbox 360 controller is attached to the machine by calling the function XInputGetState. The XInputGetState function has the following function prototype:

```
DWORD XInputGetState(
    DWORD dwUserIndex,
    XINPUT_STATE* pState
);
```

The XInputGetState function takes as parameters the player index and the out address of the XINPUT_STATE object that will store the state. The player index is zero based, so a value of 0 is for player 1, a value of 1 is for player 2, a value of 2 is for player 3, and a value of 3 is for player 4. The controller will have a light around the Xbox 360 guide button that indicates which player it is connected to.

By calling `XInputGetState` with a player index, we will receive a return value of `ERROR_SUCCESS` if the controller is plugged in. If the return value is `ERROR_DEVICE_NOT_CONNECTED`, then the controller is not plugged in. Any other return value and there is a problem with the device or obtaining its state.

Although we don't have to set up XInput, we could opt to disable it. This is done with a call to `XInputEnable`, which is used for situations when the application loses focus (which can occur if the application is minimized). The function `XInputEnable` takes a single parameter, which is a flag to enable or disable XInput. False disables XInput while true enables it. When disabled, `XInputGetState` returns neutral data as if all buttons are up and no input is occurring. The function prototype for `XInputEnable` has the following look:

```
void XInputEnable( BOOL enable );
```

Controller Vibrations

Many Xbox 360 controllers have force feedback capabilities. For game pads this occurs via a left and right motor in the controller that causes the device to vibrate. To turn on the controller vibration, we must send to the controller the vibration state with a call to `XInputSetState`. `XInputSetState` has the following function prototype:

```
DWORD XInputSetState(
    DWORD dwUserIndex,
    XINPUT_VIBRATION* pVibration
);
```

The first parameter to the `XInputSetState` function is a 0–3 player index for players 1, 2, 3, or 4. The second parameter is a `XINPUT_VIBRATION` object, which has the following structure:

```
typedef struct _XINPUT_VIBRATION {
    WORD wLeftMotorSpeed;
    WORD wRightMotorSpeed;
} XINPUT_VIBRATION, *PXINPUT_VIBRATION;
```

The `wLeftMotorSpeed` is used to set the left motor's speed and the `wRightMotorSpeed` is used to set the right motor's speed. The values for the motor speeds range between 0 and 65,535, where 0 is no speed and 65,535 is 100% power.

XInput for Input

With a call to `XInputGetState` we have all the information about the current state of a controller device. The last parameter of the `XInputGetState` function was an out address to an `XINPUT_STATE` structure object that contained an `XINPUT_GAMEPAD` structure with the following structure:

```
typedef struct _XINPUT_GAMEPAD {
    WORD wButtons;
    BYTE bLeftTrigger;
    BYTE bRightTrigger;
    SHORT sThumbLX;
    SHORT sThumbLY;
    SHORT sThumbRX;
    SHORT sThumbRY;
} XINPUT_GAMEPAD, *PXINPUT_GAMEPAD;
```

The `wButtons` is a bitmask value, meaning that each button can be tested by using bit operators. There are flags for the arrow pad buttons, the joystick buttons, the face buttons (buttons A, B, X, and Y), shoulder buttons LB and RB, and the start and select buttons. The joystick buttons are `L3` for the left stick and `R3` for the right stick, and they are pressed by pushing the joysticks inward. We'll show how to detect input from face buttons during the XInput demo.

The `bLeftTrigger` is used for the left trigger button (on top of the game pad controller), and the `bRightTrigger` is used for the right trigger. These values range between 0 and 255, where 0 is not pressed, 255 is pressed fully down, and anything between represents how much the trigger is being pressed.

The `sThumbLX`, `sThumbLY`, `sThumbRX`, and `sThumbRY` values are used for the left and right joystick positions. These values range between −32,768 and 32,767 where, for example, −32,768 for the left stick's X-axis represents the stick being moved all the way to the left, and +32,767 represents that it is pressed all the way to the right.

The `XINPUT_GAMEPAD` structure will give us all the information needed to detect and respond to input using Xbox 360 game controllers.

Controller Capabilities

Sometimes we might need to know the capabilities of a connected device. This can be achieved with a call to `XInputGetCapabilities`, which has the following prototype:

```
DWORD XInputGetCapabilities(
    DWORD dwUserIndex,
    DWORD dwFlags,
    XINPUT_CAPABILITIES* pCapabilities
);
```

The function `XInputGetCapabilities` takes as parameters the player index, the device search flags, and an out address to the structure that holds the device's capabilities. For the flags we can specify a value of 0 for all device types (e.g., game pads, steering wheels, etc.), or we can specify `XINPUT_FLAG_GAMEPAD` to limit the search to just game pads. Currently `XINPUT_FLAG_GAMEPAD` is the only flag supported.

The capabilities are stored in the `XINPUT_CAPABILITIES` object, which has the following structure:

```
typedef struct _XINPUT_CAPABILITIES {
    BYTE Type;
    BYTE SubType;
    WORD Flags;
    XINPUT_GAMEPAD Gamepad;
    XINPUT_VIBRATION Vibration;
} XINPUT_CAPABILITIES, *PXINPUT_CAPABILITIES;
```

The first member is the type of device, which currently will only be `XINPUT_DEVTYPE_GAMEPAD`.

The second member is the subtype that can further define what type of device it is and can be `XINPUT_DEVSUBTYPE_ARCADE_STICK`, `XINPUT_DEVSUB TYPE_GAMEPAD`, or `XINPUT_DEVSUBTYPE_WHEEL`. If the device is not a game pad, arcade stick, or steering wheel, it should be treated as if it is just a game pad.

The `GAMEPAD` member will store the button state of the game pad and the last member, the `VIBRATION` member, will store the current motor speeds of the device.

Battery Life

Xbox controllers that are wireless devices can have their battery information obtained via XInput. This is accomplished with a call to the function `XInput GetBatteryInformation`, which has the following function prototype:

```
DWORD XInputGetBatteryInformation(
    DWORD dwUserIndex,
    BYTE devType,
    XINPUT_BATTERY_INFORMATION* pBatteryInformation
);
```

The first parameter to the XInputGetBatteryInformation function is the player index, the second parameter is the device type (0 for all types of devices or XINPUT_FLAG_GAMEPAD), and the last parameter is the out address to the XINPUT_BATTERY_INFORMATION object that will store the battery information. The XINPUT_BATTERY_INFORMATION has the following structure:

```
typedef struct _XINPUT_BATTERY_INFORMATION {
    BYTE BatteryType;
    BYTE BatteryLevel;
} XINPUT_BATTERY_INFORMATION, *PXINPUT_BATTERY_INFORMATION;
```

The BATTERYTYPE member can be one of the following values:

- BATTERY_TYPE_DISCONNECTED for disconnected devices
- BATTERY_TYPE_WIRED for wired devices plugged into the USB port
- BATTERY_TYPE_ALKALINE for devices using alkaline batteries
- BATTERY_TYPE_NIMH for devices using nickel metal hydride batteries
- BATTERY_TYPE_UNKNOWN for devices using an unknown battery types

The BATTERYLEVEL value can be one of the following:

- BATTERY_LEVEL_EMPTY for devices with a dead battery
- BATTERY_LEVEL_LOW for devices low on power
- BATTERY_LEVEL_MEDIUM for devices with mid-levels of power
- BATTERY_LEVEL_FULL for devices with full power

Keystrokes

XInput provides a more general method of obtaining input rather than using XInputGetState via a function called XInputGetKeystroke. This function is used to obtain an input event for a connected game pad. The XInputGetKeyStroke has the following prototype:

```
DWORD XInputGetKeystroke(
    DWORD dwUserIndex,
    DWORD dwReserved,
    PXINPUT_KEYSTROKE pKeystroke
);
```

The first member is the player index, the second member is the device type we are querying for (either 0 or `XINPUT_FLAG_GAMEPAD`), and the third member is the out address to the keystroke event. The `PXINPUT_KEYSTROKE` has the following structure:

```
typedef struct _XINPUT_KEYSTROKE {
    WORD VirtualKey;
    WCHAR Unicode;
    WORD Flags;
    BYTE UserIndex;
    BYTE HidCode;
} XINPUT_KEYSTROKE, *PXINPUT_KEYSTROKE;
```

The virtual key code (`VirtualKey`) of the `XINPUT_KEYSTROKE` structure will store the ID of the button that triggered the event.

The second member is unused and is always 0.

The third member is the flag that triggered the event. This flag can be `XINPUT_KEYSTROKE_KEYDOWN` if the button was pushed, `XINPUT_ KEYSTROKE_KEYUP` if the button was released, and `XINPUT_KEYSTROKE_REPEAT` if the button is being held down.

The fourth member is the player index from 0 to 3 that caused the event, and the last parameter is an HID code value that future devices might return.

Headset Sound

Many Xbox 360 controllers have a port for the inclusion of an Xbox 360 headset. This headset is primarily used for player-to-player communications over Xbox LIVE, the online community and service Microsoft provides for the Xbox 360 game console (the Windows equivalent is Games for Windows LIVE). In XInput we could use the headset's speaker for audio output and its microphone for audio input with the help of the `XInputGetDSoundAudioDeviceGuids` function, which has the following prototype:

```
DWORD XInputGetDSoundAudioDeviceGuids(
    DWORD dwUserIndex,
    GUID* pDSoundRenderGuid,
    GUID* pDSoundCaptureGuid
);
```

The first member is the player index, the second member is the DirectSound rendering GUID, and the third member is the DirectSound capturing GUID. The GUID is for the headset device rendering (playing) or capturing sound. A headset has both a microphone for sound recording and a speaker for sound playback, and these two devices exist within all standard Xbox 360 headsets.

Using this to work with controller headsets requires knowledge of DirectSound, which is a deprecated audio API in DirectX. The DirectX SDK has samples for using DirectSound with XInput to capture headset audio.

XInput Demo

The XInput demo, which demonstrates how to detect and respond to game controller button input, can be found on the companion website in the Chapter5/XInput folder. This demo is exactly the same as the Keyboard and Mouse demos, and the Xinput-specific code can be found in the demo's Update function. Since XInput does not need to be explicitly initialized like DirectInput, all of this demo's specific code takes place in a single function.

The XInput demo class from XInputDemo.h can be seen in Listing 5.12. Like the previous input demos, we store the previous and current device states to use the combination to detect key up events.

Listing 5.12 The XInputDemo class.

```
#include"Dx11DemoBase.h"
#include<XInput.h>


class XInputDemo : public Dx11DemoBase
{
    public:
```

```
        XInputDemo( );
        virtual ~XInputDemo( );

        bool LoadContent( );
        void UnloadContent( );

        void Update( float dt );
        void Render( );

    private:
        ID3D11VertexShader* customColorVS_;
        ID3D11PixelShader* customColorPS_;

        ID3D11InputLayout* inputLayout_;
        ID3D11Buffer* vertexBuffer_;

            ID3D11Buffer* colorCB_;
            int selectedColor_;

        XINPUT_STATE controller1State_;
        XINPUT_STATE prevController1State_;
};
```

The Update function starts by obtaining the current device state. If the return value of XInputGetState is ERROR_SUCCESS, then the state was obtained successfully, and we know that device slot 0, which is player 1, has a device plugged in.

The demo uses the back button on the controller to exit the application. The demo also uses the face buttons to switch the colors, where the X button switches to blue, the A button switches to green, and the B button switches to red. The triggers in the demo are used to control the left and right motors for vibration. The more you press the triggers, the harder the device will vibrate.

The Update function can be seen in Listing 5.13.

Listing 5.13 The XInputDemo Update function.

```
void XInputDemo::Update( float dt )
{
    unsigned long result = XInputGetState( 0, &controller1State_ );
```

```
if( result == ERROR_SUCCESS )
{

}

// Button press event.
if( controller1State_.Gamepad.wButtons & XINPUT_GAMEPAD_BACK )
  {
        PostQuitMessage( 0 );
  }

// Button up event.
if( ( prevController1State_.Gamepad.wButtons & XINPUT_GAMEPAD_B ) &&
    !( controller1State_.Gamepad.wButtons & XINPUT_GAMEPAD_B ) )

  {
        selectedColor_ = 0;
  }

// Button up event.
if( ( prevController1State_.Gamepad.wButtons & XINPUT_GAMEPAD_A ) &&
    !( controller1State_.Gamepad.wButtons & XINPUT_GAMEPAD_A ) )

  {
        selectedColor_ = 1;
  }

// Button up event.
if( ( prevController1State_.Gamepad.wButtons & XINPUT_GAMEPAD_X ) &&
    !( controller1State_.Gamepad.wButtons & XINPUT_GAMEPAD_X ) )
  {
        selectedColor_ = 2;
  }

XINPUT_VIBRATION vibration;
WORD leftMotorSpeed = 0;
WORD rightMotorSpeed = 0;

float leftTriggerVal = ( float )controller1State_.Gamepad.bLeftTrigger;
float rightTriggerVal = ( float )controller1State_.Gamepad.bRightTrigger;
```

```
    if( controller1State_.Gamepad.bLeftTrigger > 0 )
      {
        leftMotorSpeed = ( WORD )( 65535.0f * ( leftTriggerVal / 255.0f ) );
      }

    if( controller1State_.Gamepad.bRightTrigger > 0 )
      {
        rightMotorSpeed = ( WORD )( 65535.0f * ( rightTriggerVal / 255.0f ) );
      }

    vibration.wLeftMotorSpeed = leftMotorSpeed;
    vibration.wRightMotorSpeed = rightMotorSpeed;

    XInputSetState( 0, &vibration );

    memcpy( &prevController1State_, &controller1State_, sizeof(XINPUT_STATE) );
}
```

Summary

Input is an integral part of any game and attention should be paid during the development cycle. When a game is reviewed, the performance of the input can make or break it. Always paying proper attention to the input system during development will only enhance the gamer's experience.

In this chapter you saw how to work with keyboards and mice in DirectInput as well as how to support a wide variety of Xbox 360 game controllers using XInput. As you can see, XInput is one of the easier DirectX libraries to work with. Quick and concise user input is vital to any gaming application. By applying the XInput functions properly, you'll enhance the user's experience with your game.

What You Have Learned

In this chapter you learned how to use XInput to read from the Xbox 360 controller. You should now understand:

- How to set up and utilize DirectInput for keyboards and mice.
- How to get user input from the Xbox 360 controller.

- Why you should detect whether the user has removed his controller.
- How to read both analog and digital controls.
- How and when to use vibration.

CHAPTER QUESTIONS

You can find the answers to chapter review questions in Appendix A on this book's companion website.

1. DirectInput allows for what type of input devices?

2. Which function creates the IDirectInput8 interface?

3. Reading from the keyboard requires what kind of buffer?

4. What is the data format type for mouse input?

5. Which function is used to get the current data from a controller?

6. How many controllers can be used at a time?

7. How is controller removal detected?

8. How is user input from a controller disabled?

9. Which structure is used to gather user input?

10. What XInput function allows you to set the vibration of a game controller?

ON YOUR OWN

1. Modify the XInput demo to use the GameSprite class from Chapter 3.

2. Build from the first exercise to enable you to move the shape in the scene with the arrow keys.

3. Modify the XInput demo so that the left trigger modulates the red color channel based on how hard it is pressed (not pressed will cause red to be 0, and fully pressed will cause red to be 100%). Do the same with the right trigger and the blue color component.

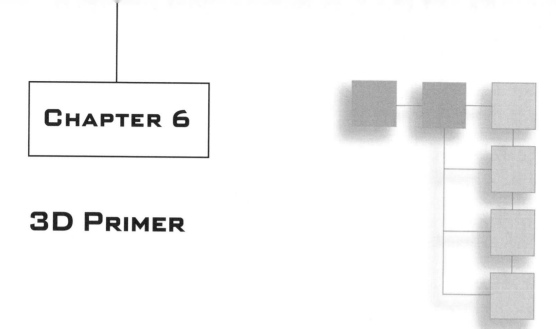

CHAPTER 6

3D PRIMER

Video games are very mathematics intensive. Everything from graphics, physics, collisions, audio, and so much more requires various levels of mathematics. Whether the application being written is by a beginner or by an experienced game developer, math is a subject that cannot be avoided.

Everything you've done up to this point has happened in a flat, two-dimensional environment. Your sprites have moved either horizontally or vertically, but there's another dimension yet to explore—the third dimension, depth. Sure, some great games can be made that take advantage of only the technology you've explored so far, but the latest cutting-edge games take place in a 3D world.

This chapter introduces the concepts and math you'll need to build a 3D world. DirectX provides a math library that is highly optimized, portable (between Windows and the Xbox 360), and very easy to use. Even if you do not have much experience with the math topics commonly seen in video games, it can at least help to understand the math structures and functions available, as well as the parameters they accept.

In this chapter:

- What coordinate systems are and how they're used
- How to define points within 3D space
- What vectors are

- The wonderful world of matrices
- How to position and move objects

XNA Math

XNA is not an acronym. XNA Math is the math library that is part of the DirectX 11 SDK. In previous versions of DirectX there was a library called D3DXMath. This library is still available in the SDK if you link to the DirectX 10 and earlier libraries, but it is recommended to learn and use XNA Math.

XNA Math is not to be confused with XNA Game Studio. XNA Game Studio is a C# framework that allows developers to create games for Windows, Zune media devices (last supported version was XNA Game Studio 3.1), Windows Phone 7 mobile devices, and the Xbox 360. Although the math library in the DirectX 11 SDK is called XNA Math, it is not in C# or part of the XNA Game Studio.

To use XNA Math we must include the xnamath.h header file. XNA Math also works on the Xbox 360 with the Xbox SDK.

Utilities

XNA Math has a set of utility functions for raising assertions, calculating the Fresnel term, and checking for CPU support. The first function, XMAssert, has the following prototype:

```
VOID XMAssert(CONST CHAR* pExpression, CONST CHAR* pFileName, UNIT LineNumber);
```

The first parameter to XMAssert is the logical expression being tested. If this logical expression results in a value of false, the code execution is halted. The second and third parameters to XMAssert are the filename of the code where the assertion was raised from and the line where the call to XMAssert can be found within the source file.

The next function is the one to calculate the Fresnel term, and it has the following function prototype:

```
XMVECTOR XMFresnelTerm( XMVECTOR CosIncidentAngle, XMVECTOR RefractionIndex );
```

The Frensel term can be used for various advanced graphical effects. As a beginner, this is not likely to be a function that you will encounter in the near future. The first parameter to the XMFresnelTerm is the cosine values of the incident angles, while the second parameter is the reflection indices for the materials for the incident angles.

The last function in the utilities section is called XMVerifyCPUSupport, and it has the following prototype:

```
BOOL XMVerifyCPUSupport( );
```

On Windows, the XMVerifyCPUSupport function is implemented using the Win32 function IsProcessorFeaturePresent to check for the necessary features required by XNA Math.

POINTS

Any position within a coordinate system can be represented using a point. A point is simply an infinitely small location in space. When locating a point in space, it is described using a single value for each axis. This value is the offset from the origin along each respective axis. For example, a point located in 2D space would need two values, an X and a Y value, to describe its location, such as <1, 3>.

For each axis added, it takes one additional value to represent the point. In 3D space, three values, X, Y, and Z, are needed to describe a point, such as <1, 2, 4>.

Points can be used in many ways in the creation of a game, from player position to the location of a planet. Even though each point is tiny, that one point can be used to represent the location of any object in your game. We have been using the position of vertex points to represent the point of a triangle throughout this book.

VECTORS

Vectors have multiple uses in 3D graphics, from describing distance and direction to describing speed. Unlike a point, which has only a position, a vector has both a direction and a length (magnitude), allowing it to be utilized to determine which direction a polygon is facing, which direction an object or particle is heading, or just describe its position. Typically, vectors are designated as arrows, with a head and tail showing the direction and magnitude. Vectors typically fall into two categories: free vectors and fixed vectors.

A free vector is a vector that can be placed in an arbitrary location within a coordinate system, and its meaning doesn't change.

A fixed vector remains fixed to the origin of the coordinate system. This places the tail of these vectors at the origin, while the head is placed at a location in space. Because fixed vectors are centered on the origin, it allows them to be used to designate a position. This position is comprised of three scalar values called components. The number of components within the vector corresponds to the number of axes. For example, if the coordinate system is describing 3D space, then three components are needed to describe a position within it. For example, the vector <3, 2, 7> corresponds to a position 3 units away from the origin on the X axis, 2 units away on the Y axis, and 7 units away on the Z axis.

The members of a vector are basic data types such as floats, integers, and so forth, and there is one for each axis of the structure. Examples of 2D, 3D, and 4D vectors can be seen as follows:

```
struct Vector2
{
    float x;
    float y;
};


struct Vector3
{
    float x;
    float y;
    float z;
};


struct Vector4
{
    float x;
    float y;
    float z;
    float w;
};
```

While you could define these types yourself, the Direct3D structures contain more than just the definitions of the embedded components. In XNA Math we can represent vectors using XMFLOAT2 for 2D vectors, XMFLOAT3 for 3D vectors, and XMFLOAT4 for 4D vectors. Additional vector types, such as XMHALF4, for example, are discussed later in this chapter in the section "Structures and Types." It is very useful to use the XNA Math library structures because they are portable (between Windows and the Xbox 360), optimized, and easy to use.

In general when using vectors you're bound to come across a few different types; here's a small list:

- **Position Vector**—A type of vector used to describe a position within a coordinate system, with the tail being at the origin and the head at a point.

- **Normal Vector**—A vector perpendicular to a plane. This is useful for determining whether a polygon is front or back facing.

- **Unit Vectors**—Vectors that have a length that equals one. Not all vectors require a large length. When creating a directional light, only the direction of the vector is important.

- **Zero Vectors**—Vectors with a length of 0.

Another structure available is the XMVECTOR, which is an optimized 4D vector. The XMVECTOR structure is not only mapped to fast hardware registers but is also portable and memory aligned.

The implementation of XMVECTOR is platform dependent, and because of this there are very efficient functions for accessing data. These functions include accessor, store, and loading functions. These functions must be used to safely access the structure's data in a portable manner.

The first function is a loading function called XMLoadFloat2. This function has a version for every type of vector, such as XMLoadInt2, XMLoadFloat3, XMLoadByte4, and so forth. The purpose of these functions is to load the corresponding vector type into an XMVECTOR. This is useful when there were times in code where you were using, let's say, XMFLOAT2 for example, and wanted to move that data into an XMVECTOR so that you can perform fast hardware operations on it.

Each of the loading functions takes as a parameter the address of the vector we want to convert to an XMVECTOR. As an example, the function prototype for taking an XMFLOAT2 and returning a XMVECTOR can be seen in XMLoadFloat2 below:

```
XMVECTOR XMLoadFloat2( CONST XMFLOAT2* pSource );
```

The simple answer is that this function copies an XMFLOAT2 to a XMVECTOR, although internally it uses fast instructions to perform the operation. If we wanted to copy a 2D vector to a 4D vector using our custom structures, it would look like the following:

```
Vector4 dest;
Vector2 src;

dest.x = src.x;
dest.y = src.y;
dest.z = <undefined>;
dest.w = <undefined>;
```

There is a large number of loading functions, and each can be found in the SDK documentation. In addition to loading functions we also have storing functions. All functions are identical to one other, with the difference of the first parameter's type. Using XMStoreFloat2, the function takes as parameters an address to an XMFLOAT2 that will receive the data as its first parameter and the XMVECTOR that has the data we want to copy. Its function prototype can be seen as follows:

```
VOID XMStoreFloat2( XMFLOAT2* pDestination, XMVECTOR V );
```

The accessor functions can be used to retrieve the value of any member of the XMVECTOR structure. These functions include XMVectorGetX, XMVectorGetY, XMVectorGetZ, and XMVectorGetW. Each of these functions takes as a parameter an XMVECTOR object and returns the value of the corresponding member. The prototypes of each of these functions can be seen as follows:

```
FLOAT XMVectorGetX( XMVECTOR V );

FLOAT XMVectorGetY( XMVECTOR V );

FLOAT XMVectorGetZ( XMVECTOR V );

FLOAT XMVectorGetW( XMVECTOR V );
```

Also available are functions that return the value via a pointer as the first parameter, which can be seen as follows:

```
VOID XMVectorGetXPtr( FLOAT* x, XMVECTOR V );

VOID XMVectorGetYPtr( FLOAT* y, XMVECTOR V );

VOID XMVectorGetZPtr( FLOAT* z, XMVECTOR V );

VOID XMVectorGetWPtr( FLOAT* w, XMVECTOR V );
```

And in addition to the functions used to get a member, we also have functions that can set them. As an example, the following are the prototypes for the setting of the X member of a XMVECTOR object:

```
XMVECTOR XMVectorSetX( XMVECTOR V, FLOAT x );
XMVECTOR XMVectorSetXPtr( XMVECTOR V, CONST FLOAT* x );
```

Vector Arithmetic

The most basic operations we can do with vectors are arithmetic operations. Adding, subtracting, multiplying, and dividing vectors with each other is as simple as performing the operation on each member in one vector to the corresponding member in a second vector. An example of this can be seen with performing various operations to a 2D vector:

```
Vector2D a, b, result;

// Adding
result.x = a.x + b.x;
result.y = a.y + b.y;

// Subtracting
result.x = a.x - b.x;
result.y = a.y - b.y;

// Multiplying
result.x = a.x * b.x;
result.y = a.y * b.y;

// Dividing
result.x = a.x / b.x;
result.y = a.y / b.y;
```

It is also common to perform these operations between a vector and a scalar (floating-point value), as well as using overloaded operators. Although overloaded operators are convenient to look at in code, they are often less optimal since they often require multiple functions to be executed (one for the equals, one for the operator, constructors for the vector parameters to the overloaded function, etc.) and multiple load/store operations. An example of adding a scalar to a vector or using an overloaded operation can be seen as follows:

```
Vector2D a, result;
float value = 100.0f;

// Adding a float
result.x = a.x + value;
result.y = a.y + value;

// Adding as an overloaded operator
result = a + value;
```

In XNA Math we have `XMVectorAdd`, `XMVectorSubtract`, `XMVectorDivide`, and `XMVectorMultiply` as a means of performing each of these operations between `XMVECTOR` objects. Their prototypes are as follows, and they use optimized instruction sets:

```
XMVECTOR XMVectorAdd( XMVECTOR V1, XMVECTOR V2 );

XMVECTOR XMVectorSubtract( XMVECTOR V1, XMVECTOR V2 );

XMVECTOR XMVectorDivide( XMVECTOR V1, XMVECTOR V2 );

XMVECTOR XMVectorMultiply( XMVECTOR V1, XMVECTOR V2 );
```

Distance Between Vectors

Occasionally you will need to determine the distance between two points. These points can be either the origin and a fixed location or two completely arbitrary points.

For example, imagine you're creating a real-time strategy game. Each of the monsters of the opposing army has the opportunity to move toward a common goal. During the turn of the AI, it can choose to move one of these monsters toward the goal, but which one? This is where the ability to figure out distance comes in handy. By calculating the relative distance between each monster and the common goal, the AI can choose which one of the creatures is more advantageous to move.

Whether you are determining the distance within a 2D or 3D space, the calculation is essentially the same. An example can be seen in the following pseudo code:

```
Vector2D x1, x2;

float xDistance = x2.x - x1.x;
float yDistance = y2.x - y1.x;

float distance = square_root( xDistance * xDistance + yDistance * yDistance );
```

In this example x2 is the X axis value of the second vector and x1 is the X axis of the first vector. The result of the distance calculation will be a single value that represents the distance between the two points. When determining the distance between two points in 3D space, make sure to take the Z value into account as well.

To put it another way, the distance between one vector and another is the square root of the dot product of the vector between the points. We'll cover dot products in the upcoming subsection titled "Dot Product." The square root of the vector between the points is also known as the vector's length. In this case the length can be used to give us the distance between vectors.

Determining the Length of a Vector

Occasionally it is useful to know the length of a vector, since the length or magnitude of the vector can be used as acceleration or velocity when applied to a game object. The length is also used as an input when normalizing the vector.

To calculate the length of a vector, each of the components must be first squared and then added together. This is known as the dot product. Finally, the square root of the dot product is taken to give the output length.

```
sqrt(vectorX * vectorX + vectorY * vectorY + vectorZ * vectorZ);
```

Direct3D provides several functions to calculate the length of a vector. The length of a 2D vector is obtained with a call to XMVector2Length, the length of a 3D vector via XMVector3Length, and a 4D vector via XMVector4Length. Additional functions also exist to estimate the length of a vector as well as to square the length. The squared-length functions end with Sq and will essentially perform length × length, while the estimation functions that end with Est are used to increase performance at the expense of accuracy. All of the length functions in XNA Math can be seen as follows:

```
XMVECTOR XMVector2Length( XMVECTOR V );
XMVECTOR XMVector3Length( XMVECTOR V );
XMVECTOR XMVector4Length( XMVECTOR V );

XMVECTOR XMVector2LengthEst( XMVECTOR V );
XMVECTOR XMVector3LengthEst( XMVECTOR V );
XMVECTOR XMVector4LengthEst( XMVECTOR V );

XMVECTOR XMVector2LengthSq( XMVECTOR V );
XMVECTOR XMVector3LengthSq( XMVECTOR V );
XMVECTOR XMVector4LengthSq( XMVECTOR V );
```

Normalize a Vector

Normalizing a vector is the process of reducing any vector into a unit vector, which as you should remember is a vector with a length equal to 1. This is best done when only the direction of a vector is needed and the length is unimportant. Vectors can be normalized simply by dividing each of the components by the vector's length—an example of which can be seen in the following:

```
Vector3 vec;

float length = Length( vec );

vec.X = vec.X / length;
vec.Y = vec.Y / length;
vec.Z = vec.Z / length;
```

The final vector will still point in the same direction, but the length of the vector is reduced to 1. In XNA Math we have XMVector2Normalize to normalize a 2D vector, XMVector2NormalizeEst to calculate an estimated normal vector (which can lead to a increase of performance at the expense of accuracy), and versions of each for 3D and 4D vectors. The function prototypes are as follows:

```
XMVECTOR XMVector2Normalize( XMVECTOR V );
XMVECTOR XMVector3Normalize( XMVECTOR V );
XMVECTOR XMVector4Normalize( XMVECTOR V );

XMVECTOR XMVector2NormalizeEst( XMVECTOR V );
XMVECTOR XMVector3NormalizeEst( XMVECTOR V );
XMVECTOR XMVector4NormalizeEst( XMVECTOR V );
```

Cross Product

A cross product of a vector is used to calculate a vector that is perpendicular to two other vectors. One common use for this is to calculate the normal of a triangle. In this situation you can use the cross product of each edge vector to obtain the triangle's normal. An edge vector is essentially point A of the triangle − point B for edge 1, and point B − point C for the second edge. The cross product is also known as the vector product.

An example of calculating the cross product can be seen in the following, where a new vector is created by multiplying the components of the two input vectors:

```
newVectorX = (vector1Y * vector2Z) -(vector1Z * vector2Y);
newVectorY = (vector1Z * vector2X) -(vector1X * vector2Z);
newVectorZ = (vector1X * vector2Y) -(vector1Y * vector2X);
```

In XNA Math we have XMVector2Cross, XMVector3Cross, and XMVector4Cross for calculating the cross product of 2D, 3D, and 4D vectors. Their function prototypes are as follows:

```
XMVECTOR XMVector2Cross( XMVECTOR V1, XMVECTOR V2 );
XMVECTOR XMVector3Cross( XMVECTOR V1, XMVECTOR V2 );
XMVECTOR XMVector4Cross( XMVECTOR V1, XMVECTOR V2 );
```

Dot Product

The final vector calculation we'll go over is the dot product. The dot product, also known as the scalar product, is used to determine the angle between two vectors and is commonly used for many calculations in computer graphics such as back-face culling, lighting, and more.

Back-face culling is the process by which polygons that are not visible are removed to reduce the number of polygons being drawn. If two vectors have an angle less than 90 degrees, then the dot product is a positive value; otherwise, the dot product is negative. The sign of the dot product is what's used to determine whether a polygon is front or back facing. If we use the view vector as one vector, the dot product between the view vector and the polygon's normal tells us which direction it is facing, and thus which polygons we should draw or not. This is usually handled internally by the graphics hardware and is not anything we would do manually when using Direct3D.

We could also use this for lighting, which we'll discuss in more detail in Chapter 7 in the section titled "Lighting." One way we can use the dot product for lighting is to use the value to see how much diffuse light is reaching the surface. Light sources directly above a surface will be fully lit, surfaces at an angle will be partially lit, and surfaces where the light is behind it will receive no light. The vector used for the dot product is usually the surface normal and the light vector, where the light vector is calculated as the light's position − the vertex position (or the pixel's position when doing per-pixel lighting).

The dot product is calculated by squaring each axis of the vector and adding together their results to form a single scalar value. An example of this can be seen in the following:

```
float dotProduct = vec1.X * vec2.X + vec1.Y * vec2.Y + vec1.Z * vec2.Z;
```

XNA Math has `XMVector2Dot` for the dot product between 2D vectors, `XMVector3Dot` for 3D vectors, and `XMVector4Dot` for 4D vectors. Their prototypes are shown as follows:

```
XMVECTOR XMVector2Dot( XMVECTOR V1, XMVECTOR V2 );
XMVECTOR XMVector3Dot( XMVECTOR V1, XMVECTOR V2 );
XMVECTOR XMVector4Dot( XMVECTOR V1, XMVECTOR V2 );
```

Although the dot product returns a scalar, in XNA Math it seems to be returning a vector of `XMVECTOR`. This is because the result is copied into all components of `XMVECTOR`. Since the optimized instruction set used in XNA Math uses vectors for stream parallel processing, technically that is what we are using even if we ultimately only really use one component. SIMD instructions work on four floating-point values at a time with a single instruction, so in a case such as this we only need to access one of them to get our scalar result.

3D Space

The basis to any three-dimensional world is the space it takes place in. Look around you. The keyboard and monitor on your desk, the chair on the floor, all of these items exist in a 3D space. If you had to describe the location of one of these objects to someone over the phone, how would you do it? Would you describe your desk as located in front of you or would you say it was near a certain wall? If the person on the phone knew absolutely nothing about the room you were in, from that description, would they understand? Probably not; they're missing a point of reference.

Coordinate Systems

A point of reference is a location that both you and the other person understand. For instance, if the point of reference was a doorway, you could then explain that the desk was located about 10 feet from the door on the left side. When you're building a 3D world, a point of reference is crucial.

You need to be able to place objects in relation to a point of reference that both you and the computer understand. When working with 3D graphics, this point of reference is the coordinate system. A coordinate system is a series of imaginary lines that run through space and are used to describe locations within it. The center of this coordinate system is called the origin; this is the core of your point of reference. Any location within this space can be described precisely in relation to the origin.

For example, you can describe the location of an object by saying it is four units up from the origin and two units to the left. By using the origin as the point of reference, any point within the defined space can be described.

If you remember from working with sprites, any point on the screen can be explained using X and Y coordinates. The X and Y coordinates determine the sprite's position in a coordinate system consisting of two perpendicular axes, a horizontal and a vertical. Figure 6.1 shows an example of a 2D coordinate system.

When working with three dimensions, a third axis will be needed: the Z axis. The Z axis extends away from the viewer, giving the coordinate system a way to describe depth. So now you have three dimensions, width, height, and depth, as well as three axes.

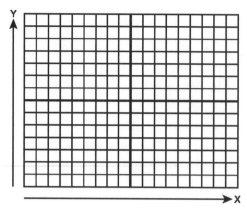

Figure 6.1
A 2D coordinate system.

When dealing with 3D coordinate systems, you have to be aware that they come in two flavors: left-handed and right-handed. The handedness of the system determines the direction the axes face in relation to the viewer.

Left-Handed Coordinate Systems

A left-handed coordinate system extends the positive X axis to the left and the positive Y axis upward. The Z axis in a left-handed system is positive in the direction away from the viewer, with the negative portion extending toward them. Figure 6.2 shows how a left-handed coordinate system is set up.

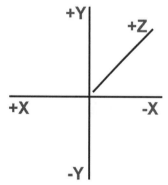

Figure 6.2
A left-handed coordinate system.

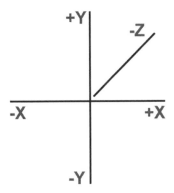

Figure 6.3
A right-handed coordinate system.

Right-Handed Coordinate Systems

The right-handed coordinate system extends the X and Y axes similarly to the left-handed system, but it reverses the X and Z axis directions. The positive Z values extend toward the viewer, whereas the negative values continue away. For the X axis, the positive X axis increases to the right, whereas the positive X axis in the left-handed system is to the left. Figure 6.3 shows a right-handed system.

Transformations

3D models are for the most part created outside of your game code. For instance, if you're creating a racing game, you'll probably create the car models in a 3D art package. During the creation process, these models will be working off of the coordinate system provided to them in the modeler. This causes the objects to be created with a set of vertices that aren't necessarily going to place where the model will end up in the game and how you want it oriented in your game environment. Because of this, you will need to move and rotate the model yourself. You can do this by using the geometry pipeline. The geometry pipeline is a process that allows you to transform an object from one coordinate system into another. Figure 6.4 shows the transformations a vertex goes through.

When a model starts out, it is centered on the origin. This causes the model to be centered in the environment with a default orientation. Not every model you load needs to be at the origin, so how do you get models where they need to be? The answer to that is through transformations.

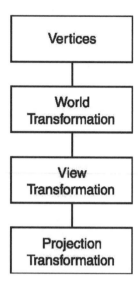

Figure 6.4
Geometry pipeline.

Transformations refer to the actions of translating (moving), rotating, and scaling an object. By applying these actions, you can make an object appear to move around. These actions are handled as your objects progress through the stages of the geometry pipeline.

When you load a model, its vertices are in a local coordinate system called model space. Model space refers to a coordinate system where the parts of an object are relative to a local origin. For instance, upon creation, a model's vertices are in reference to the origin point around which they were created. A cube that is two units in size centered on the origin would have its vertices one unit on either side of the origin. If you then wanted to place this cube somewhere within your game, you would need to transform its vertices from model space into the global system used by all the objects in your world. This global coordinate system is called world space, where all objects are relative to a single fixed origin. The process of transforming an object from model space into world space is called the world transformation.

World Transformations

The world transformation stage of the geometry pipeline takes an existing object with its own local coordinate system and transforms that object into the world coordinate system. The world coordinate system is the system that contains the position and orientation of all objects within the 3D world. The world system has a single origin point that all models transformed into this system become relative to.

The transformation from model space to world space usually occurs within the vertex shader when it comes to rendering geometry. You could transform the geometry yourself outside of shaders, but that will require repopulating vertex buffers with dynamic information, which would not always be the best course of action (especially for static geometry).

The next stage of the geometry pipeline is the view transformation. Because all objects at this point are relative to a single origin, you can only view them from this point. To allow you to view the scene from any arbitrary point, the objects must go through a view transformation.

View Transformations

The view transformation transforms the coordinates from world space into view space. View space refers to the coordinate system that is relative to the position of a virtual camera. In other words, the view transformation is used to simulate a camera that is applied to all objects in the game world with the exception of the graphical user interface (e.g., screen elements for the health bar, timers, ammo counter, etc.). When you choose a point of view for your virtual camera, the coordinates in world space get reoriented in respect to the camera. For instance, the camera remains at the origin, while the world itself is moved into the camera's view.

At this point, you have the camera angle and view for your scene, and you're ready to display it to the screen.

Projection Transformations

The next stage in the geometry pipeline is the projection transformation. The projection transformation is the stage of the pipeline where depth is applied. When you cause objects that are closer to the camera to appear larger than those farther away, you create an illusion of depth. This type of projection is known as perspective projection and is used for 3D games. Another type of projection will keep all rendered objects looking like they are the same distance apart from each other even when they are not. This is done through orthographic projection. A final type of projection is isometric projection, which is a projection used to display 3D objects in 2D technical drawings. This type of projection is simulated and not actually done in graphics APIs, where we usually just have either perspective projection or orthographic projection.

Finally, the vertices are scaled to the viewport and projected into 2D space. The resulting 2D image appears on your monitor with the illusion of being a 3D scene.

Transforming an Object

Now that you're aware of the transformations, what are they really used for? As an example, say you were modeling a city. This city is made up of houses, office buildings, and a few cars here and there. Now, you load in a model of a new car and need to add it to your existing scene. When the model comes in, though, it's centered on the origin and facing the wrong way. To get the car to the correct spot and orientation in the scene, the car model will have to be rotated properly and then translated to its world space location.

When putting an object through the transformation pipeline, you're really transforming each vertex individually. In the case of the car, every vertex that makes up the car will be moved individually by a certain amount and then rotated. After each vertex is complete, the object appears in the new position. These transformations take place by multiplying each vertex in the model by a transformation matrix.

The world matrix used for the world transformation is created by combining the scale, rotation, and translation (positioning) matrices for that specific game object. Although we usually use these three matrices to create the world matrix, if the object doesn't use one or more of these properties, you could just leave it out, since combining one matrix with an identity matrix is similar to multiplying a number by 1; it doesn't change its value. An identity matrix is similar to a matrix with nothing applied to it.

Combining the world matrix and the view matrix will create a new matrix called the world-view matrix. Combining the world-view and projection matrices will create another matrix called the world-view-projection matrix. This matrix is often used by the vertex shader and is the one we've been working with throughout this book.

Transforming a vector by a transformation matrix is done by multiplying the vector by the matrix. This is an operation we've done in the large majority of demos in the vertex shader where we used the HLSL keyword mul to perform the multiplication. In XNA Math we can call, using 2D vectors as an example, the function XMVector2Transform to transform a vector by a matrix. There is also a version of this called XMVector2TransformCoord, which is used to transform a vector and then project it onto w = 1. The third type of transformation function, called XMVector2TransformNormal, is used to transform a vector by all parts of the matrix with the exception of its translational part. Each of these types of functions for 2D, 3D, and 4D vectors can be seen as follows:

```
XMVECTOR XMVector2Transform( XMVECTOR V, XMMATRIX M );
XMVECTOR XMVector3Transform( XMVECTOR V, XMMATRIX M );
XMVECTOR XMVector4Transform( XMVECTOR V, XMMATRIX M );

XMVECTOR XMVector2TransformCoord( XMVECTOR V, XMMATRIX M );
XMVECTOR XMVector3TransformCoord( XMVECTOR V, XMMATRIX M );
XMVECTOR XMVector4TransformCoord( XMVECTOR V, XMMATRIX M );

XMVECTOR XMVector2TransformNormal( XMVECTOR V, XMMATRIX M );
XMVECTOR XMVector3TransformNormal( XMVECTOR V, XMMATRIX M );
XMVECTOR XMVector4TransformNormal( XMVECTOR V, XMMATRIX M );
```

There is also a stream version of each of these functions. Using the 2D vector version of this function as an example, the parameters include the address to the output array the data will be saved, the size in bytes between each output vector, the input array of vectors you are supplying to be transformed, the size in bytes between each input vector, the total number of vectors being transformed, and the matrix by which these vectors will be transformed. The function prototype for the XMVector2TransformStream function can be seen as follows:

```
XMFLOAT4* XMVector2TransformStream(
    XMFLOAT4 *pOutputStream,
    UINT OutputStride,
    CONST XMFLOAT2 *pInputStream,
    UINT InputStride,
    UINT VectorCount,
    XMMATRIX M
);
```

An alternative to `XMVector2Transform` is `XMVector2TransformNC`, where `NC` refers to non-cached memory.

MATRICES

You've probably come across matrices in a math class along the way and wondered what they would ever be used for. Well, here it is: game programming. Matrices are used to transform objects from one coordinate system to another. By applying a matrix to an existing point, it is transformed from its original coordinate system to the new one. For example, most objects start out in their own local coordinate system. This means that all the points that make up that object are relative to a local origin. To convert those points into a common world coordinate system, they must be transformed using a matrix.

You will probably find matrices to be the single most confusing concept to wrap your thoughts around when just starting out with 3D graphics. Matrices and the math involved can feel very daunting and overwhelming at the start. The important thing to take away from this section on matrices isn't necessarily how they work, but what they're for and how to use them. No one should expect you to be able to perform all the math required right off the bat; luckily, Direct3D provides optimized functionality to do a lot of this work for you. If you ever want to know all the details behind matrices, there is a ton of good math resources available on the web. Simply put, a matrix is used to represent a system of values where, in the case of graphics and game programming, we use these objects to store the necessary information to transform vectors to the system the matrix represents.

Mathematically, a matrix is a 4×4 grid of numbers that are arranged in columns and rows. Each row in the matrix corresponds to the three major axes. The first row is used for the X axis, the second row for the Y axis, and the third row for the Z axis. The final row is used to contain the translation offset values.

If you wanted to create your own matrix in code, you could define it as a simple 4×4 array of float values.

```
float matrix [4][4] =
{
    1.0f, 0.0f, 0.0f, 0.0f,
    0.0f, 1.0f, 0.0f, 0.0f,
```

```
    0.0f, 0.0f, 1.0f, 0.0f,
    0.0f, 0.0f, 0.0f, 1.0f
};
```

XNA Math has several structures for matrices. There is `XMFLOAT3X3` for 3×3 matrices, `XMFLOAT4X3` for 4×3 matrices, and `XMFLOAT4X4` for 4×4 matrices. Using `XMFLOAT3X3` as an example, the structure looks as follows:

```
typedef struct _XMFLOAT3X3
{
    union
    {
        struct
        {
            FLOAT _11;
            FLOAT _12;
            FLOAT _13;
            FLOAT _21;
            FLOAT _22;
            FLOAT _23;
            FLOAT _31;
            FLOAT _32;
            FLOAT _33;
        };

        FLOAT m[3][3];
    };

} XMFLOAT3X3;
```

There is also `XMMATRIX`, which like `XMVECTOR` is the memory-aligned structure that maps to hardware registers. Additional variations of these types we'll discuss later on in this chapter in the section titled "Structures and Types."

The Identity Matrix

There is a special matrix that you should be aware of called the identity matrix. This is the default matrix. It contains values that reset scaling to 1, with no rotations and no translation taking place. The identity matrix is created by zeroing out all 16 values in the matrix and then applying ones along the diagonal. The identity matrix can be used as a starting point for all matrix operations. Multiplying a matrix with an identity matrix has no affect, and transforming an object by an identity matrix does nothing, since the matrix has no translation, no scaling, and no rotation.

Following is an identity matrix:

```
float matrix [4][4] =
{
    1.0f, 0.0f, 0.0f, 0.0f,
    0.0f, 1.0f, 0.0f, 0.0f,
    0.0f, 0.0f, 1.0f, 0.0f,
    0.0f, 0.0f, 0.0f, 1.0f
};
```

Creating an identity matrix in XNA Math is as simple as calling the XMMatrixIdentity function. This function takes no parameters and returns an XMMATRIX object loaded as an identity matrix. The function prototype for this function is:

```
XMMATRIX XMMatrixIdentity( );
```

Matrix Scaling

One of the transformations you can apply to an object is scaling. Scaling is the ability to shrink or enlarge an object by a certain factor. For instance, if you have a square centered on the origin that was two units wide and two units tall and you scaled it twice in size, you would have a square that now went four units in each direction (i.e., twice its original size).

Remember the ones that were placed into the identity matrix? Those ones control the scaling on each of the three axes. When vertices are transformed using this matrix, their X, Y, and Z values are altered based on the scaling values. By changing the X axis value to 2 and the Y axis to 3, the objects will be scaled twice their size in the X direction and three times their size in the Y. An example ScaleMatrix array is shown next. The variables scaleX, scaleY, and scaleZ show where the appropriate scaling values would go.

```
float ScaleMatrix [4][4] =
{
    scaleX, 0.0f, 0.0f, 0.0f,
    0.0f, scaleY, 0.0f, 0.0f,
    0.0f, 0.0f, scaleZ, 0.0f,
```

```
    0.0f, 0.0f, 0.0f, 1.0f
};
```

In XNA Math we can use the function `XMMatrixScaling` to create a scaling matrix. This function takes as parameters the X, Y, and Z scaling factors and returns an `XMMATRIX` that represents this scale in matrix form. The function prototype can be seen as follows:

```
XMMATRIX XMMatrixScaling( FLOAT ScaleX, FLOAT ScaleY, FLOAT ScaleZ );
```

Matrix Translation

The act of moving an object is called translation. Translation allows for an object to be moved along any of the three axes by specifying the amount of movement needed. For example, if you want to move an object right along the X axis, you would need to translate that object an appropriate number of units in the positive X direction. To do so, you would need to create a translation matrix.

Again, we'll start with the identity matrix and change it to add in the variables that affect translation. Take a look at the following translation matrix; the variables `moveX`, `moveY`, and `moveZ` show you where the translation values would go. If you wanted to translate an object four units to the right, you would replace `moveX` with the value 4.

```
float matrix [4][4] =
{
    1.0f, 0.0f, 0.0f, 0.0f,
    0.0f, 1.0f, 0.0f, 0.0f,
    0.0f, 0.0f, 1.0f, 0.0f,
    moveX, moveY, moveZ, 1.0f
};
```

In XNAMath we create a translation matrix by calling `XMMatrixTranslation`, which takes as parameters the X, Y, and Z translation values and has the following function prototype:

```
XMMATRIX XMMatrixTranslation( FLOAT OffsetX, FLOAT OffsetY, FLOAT OffsetZ );
```

Matrix Rotation

The final effect we'll describe is rotation. Rotation is the act of turning an object around a certain axis. This allows objects to change their orientation within space. For instance, if you wanted to rotate a planet, you would create a rotation matrix and apply it to the planet.

Rotation matrices take a little more explanation because the matrix needs to change based on the axis you're trying to rotate around.

When rotating around any axis, it will require you to convert the angle of rotation into both a sine and a cosine value. These values are then plugged into the matrix to cause the proper amount of rotation. When rotating around the X axis, the sine and cosine values are placed into the matrix in the following manner.

```
float rotateXMatrix[4][4] =
{
    1.0f, 0.0f, 0.0f, 0.0f
    0.0f, cosAngle, sinAngle, 0.0f,
    0.0f, -sinAngle, cosAngle, 0.0f,
    0.0f, 0.0f, 0.0f, 1.0f
};
```

Rotating around the Y axis requires only that the sine and cosine values be moved to different positions within the matrix. In this instance, the values are moved to affect the X and Z axes as shown in the following manner.

```
float rotateYMatrix[4][4] =
{
    cosAngle, 0.0f, -sinAngle, 0.0f,
    0.0f, 1.0f, 0.0f, 0.0f,
    sinAngle, 0.0f, cosAngle, 0.0f,
    0.0f, 0.0f, 0.0f, 1.0f
};
```

The final rotation matrix allows for rotation around the Z axis. In this instance, the sine and cosine values affect the X and Y axes.

```
float rotateZMatrix[4][4] =
{
    cosAngle, sinAngle, 0.0f, 0.0f,
    -sinAngle, cosAngle, 0.0f, 0.0f,
    0.0f, 0.0f, 1.0f, 0.0f,
    0.0f, 0.0f, 0.0f, 1.0f
};
```

In XNA Math we have quite a few different options for creating a rotation matrix. We can rotate along a single axis as we've already discussed to create three separate rotation matrices, which we can then combine into one with the following functions:

```
XMMATRIX XMMatrixRotationX( FLOAT Angle );
XMMATRIX XMMatrixRotationY( FLOAT Angle );
XMMATRIX XMMatrixRotationZ( FLOAT Angle );
```

We can also rotate using Yaw, Pitch, and Roll values by using the following XNA Math functions:

```
XMMATRIX XMMatrixRotationRollPitchYaw(
    FLOAT Pitch,
    FLOAT Yaw,
    FLOAT Roll
);


XMMATRIX XMMatrixRotationRollPitchYawFromVector(
    XMVECTOR Angles
);
```

Pitch is the rotation in radians (not degrees) for the X axis, Yaw is the rotation in radians for the Y axis, and Roll is the rotation in radians for the Z axis. By specifying all three of these angles in radians we can use the XMMatrixRotationRollPitchYaw function to build one rotation matrix that combines all three axis rotations instead of creating three separate rotation matrices using XMMatrixRotationX etc. and combining the three together into one final rotation matrix.

Other options of rotation include rotating around an axis where we provide an axis to rotate about and an angle in radians that describes by how much to rotate. This is done using XMMatrixRotationAxis:

```
XMMATRIX XMMatrixRotationAxis( XMVECTOR Axis, FLOAT Angle );
```

We can also rotate around a normal vector by using XMMatrixRotationNormal:

```
XMMATRIX XMMatrixRotationNormal( XMVECTOR NormalAxis, FLOAT Angle );
```

And we can also rotate around a quaternion using XMMatrixRotationQuaternion:

```
XMMATRIX XMMatrixRotationQuaternion( XMVECTOR Quaternion );
```

A quaternion is another mathematical object we can use to represent rotation in graphics programming. The topic of quaternions is more advanced than matrices and is definitely something you will encounter when you touch upon advanced character animation techniques, such as skinned animation using bones (skeleton).

Matrix Concatenation

The last thing you need to learn about matrices is how to combine them. Most of the time, you won't need to only translate an object, you'll need to scale it or maybe rotate it all in one go. Multiple matrices can be multiplied, or concatenated, together to create a single matrix that is capable of containing the previously single calculations. This means that instead of needing a matrix for rotation as well as one for translation, these two can be combined into one.

Depending on the platform and intrinsic used, in XNA Math we could use the overloaded multiplication operator. The following single line of code demonstrates this.

```
XMMATRIX finalMatrix = rotationMatrix * translationMatrix;
```

A new matrix called finalMatrix is created, which now contains both the rotation and translation. This new matrix can then be applied to any object going through the pipeline. One thing to mention though is to watch out for the order in which you multiply matrices. Using the previous line of code, objects will be rotated first and then translated away from that position. For example, rotating the object 90 degrees around the Y axis and then translating it four units along the X axis would cause the object to be rotated in place at the origin and then moved four units to the right. When creating a world matrix, you should combine the various matrices as scaling × rotation × translation.

If the translation appeared first, the object would be translated four units to the right of the origin first and then rotated 90 degrees. Think what would happen if you extended your hand to your right and then turned your body 90 degrees— where would your hand end up? Not exactly in the same place as before; you need to make sure that the order in which you multiply the matrices is the order you really want them applied.

In XNA Math we can also multiply matrices using the function `XMMatrixMultiply`, which takes as parameters two matrices to multiply together and returns the resulting matrix. Its prototype can be seen as follows:

```
XMMATRIX XMMatrixMultiply( XMMATRIX M1, XMMATRIX M2 );
```

Matrix concatenation is another term for matrix multiplication.

CUBE DEMO

In this chapter we will create our first true 3D demo, called the Cube demo, which is located on the companion website in the Chapter6/CubeDemo folder. By "first true 3D demo" we are referring to the fact that all demos up to this point have created a flat-colored or textured surface (e.g., triangles, sprites, etc.). Although technically these demos are 3D, since there was nothing to stop us from utilizing the Z axis of the vertices, we did not create a mesh with an actual volume. Let's start with the "Hello World" of 3D demos by creating a 3D cube.

To begin we will update our base DirectX 11 class by adding a depth/stencil view. This is related to depth and stencil testing. A stencil buffer is used primarily to render to a destination where you can increment or decrement the values in the buffer for pixels that passed the stencil test. This is often used for more advanced rendering topics, with one very famous technique being stencil shadow volumes.

Depth testing, as we mentioned in Chapter 2, is used to ensure that surfaces are properly drawn and displayed in the correct order without the need to sort polygons. For example, if we have two triangles with the same X and Y axis but separated by 100 units along the Z axis, then the triangles are not touching or overlapping. If we draw the closer triangle first and the further triangle second, the second triangle's color data will overwrite the triangle that is closer to the camera. This is not what we want, and if we want to draw those triangles properly, where the closer one is displayed to be closer than the further triangle, we'd have to spend precious resources sorting those polygons so we know the proper rendering order.

But sorting polygons is no cheap operation, and a scene can have millions of them, or at least thousands, that are visible in any given frame. The depth buffer is a simple concept that eliminates the need to presort all polygons before submitting them to the graphics hardware. Every time a surface is rendered, its vertices are transformed by the model-view projection matrix. The depth of each of these vertices as well as the interpolated depths of the pixels that lie within the surface is calculated by the hardware. The depth buffer stores the depths for each rendered pixel as long as the depth is determined (by hardware) to be closer to the viewer than what was previously rendered. If the depth is closer, then the various buffers are updated appropriately. In other words, the final rendered scene's color buffer, depth buffer, and whatever other destination targets attached are updated for those pixels that pass the depth test. Pixels that do not pass the depth test are discarded.

Note

Early 3D games like *Wolfenstein 3D* by Id Software were sorting polygons before rendering the scenes. This was one of the early uses for Binary Space Partitioning (BSP) Trees.

We can represent a depth/stencil view as an ID3D11DepthStencilView object. As we already know, in Direct3D a view is simply a way for our hardware to access a resource. In the case of a depth buffer that resource is going to be a 2D texture, and that means that in addition to creating a new ID3D11DepthStencilView object in our base class, we'll also need to create a ID3D11Texture2D object to store the contents of the depth buffer. Listing 6.1 shows our updated Dx11De-moBase class definition, where the new objects for a ID3D11DepthStencilView and a ID3D11Texture2D are added as member pointers.

Listing 6.1 Our updated Dx11DemoBase class that includes depth buffer objects.

```
class Dx11DemoBase
{
    public:
        Dx11DemoBase( );
        virtual ~Dx11DemoBase( );

        bool Initialize( HINSTANCE hInstance, HWND hwnd );
        void Shutdown( );
```

```
        bool CompileD3DShader( char* filePath, char* entry,
                               char* shaderModel, ID3DBlob** buffer );

        virtual bool LoadContent( );
        virtual void UnloadContent( );

        virtual void Update( float dt ) = 0;
        virtual void Render( ) = 0;

    protected:
        HINSTANCE hInstance_;
        HWND hwnd_;

        D3D_DRIVER_TYPE driverType_;
        D3D_FEATURE_LEVEL featureLevel_;

        ID3D11Device* d3dDevice_;
        ID3D11DeviceContext* d3dContext_;
        IDXGISwapChain* swapChain_;
        ID3D11RenderTargetView* backBufferTarget_;

        ID3D11Texture2D* depthTexture_;
        ID3D11DepthStencilView* depthStencilView_;
};
```

The base class's Initialize function must be updated to create the depth buffer. In Listing 6.2 we will omit the code from the Initialize function that we've been using in every demo of this book and only focus on the code that is new. This new code includes creating the 2D texture, creating the depth/stencil view, and attaching that view to Direct3D.

We create the 2D texture that will act as the depth buffer by simply filling out a D3D11_TEXTURE2D_DESC object with the properties necessary for the depth buffer. The depth buffer must match our rendering width and height, have a bind flag of D3D11_BIND_DEPTH_STENCIL, allow for default usage, and have a format of DXGI_FORMAT_D24_UNORM_S8_UINT. The format essentially says that we are using 24 bits for a single component that will store the depth. Since a depth is a single value, we do not need an RGB or RGBA texture image and only need to create a single component (R) texture.

Once we have the depth texture, we then create the depth/stencil view. This is done by filling out a D3D11_DEPTH_STENCIL_VIEW_DESC object with the properties that define what we are viewing, which in our case requires us to set the format to match that of the depth texture (our examples use DXGI_FORMAT_D24_UNORM_S8_UINT) and to use a view dimension flag of D3D11_DSV_DIMENSION_TEXTURE2D. The depth/stencil target is created with a call to CreateDepthStencilView, which takes as parameters the depth texture, the view description object, and a pointer to the object that will store the depth/stencil view.

Listing 6.2 shows the new code added to the Initialize function to create the depth texture and to create the render target view for the depth/stencil buffer.

Listing 6.2 The updated Initialize function.

```
bool Dx11DemoBase::Initialize( HINSTANCE hInstance, HWND hwnd )
{
    // ... Previous initialize code ...

    D3D11_TEXTURE2D_DESC depthTexDesc;
    ZeroMemory( &depthTexDesc, sizeof( depthTexDesc ) );
    depthTexDesc.Width = width;
    depthTexDesc.Height = height;
    depthTexDesc.MipLevels = 1;
    depthTexDesc.ArraySize = 1;
    depthTexDesc.Format = DXGI_FORMAT_D24_UNORM_S8_UINT;
    depthTexDesc.SampleDesc.Count = 1;
    depthTexDesc.SampleDesc.Quality = 0;
    depthTexDesc.Usage = D3D11_USAGE_DEFAULT;
    depthTexDesc.BindFlags = D3D11_BIND_DEPTH_STENCIL;
    depthTexDesc.CPUAccessFlags = 0;
    depthTexDesc.MiscFlags = 0;

    result = d3dDevice_->CreateTexture2D( &depthTexDesc, NULL, &depthTexture_ );

    if( FAILED( result ) )
    {
        DXTRACE_MSG( "Failed to create the depth texture!" );
```

```
        return false;
    }

    // Create the depth stencil view
    D3D11_DEPTH_STENCIL_VIEW_DESC descDSV;
    ZeroMemory( &descDSV, sizeof( descDSV ) );
    descDSV.Format = depthTexDesc.Format;
    descDSV.ViewDimension = D3D11_DSV_DIMENSION_TEXTURE2D;
    descDSV.Texture2D.MipSlice = 0;

    result = d3dDevice_->CreateDepthStencilView( depthTexture_, &descDSV,
        &depthStencilView_ );

    if( FAILED( result ) )
    {
        DXTRACE_MSG( "Failed to create the depth stencil target view!" );
        return false;
    }

    d3dContext_->OMSetRenderTargets( 1, &backBufferTarget_, depthStencil-
View_ );

    D3D11_VIEWPORT viewport;
    viewport.Width = static_cast<float>( width );
    viewport.Height = static_cast<float>( height );
    viewport.MinDepth = 0.0f;
    viewport.MaxDepth = 1.0f;
    viewport.TopLeftX = 0.0f;
    viewport.TopLeftY = 0.0f;

    d3dContext_->RSSetViewports( 1, &viewport );

    return LoadContent( );
}
```

Since our depth texture and view are objects that consume resources, we must remember to release these resources in the base class's Shutdown function, which can be seen in Listing 6.3.

Listing 6.3 The updated Shutdown function.

```
void Dx11DemoBase::Shutdown( )
{
    UnloadContent( );

    if( depthTexture_ ) depthTexture_->Release( );
    if( depthStencilView_ ) depthStencilView_->Release( );
    if( backBufferTarget_ ) backBufferTarget_->Release( );
    if( swapChain_ ) swapChain_->Release( );
    if( d3dContext_ ) d3dContext_->Release( );
    if( d3dDevice_ ) d3dDevice_->Release( );

    depthTexture_ = 0;
    depthStencilView_ = 0;
    backBufferTarget_ = 0;
    swapChain_ = 0;
    d3dContext_ = 0;
    d3dDevice_ = 0;
}
```

Our demo class will be called CubeDemo. This CubeDemo class will create three constant buffers for the model, view, and projection matrices. Since our demos really only need to combine these matrices into a model-view projection matrix, we'll keep them separate to show an example of utilizing multiple constant buffers. Later in this section you'll see how this relates to HLSL and setting usage trends.

Also in the demo we create an index buffer. In Chapter 3 we mentioned that an index buffer is used to specify array indices into a vertex list to specify which vertices form triangles. With large polygon count (closed volume) models this can save a lot of memory when representing our geometry. Knowing how to create an index buffer is important when it comes to 3D rendering, so we will cover this in this demo.

The CubeDemo can be seen in Listing 6.4. It builds off of the Texture Mapping demo of Chapter 3. We are also storing the view and projection matrices on the class level, since these never change in this specific demo and don't need to be recalculated for each frame. In Chapter 8, when we talk about cameras, we will update the view matrix each frame in the Update function, and that camera demo will build directly off of this demo's code.

Listing 6.4 The CubeDemo class.

```
#include"Dx11DemoBase.h"
#include<xnamath.h>


class CubeDemo : public Dx11DemoBase
{
    public:
        CubeDemo( );
        virtual ~CubeDemo( );

        bool LoadContent( );
        void UnloadContent( );

        void Update( float dt );
        void Render( );

    private:
        ID3D11VertexShader* solidColorVS_;
        ID3D11PixelShader* solidColorPS_;

        ID3D11InputLayout* inputLayout_;
        ID3D11Buffer* vertexBuffer_;
        ID3D11Buffer* indexBuffer_;

        ID3D11ShaderResourceView* colorMap_;
        ID3D11SamplerState* colorMapSampler_;

        ID3D11Buffer* viewCB_;
        ID3D11Buffer* projCB_;
        ID3D11Buffer* worldCB_;
        XMMATRIX viewMatrix_;
        XMMATRIX projMatrix_;
};
```

We must update the LoadContent function to load a 3D cube into the vertex buffer instead of the square that we were loading in the Texture Mapping demo. This is done simply by specifying each triangle one at a time in the vertices list for the triangles of the cube. We also create an index buffer that specifies which vertices form which triangles. If you look up the vertices manually (as an exercise) using the array indices in the index buffer, then you can clearly see how each triangle is specified.

Creating the index buffer is done the exact same way as the vertex buffer, with the exception that we are using a bind flag of D3D11_BIND_INDEX_BUFFER. That's it! At the end of the LoadContent function we create our three constant buffers, and we initialize our view and projection matrices. Since we don't have a camera yet, the view matrix will equal an identity matrix (this will change in Chapter 8). The projection matrix is created as a perspective projection, which can be done with a call to XMMatrixPerspectiveFovLH. The XMMatrixPerspectiveFovLH function takes as parameters the field of view of the camera in radians, the aspect ratio of the camera, and the near and far clip planes. If you wish to specify the field of view in degrees, you'll have to convert those degrees to radians yourself before passing it as a parameter to this function. Also, the aspect ratio is measured as the width divided by the height.

The updated LoadContent function can be seen in Listing 6.5. The bulk of the code deals with defining the triangle data manually. In Chapter 8 we will explore loading models from files exported by tools such as 3D Studio Max, which is necessary for complex and detailed models.

Listing 6.5 The updated LoadContent function.

```
bool CubeDemo::LoadContent( )
{
    // ... Previous demo's LoadContent code ...


    VertexPos vertices[] =
    {
        { XMFLOAT3( -1.0f,  1.0f, -1.0f ), XMFLOAT2( 0.0f, 0.0f ) },
        { XMFLOAT3(  1.0f,  1.0f, -1.0f ), XMFLOAT2( 1.0f, 0.0f ) },
        { XMFLOAT3(  1.0f,  1.0f,  1.0f ), XMFLOAT2( 1.0f, 1.0f ) },
        { XMFLOAT3( -1.0f,  1.0f,  1.0f ), XMFLOAT2( 0.0f, 1.0f ) },

        { XMFLOAT3( -1.0f, -1.0f, -1.0f ), XMFLOAT2( 0.0f, 0.0f ) },
        { XMFLOAT3(  1.0f, -1.0f, -1.0f ), XMFLOAT2( 1.0f, 0.0f ) },
        { XMFLOAT3(  1.0f, -1.0f,  1.0f ), XMFLOAT2( 1.0f, 1.0f ) },
        { XMFLOAT3( -1.0f, -1.0f,  1.0f ), XMFLOAT2( 0.0f, 1.0f ) },
```

```
    { XMFLOAT3( -1.0f, -1.0f,  1.0f ), XMFLOAT2( 0.0f, 0.0f ) },
    { XMFLOAT3( -1.0f, -1.0f, -1.0f ), XMFLOAT2( 1.0f, 0.0f ) },
    { XMFLOAT3( -1.0f,  1.0f, -1.0f ), XMFLOAT2( 1.0f, 1.0f ) },
    { XMFLOAT3( -1.0f,  1.0f,  1.0f ), XMFLOAT2( 0.0f, 1.0f ) },

    { XMFLOAT3(  1.0f, -1.0f,  1.0f ), XMFLOAT2( 0.0f, 0.0f ) },
    { XMFLOAT3(  1.0f, -1.0f, -1.0f ), XMFLOAT2( 1.0f, 0.0f ) },
    { XMFLOAT3(  1.0f,  1.0f, -1.0f ), XMFLOAT2( 1.0f, 1.0f ) },
    { XMFLOAT3(  1.0f,  1.0f,  1.0f ), XMFLOAT2( 0.0f, 1.0f ) },

    { XMFLOAT3( -1.0f, -1.0f, -1.0f ), XMFLOAT2( 0.0f, 0.0f ) },
    { XMFLOAT3(  1.0f, -1.0f, -1.0f ), XMFLOAT2( 1.0f, 0.0f ) },
    { XMFLOAT3(  1.0f,  1.0f, -1.0f ), XMFLOAT2( 1.0f, 1.0f ) },
    { XMFLOAT3( -1.0f,  1.0f, -1.0f ), XMFLOAT2( 0.0f, 1.0f ) },

    { XMFLOAT3( -1.0f, -1.0f,  1.0f ), XMFLOAT2( 0.0f, 0.0f ) },
    { XMFLOAT3(  1.0f, -1.0f,  1.0f ), XMFLOAT2( 1.0f, 0.0f ) },
    { XMFLOAT3(  1.0f,  1.0f,  1.0f ), XMFLOAT2( 1.0f, 1.0f ) },
    { XMFLOAT3( -1.0f,  1.0f,  1.0f ), XMFLOAT2( 0.0f, 1.0f ) },
};

D3D11_BUFFER_DESC vertexDesc;
ZeroMemory( &vertexDesc, sizeof( vertexDesc ) );
vertexDesc.Usage = D3D11_USAGE_DEFAULT;
vertexDesc.BindFlags = D3D11_BIND_VERTEX_BUFFER;
vertexDesc.ByteWidth = sizeof( VertexPos ) * 24;

D3D11_SUBRESOURCE_DATA resourceData;
ZeroMemory( &resourceData, sizeof( resourceData ) );
resourceData.pSysMem = vertices;

d3dResult = d3dDevice_->CreateBuffer( &vertexDesc,
    &resourceData, &vertexBuffer_ );

if( FAILED( d3dResult ) )
{
    DXTRACE_MSG( "Failed to create vertex buffer!" );
    return false;
}
```

```
WORD indices[] =
{
    3,   1,  0,  2,  1,  3,
    6,   4,  5,  7,  4,  6,
    11,  9,  8, 10,  9, 11,
    14, 12, 13, 15, 12, 14,
    19, 17, 16, 18, 17, 19,
    22, 20, 21, 23, 20, 22
};

D3D11_BUFFER_DESC indexDesc;
ZeroMemory( &indexDesc, sizeof( indexDesc ) );
indexDesc.Usage = D3D11_USAGE_DEFAULT;
indexDesc.BindFlags = D3D11_BIND_INDEX_BUFFER;
indexDesc.ByteWidth = sizeof( WORD ) * 36;
indexDesc.CPUAccessFlags = 0;
resourceData.pSysMem = indices;

d3dResult = d3dDevice_->CreateBuffer( &indexDesc,
    &resourceData, &indexBuffer_ );

if( FAILED( d3dResult ) )
{
    DXTRACE_MSG( "Failed to create index buffer!" );
    return false;
}

d3dResult = D3DX11CreateShaderResourceViewFromFile( d3dDevice_,
    "decal.dds", 0, 0, &colorMap_, 0 );

if( FAILED( d3dResult ) )
{
    DXTRACE_MSG( "Failed to load the texture image!" );
    return false;
}

D3D11_SAMPLER_DESC colorMapDesc;
ZeroMemory( &colorMapDesc, sizeof( colorMapDesc ) );
colorMapDesc.AddressU = D3D11_TEXTURE_ADDRESS_WRAP;
colorMapDesc.AddressV = D3D11_TEXTURE_ADDRESS_WRAP;
```

```
colorMapDesc.AddressW = D3D11_TEXTURE_ADDRESS_WRAP;
colorMapDesc.ComparisonFunc = D3D11_COMPARISON_NEVER;
colorMapDesc.Filter = D3D11_FILTER_MIN_MAG_MIP_LINEAR;
colorMapDesc.MaxLOD = D3D11_FLOAT32_MAX;

d3dResult = d3dDevice_->CreateSamplerState( &colorMapDesc,
    &colorMapSampler_ );

if( FAILED( d3dResult ) )
{
    DXTRACE_MSG( "Failed to create color map sampler state!" );
    return false;
}


D3D11_BUFFER_DESC constDesc;
ZeroMemory( &constDesc, sizeof( constDesc ) );
constDesc.BindFlags = D3D11_BIND_CONSTANT_BUFFER;
constDesc.ByteWidth = sizeof( XMMATRIX );
constDesc.Usage = D3D11_USAGE_DEFAULT;

d3dResult = d3dDevice_->CreateBuffer( &constDesc, 0, &viewCB_ );

if( FAILED( d3dResult ) )
{
    return false;
}

d3dResult = d3dDevice_->CreateBuffer( &constDesc, 0, &projCB_ );

if( FAILED( d3dResult ) )
{
    return false;
}

d3dResult = d3dDevice_->CreateBuffer( &constDesc, 0, &worldCB_ );

if( FAILED( d3dResult ) )
{
    return false;
```

```
    }

    viewMatrix_ = XMMatrixIdentity( );
    projMatrix_ = XMMatrixPerspectiveFovLH( XM_PIDIV4, 800.0f / 600.0f,
        0.01f, 100.0f );

    viewMatrix_ = XMMatrixTranspose(viewMatrix_ );
    projMatrix_ = XMMatrixTranspose( projMatrix_ );

    return true;
}
```

Remember that all of our new objects need to be released by the UnloadContent function. This includes our three constant buffers and well as our newly created index buffer. This can be seen in Listing 6.6 in the updated UnloadContent function.

Listing 6.6 The updated UnloadContent function.

```
void CubeDemo::UnloadContent( )
{
    if( colorMapSampler_ ) colorMapSampler_->Release( );
    if( colorMap_ ) colorMap_->Release( );
    if( solidColorVS_ ) solidColorVS_->Release( );
    if( solidColorPS_ ) solidColorPS_->Release( );
    if( inputLayout_ ) inputLayout_->Release( );
    if( vertexBuffer_ ) vertexBuffer_->Release( );
    if( indexBuffer_ ) indexBuffer_->Release( );
    if( viewCB_ ) viewCB_->Release( );
    if( projCB_ ) projCB_->Release( );
    if( worldCB_ ) worldCB_->Release( );

    colorMapSampler_ = 0;
    colorMap_ = 0;
    solidColorVS_ = 0;
    solidColorPS_ = 0;
    inputLayout_ = 0;
    vertexBuffer_ = 0;
    indexBuffer_ = 0;
    viewCB_ = 0;
```

```
    projCB_ = 0;
    worldCB_ = 0;
}
```

The last code to cover is the HLSL shader and the rendering function. The rendering function adds a line of code to clear the depth buffer by calling the device context's `ClearDepthStencilView` function, which takes as parameters the depth/stencil view, what we are clearing (in this case we use the clear depth flag of `D3D11_CLEAR_DEPTH`), a value between 0 and 1 to clear the depth buffer to, and a value to clear the stencil buffer to.

Before we begin rendering, we must set the index buffer to the input assembler, since we are making use of it. This is done with a call to `IASetIndexBuffer`, which takes as parameters the index buffer, the data format of the buffer, and a starting offset in bytes. The format we used to create the index buffer is a 16-bit unsigned integer, which means we must use `DXGI_FORMAT_R16_UINT` for the data format parameter of this function. Whatever format you use for the index buffer array must be passed to this function so that Direct3D knows how to properly access the elements of the buffer.

The last steps we take are to bind our constant buffer and draw our geometry. We bind each constant buffer to `b0`, `b1`, and `b2`, which are specified in the HLSL shader file. To draw the data, we don't use a call to the `Draw` function but instead we call the `DrawIndexed` function. `DrawIndexed` takes as parameters the number of indices in the index buffer, the starting index we are drawing, and the base vertex location, which is an offset added to each index before reading from the vertex buffer. This can be useful when only drawing portions of the vertex buffer, which can happen if you batched multiple models in one larger vertex buffer. That is a topic for advanced rendering optimizations.

The updated rendering function can be seen in Listing 6.7.

Listing 6.7 The updated `Render` function.

```
void CubeDemo::Render( )
{
    if( d3dContext_ == 0 )
        return;

    float clearColor[4] = { 0.0f, 0.0f, 0.25f, 1.0f };
```

```
    d3dContext_->ClearRenderTargetView( backBufferTarget_, clearColor );
    d3dContext_->ClearDepthStencilView( depthStencilView_,
        D3D11_CLEAR_DEPTH, 1.0f, 0 );

    unsigned int stride = sizeof( VertexPos );
    unsigned int offset = 0;

    d3dContext_->IASetInputLayout( inputLayout_ );
    d3dContext_->IASetVertexBuffers( 0, 1, &vertexBuffer_, &stride, &offset );
    d3dContext_->IASetIndexBuffer( indexBuffer_, DXGI_FORMAT_R16_UINT, 0 );
    d3dContext_->IASetPrimitiveTopology(D3D11_PRIMITIVE_TOPOLOGY_TRIANGLE
LIST);

    d3dContext_->VSSetShader( solidColorVS_, 0, 0 );
    d3dContext_->PSSetShader( solidColorPS_, 0, 0 );
    d3dContext_->PSSetShaderResources( 0, 1, &colorMap_ );
    d3dContext_->PSSetSamplers( 0, 1, &colorMapSampler_ );

    XMMATRIX rotationMat = XMMatrixRotationRollPitchYaw( 0.0f, 0.7f, 0.7f );
    XMMATRIX translationMat = XMMatrixTranslation( 0.0f, 0.0f, 6.0f );

    XMMATRIX worldMat = rotationMat * translationMat;
    worldMat = XMMatrixTranspose( worldMat );


    d3dContext_->UpdateSubresource( worldCB_, 0, 0, &worldMat, 0, 0 );
    d3dContext_->UpdateSubresource( viewCB_, 0, 0, &viewMatrix_, 0, 0 );
    d3dContext_->UpdateSubresource( projCB_, 0, 0, &projMatrix_, 0, 0 );

    d3dContext_->VSSetConstantBuffers( 0, 1, &worldCB_ );
    d3dContext_->VSSetConstantBuffers( 1, 1, &viewCB_ );
    d3dContext_->VSSetConstantBuffers( 2, 1, &projCB_ );

    d3dContext_->DrawIndexed( 36, 0, 0 );

    swapChain_->Present( 0, 0 );
}
```

In the HLSL code we create three constant buffers that we register to b0, b1, and b2. We must keep in mind that the buffers must be consistent to what we've specified in the Render function so that the correct buffer is registered to the correct HLSL object.

For the constant buffer we have cbChangesEveryFrame, cbNeverChanges, and cbChangeOnResize. This is done a lot in the DirectX SDK, and by grouping our constant buffer objects by how often they are updated, we can update all the necessary constants for a particular update frequency at the same time. Again, for our purposes we can do what we've done in past demos and use one constant buffer for the model-view projection matrix. The naming convention used for the constant buffers simply allows us to easily see how often the objects within are updated by the outside program.

The remainder of the HLSL code is essentially the same as the Texture Mapping demo, with the exception of the fact that we are transforming the incoming vertex by the model, view, and projection matrices separately. The demo's HLSL shader file can be seen in Listing 6.8. A screenshot of the demo can be seen in Figure 6.5.

Figure 6.5
3D Cube demo screenshot.

Listing 6.8 The HLSL shader for the CubeDemo.

```
Texture2D colorMap_ : register( t0 );
SamplerState colorSampler_ : register( s0 );


cbuffer cbChangesEveryFrame : register( b0 )
{
    matrix worldMatrix;
};

cbuffer cbNeverChanges : register( b1 )
{
    matrix viewMatrix;
};

cbuffer cbChangeOnResize : register( b2 )
{
    matrix projMatrix;
};


struct VS_Input
{
    float4 pos   : POSITION;
    float2 tex0 : TEXCOORD0;
};

struct PS_Input
{
    float4 pos   : SV_POSITION;
    float2 tex0 : TEXCOORD0;
};


PS_Input VS_Main( VS_Input vertex )
{
    PS_Input vsOut = ( PS_Input )0;
    vsOut.pos = mul( vertex.pos, worldMatrix );
    vsOut.pos = mul( vsOut.pos, viewMatrix );
    vsOut.pos = mul( vsOut.pos, projMatrix );
```

```
    vsOut.tex0 = vertex.tex0;

    return vsOut;
}


float4 PS_Main( PS_Input frag ) : SV_TARGET
{
    return colorMap_.Sample( colorSampler_, frag.tex0 );
}
```

ADDITIONAL XNA MATH TOPICS

XNA Math has hundreds of functions and structures. There would be too much to cover in just one chapter, and the math behind it could span multiple books. In the remainder of this chapter we will look at other areas of XNA Math that might be important to know for a user at the beginner level of working with DirectX 11.

Compiler Directives

XNA Math has a list of compiler directives used to tune how XNA Math is compiled and used within an application. These compiler directives give developers the ability to specify their applications' functionality and include the following:

- _XM_NO_INTRINSICS_
- _XM_SSE_INTRINSICS_
- _XM_VMX128_INTRINSICS_
- XM_NO_ALIGNMENT
- XM_NO_MISALIGNED_VECTOR_ACCESS
- XM_NO_OPERATOR_OVERLOADS
- XM_STRICT_VECTOR4

_XM_NO_INTRINSICS_ defines that no intrinsic types are to be used and that the XNA Math library will only use standard floating-point precision when performing its operations. This can be seen as the behavior that will allow an application to use XNA Math with no special optimizations or functionality.

_XM_SSE_INTRINSICS_ is used to enable the use of SSE and SSE2 intrinsic types on platforms that support it. This define has no effect on platforms that do not support SSE and SSE2. SSE and SSE2 are types of SIMD (single-instruction multiple data) operations that aim to boost performance by providing instruction-level parallelism, or in other words allow multiple operations to be done on multiple pieces of data at the same time. SIMD is discussed in more detail later in this chapter under the subsection "SIMD." SSE stands for Streaming SIMD Extension.

_XM_VMX128_INTRINSICS_ is used to define that the Xbox 360 target use the VMX128 intrinsic but has no effect on other platforms. VMX is another SIMD set of instructions. VMX128 is an extension of the VMX set for use in Xenon processors, which is found inside the Xbox 360. Using this intrinsic should be done if the game is being targeted toward the Xbox 360.

XM_NO_ALIGNMENT is used to define that no alignment should be made to the data. For example, the XMMATRIX type structure will not be aligned to 16 bytes using this directive. This is not defined by default since by default alignment takes places.

XM_NO_MISALIGNED_VECTOR_ACCESS is used to improve the performance of the VMX128 intrinsic when operating on write-combined memory. This affects the Xbox 360's Xenon processor.

XM_NO_OPERATOR_OVERLOADS is used to disable the use of C++ style operator overloads. By default this is not defined, but it can be used to force the omission of overloaded operators.

XM_STRICT_VECTOR4 is used to determine if the X, Y, Z, and W components of the XMVECTOR and XMVECTORI types can be directly accessed (e.g., float $\times$ Val = vec.x). This only affects Xbox 360 targets that are defined using the __vector4 intrinsic type and has no effect on Windows targets using the __m128 type. Accessor functions can be used to access members of these structures when this strict directive is used.

Constants

Compiler constants provide useful information to developers using the XNA Math library. The list of constants and what each one represents can be seen in the following:

- XNAMATH_VERSION—Used to obtain the XNA Math library version.

- XM_CACHE_LINE_SIZE—The size in bytes of the cache line used by stream operations within the XNA Math library.

- XM_PI—Represents the value of PI.

- XM_2PI—Represents the value of $2 \times$ PI.

- XM_1DIVPI—Represents the value of 1 / PI.

- XM_1DIV2PI—Represents the value of 2 / PI.

- XM_PIDIV2—Represents the value of PI / 2.

- XM_PIDIV4—Represents the value of PI / 4.

- XM_PERMUTE_0X—This is a constant used to create a control vector that controls how data is copied using the XMVectorPermute function. For this constant the first vector's X component is copied to the result vector's location dictated by the control vector.

- XM_PERMUTE_0Y—This is a constant used to create a control vector that controls how data is copied using the XMVectorPermute function. For this constant the first vector's Y component is copied to the result vector's location dictated by the control vector.

- XM_PERMUTE_0Z—This is a constant used to create a control vector that controls how data is copied using the XMVectorPermute function. For this constant the first vector's Z component is copied to the result vector's location dictated by the control vector.

- XM_PERMUTE_0W—This is a constant used to create a control vector that controls how data is copied using the XMVectorPermute function. For this constant the first vector's W component is copied to the result vector's location dictated by the control vector.

- XM_PERMUTE_1X—This is a constant used to create a control vector that controls how data is copied using the XMVectorPermute function. For this constant the second vector's X component is copied to the result vector's location dictated by the control vector.

- XM_PERMUTE_1Y—This is a constant used to create a control vector that controls how data is copied using the XMVectorPermute function. For this constant the second vector's Y component is copied to the result vector's location dictated by the control vector.

- XM_PERMUTE_1Z—This is a constant used to create a control vector that controls how data is copied using the XMVectorPermute function. For this constant the second vector's Z component is copied to the result vector's location dictated by the control vector.

- XM_PERMUTE_1W—This is a constant used to create a control vector that controls how data is copied using the XMVectorPermute function. For this constant the second vector's W component is copied to the result vector's location dictated by the control vector.

- XM_SELECT_0—Used to construct a control vector that controls how components are copied when using XMVectorSelect. The first vector's component is copied to the index location in the result vector that is specified by the control vector.

- XM_SELECT_1—Used to construct a control vector that controls how components are copied when using XMVectorSelect. The second vector's component is copied to the index location in the result vector that is specified by the control vector.

- XM_CRMASK_CR6—A mask used to obtain a comparison result.

- XM_CRMASK_CR6TRUE—A mask used to obtain a comparison result and indicate if it is logically true.

- XM_CRMASK_CR6FALSE—A mask used to obtain a comparison result and indicate if it is logically false.

- XM_CRMASK_CR6BOUNDS—A mask used to obtain a comparison result and to verify if the results indicate some of the inputs were out of bounds.

Macros

Macros are available in XNA Math to provide extra functionality for common operations such as comparison operations, min and max determination, asserts, and the ability to mark objects as global. The complete list of XNA Math macros is seen in the following:

- XMASSERT

- XMGLOBALCONST

- XMComparisonAllFalse

- XMComparisonAllTrue

- XMComparisonAllInBounds

- XMComparisonAnyFalse

- XMComparisonAnyOutOfBounds

- XMComparisonAnyTrue

- XMComparisonMixed

- XMMax

- XMMin

XMASSERT provides debugging information by using assertions that are raised when a condition is false. This macro takes the expression to test and will include the file and line information for you.

XMGLOBALCONST is used to specify an object as a "pick-any" global constant and is used to reduce the size of the data segment and avoid reloads of global constants that are used and declared in multiple places within the XNA Math library.

XMComparisonAllFalse is used to compare all components and to return true if they all evaluate to false.

XMComparisonAllTrue is used to compare all components and to return true if they all evaluate to true.

XMComparisonAllInBounds is used to test if all components are within the allowed bounds. True is returned if they are all within the bounds.

XMComparisonAnyFalse returns true if any, not necessarily all, of the components evaluate to false.

XMComparisonAnyOutOfBounds returns true if any, not necessarily all, of the components are out of bounds.

XMComparisonAnyTrue returns true if any component, not necessarily all, evaluates to true.

XMComparisonMixed returns true if some of the components evaluated to true while others evaluated to false.

XMMax compares two types and returns the one determined to be larger using the operator <.

XMMin compares two types and returns the one determined to be smaller using the operator <.

Structures and Types

The goal of these various structures and types is to encapsulate their functionality to make them easier to code with, easier to obtain portability, and allows for data optimizations. All of these structures and types are exposed via the header file xnamath.h. So far we've briefly touched upon a few vector and matrix structures, but in this section we will look at all of them.

The first sets of structures we will look at are the following:

- XMBYTE4
- XMBYTEN4
- XMCOLOR
- XMDEC4
- XMDECN4
- XMDHEN3
- XMDHENN3

The XMBYTE4 structure is used to create a four-component vector where each component is 1 byte (using the char data type). The XMBYTEN4 is similar to the XMBYTE4 structure with the exception that XMBYTEN4 is used to store normalized input. When XMBYTEN4 is initialized, its inputs are multiplied by 127.0f and scaled to fit the range 0.0 – 1.0f. Input data are to be in the range of -127.0f and 127.0f when using XMBYTEN4.

XMCOLOR is a 32-bit color structure that stores red, blue, green, and alpha color channels. Each channel is an unsigned 8-bit value, where all four 8-bit channels total 32 bits for the entire structure. This is the same as XMBYTE4.

The XMDEC4 structure uses 10 bits for the X, Y, and Z components and uses 2 bits for the W. This totals 32 bits for the structure. XMDECN4 stores normalized values. On the other hand, XMDHEN3 stores 10 bits for the X component and stores 11 bits for the Y and Z components. XMDHENN3 stores the normalized values of a XMDHEN3. These can be used if you need structures that provide more bits per component while totaling 32 bits in all.

The next set of structures deals with 2D components:

- XMFLOAT2
- XMFLOAT2A
- XMHALF2
- XMSHORT2
- XMSHORTN2
- XMUSHORT2
- XMUSHORTN2

XMFLOAT2 was mentioned earlier in this chapter and is used to represent a 2D floating-point vector. XMFLOAT2A represents a 16-byte boundary aligned XMFLOAT2.

XMHALF2 is a 2D vector used to store half-precision 16-bit floating-point components (instead of 32 bits per component), whereas XMSHORT2 is a 2D vector storing half-precision 16-bit integer components. The U after XM for these structures are used to specify that they are unsigned, and the N that follows the number of components at the end of the names represents that they store normalized values. Therefore the appearance of a U and N represents an unsigned normalized structure.

The next list displays all structures that are based on three components:

- XMFLOAT3
- XMFLOAT3A

- XMFLOAT3PK

- XMFLOAT3SE

- XMHEND3

- XMHENDN3

- XMDHEN3

- XMDHENN3

- XMU555

- XMU565

- XMUDHEN3

- XMUDHENN3

- XMUHEND3

- XMUHENDN3

XMFLOAT3, which was mentioned in the "Vectors" section earlier in this chapter, is a three-component structure of floating-point values. XMFLOAT3A is used for 16-byte aligned three-component vectors. XMFLOAT3PK is used for three-component vectors, where the X and Y components are 10 bits each, and the Z is 11 bits, whereas XMFLOAT3SE is a vector where the components use nine bits for the mantissa and five bits for the exponent.

XMDHEN3 (and its normalized form XMDHENN3) are 3D integer vectors with 10 bits for the X components and 11 bits for the Y and Z. The XMHEND3 and XMHENDN3 are used to store 11 bits for the X and Y and 10 bits for the Z components. The unsigned versions of these are XMUDHEN3 and XMUDHENN3.

The XMU555 is used to create a three-component vector that uses five bits for each component. The XMU565 creates a three-component vector that uses five bits for the X and Z components but uses six bits for the Y.

The next list displays the 4D vector structures in the XNA Math library:

- XMFLOAT4

- XMFLOAT4A

- XMHALF4

- XMICO4

- XMICON4

- XMSHORT4

- XMSHORTN4

- XMUBYTE4

- XMUBYTEN4

- XMUDEC4

- XMUDECN4

- XMUICO4

- XMUICON4

- XMUNIBBLE4

- XMUSHORT4

- XMUSHORTN4

- XMXDEC4

- XMXDECN4

- XMXICO4

- XMXICON4

XMFLOAT4 is a four-component floating-point vector that was mentioned in the "Vectors" section of this chapter. XMHALF4 is a half-precision 4D vector, and XMSHORT4 is half-precision using short integers. Again, the A that follows the structure names is for byte-aligned structures, while N is for normalized versions of them.

XMUBYTE4 is for a four-component unsigned byte (char) structure, and XMUNIB-BLE4 uses four 4-bit integer components. The structures with ICO in their names use 20 bits for the X, Y, and Z components while using four bits for the W, which totals 64 bits for the ICO structures. The structures with DEC in their names use 10 bits for the X, Y, and Z components and two bits for the W, which totals 32 bits for the DEC structures. The XICO and XDEC structures use signed values, whereas UICO and UDEC use unsigned values.

The next list of structures is related to matrices:

- XMFLOAT3x3

- XMFLOAT4x3

- XMFLOAT4x3A

- XMFLOAT4x4

- XMFLOAT4x4A

- XMMATRIX

XMFLOAT3x3 represents a 3×3 matrix of floating-point values (9 in total) and is usually used to represent rotation matrices. XMFLOAT4x3 represents 4×3 matrices (12 elements in total), and XMFLOAT4x4 represents 4×4 matrices (16 elements in total). The A that follows the structure names indicates that they are aligned structures. XMMATRIX is a row-major 4×4 byte-aligned matrix that maps to four vector hardware registers.

The final list that we'll look at includes the additional types available using XNA Math. These additional types are listed as follows:

- HALF

- XMVECTOR

- XMVECTORF32

- XMVECTORI32

- XMVECTORU32

- XMVECTORU8

The HALF data type, which is aliased by USHORT, is a 16-bit floating-point number. It uses five bits for the exponent and 10 for the mantissa and has a sign bit.

The XMVECTOR structure is a four-component structure where each component is represented by 32 bits. This structure can use floating-point numbers or integers and is also optimally aligned and mapped to a hardware vector register. XMVECTOR was discussed in the "Vectors" section of this chapter.

The XMVECTORF32 is a portable 32-bit floating-point structure used by C++ initializer syntax to initialize a XMVECTOR structure to use floating-point values.

The XMVECTORI32 is a portable 32-bit integer structure used by C++ initializer syntax to initialize a XMVECTOR structure to use integer values.

The XMVECTORU32 is a portable structure used by C++ initializer syntax to initialize a XMVECTOR structure to use unsigned integer values (UINT).

The XMVECTORI32 is a portable 8-bit structure used by C++ initializer syntax to initialize a XMVECTOR structure to use byte values (char).

Additional Functions

In this section we will briefly discuss the additional functions available through XNA Math that we have yet to touch upon. These functions deal with colors, conversions, and scalars. The first type we'll discuss is the color functions.

Color Functions

XNA Math has several functions useful for performing color manipulation on data. The first is used to adjust the contrast of a single color and is called XMColorAdjustContrast, whose prototype can be seen as follows:

XMVECTOR XMColorAdjustContrast(XMVECTOR C, FLOAT Contrast);

The first parameter of the XMColorAdjustContrast function is an XMVECTOR that represents a color value, where each component is to be in the range of 0.0 to 1.0f. If the contrast is 0.0f, then the color is adjusted by 50% gray; if the contrast is 1.0f, then the full color is returned. Anything between the two extremes will return a contrasted color.

The next function is called XMColorAdjustSaturation, and it is used to adjust the saturation of a color value. Its prototype is:

XMVECTOR XMColorAdjustSaturation(XMVECTOR C, FLOAT Saturation);

The first parameter of the function XMColorAdjustSaturation is also a XMVECTOR that represents a color value, where each component is to be in the range of 0.0 to 1.0f. If the saturation is 0.0f, then a gray color is returned; if the saturation is 1.0f, then the full color is returned. Anything between 0.0 and 1.0 for the saturation will return a value that linearly interpolates between the two (i.e., gray and the original color).

The next six functions are comparison functions. These functions include testing if two vectors are equal, not equal, greater than, less than, greater than or equal to, or less than or equal to. The functions test the first parameter with the second and return a true/false result. Each of the comparison functions can be seen as follows:

```
BOOL XMColorEqual( XMVECTOR C1, XMVECTOR C2 );
BOOL XMColorNotEqual( XMVECTOR C1, XMVECTOR C2 );

BOOL XMColorGreater( XMVECTOR C1, XMVECTOR C2 );
BOOL XMColorGreaterOrEqual( XMVECTOR C1, XMVECTOR C2 );

BOOL XMColorLess( XMVECTOR C1, XMVECTOR C2 );
BOOL XMColorLessOrEqual( XMVECTOR C1, XMVECTOR C2 );
```

Another two functions that deal with comparison are XMColorIsInfinite, which tests if a color is equal to infinity, and XMColorIsNaN which looks to see if one of the components is defined as NaN (not a number).

```
BOOL XMColorIsInfinite( XMVECTOR C );
BOOL XMColorIsNaN( XMVECTOR C );
```

The next function is called XMColorModulate, and it is used to blend two colors together. The last color function is XMColorNegative, which is used to negate a color. The function prototypes for these last two color functions are:

```
XMVECTOR XMColorModulate( XMVECTOR C1, XMVECTOR C2 );
XMVECTOR XMColorNegative( XMVECTOR C );
```

The XMColorNegative function is similar to performing the following:

```
XMVECTOR col, result;

result.x = 1.0f - col.x;
result.y = 1.0f - col.y;
result.z = 1.0f - col.z;
result.w = 1.0f - col.w;
```

A black color component would become white using XMColorNegative, while white would become black. The same goes for intensities between 0.0 and 1.0, where their intensity of light and dark will be swapped.

Conversion Functions

The conversion set of XNA Math functions is used to convert values from one type to another. The XMConvertFloatToHalf function, the prototype of which can be seen below, converts a 32-bit floating-point value to a HALF (half-precision). All floating-point exceptions such as NaN, negative and positive infinity, etc., are converted to the value of 0x7FFF.

```
HALF XMConvertFloatToHalf( FLOAT Value );
```

To convert a HALF back to a floating-point value, we could use the following function:

```
FLOAT XMConvertHalfToFloat( HALF Value );
```

Values passed to XMConvertHalfToFloat that equal 0x7FFF are converted to 131008.0f, according to the XNA Math documentation.

If an array of values needs to be converted, we can use the XMConvertFloatTo-HalfStream and XMConvertHalfToFloatStream. These functions take as parameters the address of the first value in the output stream array, the stride in bytes between each output value, the address of the first element in the input array, the stride in bytes between each input value, and the total number of elements we are converting. Both of these functions also return the first address of the output stream, and their prototypes can be seen as follows:

```
HALF* XMConvertFloatToHalfStream( HALF* pOutputStream, UINT OutputStride,
    CONST FLOAT* pInputStream, UINT InputStride, UINT FloatCount );

FLOAT* XMConvertHalfToFloatStream( FLOAT *pOutputStream, UINT OutputStride,
    CONST HALF* pInputStream, UINT InputStride, UINT HalfCount );
```

Another set of useful functions is those dedicated to converting degrees to radians and vice-versa. In games we often use one or the other, and sometimes it might be convenient to take one representation and adopt it to another. The functions to perform this conversion are XMConvertToDegrees and XMConvert-ToRadians, both of which take a floating-point value as a parameter and return the result as a floating-point value. Their prototypes are the following:

```
FLOAT XMConvertToDegrees( FLOAT fRadians );
FLOAT XMConvertToRadians( FLOAT fDegrees );
```

The last conversion functions are used to convert a float vector to an integer vector and vice-versa while performing a uniform bias. XMConvertVectorIntToFloat and

XMConvertVectorUIntToFloat will perform the conversion of the first parameter and divide the results by the two raised to the DivExponent power. XMConvertVectorFloatToInt and XMConvertVectorFloatToUInt will do something similar but will multiply the two to the MulExponent power. Their prototypes can be seen as follows:

```
XMVECTOR XMConvertVectorFloatToInt( XMVECTOR VFloat, UINT MulExponent );
XMVECTOR XMConvertVectorFloatToUInt( XMVECTOR VFloat, UINT MulExponent );

XMVECTOR XMConvertVectorIntToFloat( XMVECTOR VInt, UINT DivExponent );
XMVECTOR XMConvertVectorUIntToFloat( XMVECTOR VUInt, UINT DivExponent );
```

Scalar Functions

Next are the scalar functions. These functions take floating-point values and perform a specific operation on them. There are functions for calculating the cosine of a value, such as XMScalarCos, functions for calculating the sine of a value, such as XMScalarSin, functions to calculate the arccosine (XMScalarACos) and arcsine (XMScalarASin), and functions to calculate the estimation of these values. The function prototypes of these functions are as follows:

```
FLOAT XMScalarCos( FLOAT Value );
FLOAT XMScalarCosEst( FLOAT Value );

FLOAT XMScalarSin( FLOAT Value );
FLOAT XMScalarSinEst( FLOAT Value );

FLOAT XMScalarACos( FLOAT Value );
FLOAT XMScalarACosEst( FLOAT Value );

FLOAT XMScalarASin( FLOAT Value );
FLOAT XMScalarASinEst( FLOAT Value );

FLOAT XMScalarSinCos( FLOAT Value );
FLOAT XMScalarSinCosEst( FLOAT Value );
```

In addition to the trigonometry functions, we also have XMScalarModAngle and XMScalarNearEqual. XMScalarModAngle will compute an angle between –PI and +PI that is congruent to Value modulo 2PI. XMScalarNearEqual will test two values to see if they are close to being equal. Both function prototypes can be seen as follows:

```
FLOAT XMScalarModAngle( FLOAT Value );
BOOL XMScalarNearEqual( FLOAT S1, FLOAT S2, FLOAT Epsilon )
```

ADDITIONAL MATH STRUCTURES AND TOPICS

XNA Math has support for colors, vectors, matrices, planes, and quaternions. All of these can be represented using 4D vectors, where a 4×4 matrix is four vectors representing each row. Planes and quaternions touch upon more advanced concepts that we won't get to explore in this book, but XNA Math has functions to work with them.

A plane can be represented using a 4D vector. A plane is an infinitely small surface that extends along two axes infinitely. A plane is defined simply as a normal vector that specifies the direction the plane is facing (X, Y, and Z) and a distance value (stored in W) that represents how far from the origin this plane is.

Planes are commonly used for culling and collision detection, trigger volumes, and other concepts along those lines. We do not render planes like we do triangles, points, and lines.

Unit quaternions can be used to represent rotations and orientations. A quaternion has four floating-point members, so therefore a 4D vector such as `XMFLOAT4` or `XMVECTOR` can be used as a quaternion.

Game Physics and Collision Detection

Everything in this chapter is related not only to graphics but also to game physics. Physics is a huge part of 3D game development and cannot be avoided when creating realistic simulations. Physics in games usually deals with point masses, rigid bodies, and soft bodies.

Point masses are physics objects that have their linear velocities and positions updated but have no applied rotations. These are often the easiest to start with for beginners and are common for many simulations in games, including particle systems.

Rigid bodies are often used for objects in the scene that can have forces acting upon them that causes them to not only have forces applied to their position and velocity but also their angular movements. This is used for things like crates and other objects as they react to explosions and other forces that cause them to realistically move throughout the scene by moving and rotating as they interact with the world. Another example can be seen with rag-doll bodies, where enemies can fall down a flight of stairs realistically as they collide with the environment. Rigid bodies do not deform in shape.

Soft bodies are not used as often as the other two but are used to simulate objects that can deform in shape. Epic's *Unreal* game engine has support for soft bodies.

Collision detection and response is the act of detecting when one or more objects collide and resolving those collisions by applying forces on them or restricting their movements. This is done so that objects never penetrate one another and so that they react as you would expect them to when they touch. Physics in games is applying forces on objects so that they behave as designed within the environment. Collision detection allows us to catch objects that start to penetrate each other as a result of these forces acting upon them, and the response to collision allows us to deal with that collision realistically to add further to the simulation. Although they can go hand in hand, physics and collision detection are separate subjects that meet to create the complete simulation the designers intended.

Summary

Math is an important topic in video game development. XNA Math, which is part of the DirectX 11 SDK, is a huge library of optimized code that we have at our disposal. In this chapter we mainly covered the topics in XNA Math that were important for this book, but the library itself is made up of hundreds of structures and functions. It is a huge library and is definitely a very useful tool to have at our disposal. When it is used properly, you can obtain great performance using XNA Math.

What You Have Learned

- Learned about vectors
- Learned about matrices
- Learned about coordinate systems and transformations

- Learned about the various functions and structures available through XNA Math
- Learned about projections

CHAPTER QUESTIONS

You can find the answers to the chapter review questions in Appendix A on this book's companion website.

1. Define a vector.

2. Define a matrix.

3. What is the difference between XMVECTOR and XMFLOAT4?

4. What is the difference between XMFLOAT4 and XMFLOAT4A?

5. How is a point defined in a 3D coordinate system?

6. What does normalizing a vector do?

7. What is the purpose of the dot product calculation?

8. What primitive type consists of a series of connected lines?

9. What is the identity matrix?

10. What is another term for multiplying matrices?

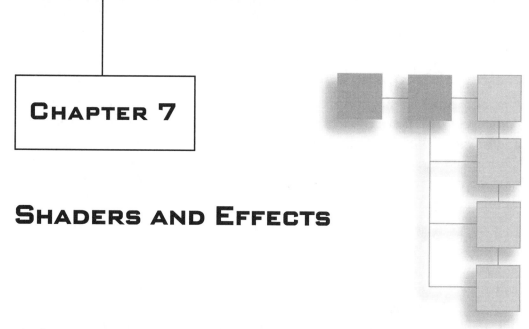

CHAPTER 7

SHADERS AND EFFECTS

Shaders have been a part of Direct3D for a while now. Vertex and pixel shaders have given developers the power to control every detail of how their data is manipulated in multiple stages of the pipeline, giving them increased realism. Now with Direct3D 11, the next iteration of shader technology is being released: shader model 5.0.

In this chapter:

- What an effect file is
- How to use the High Level Shading Language
- What the various types of shaders are
- A basic understanding of lighting
- HLSL reference

SHADERS IN DIRECT3D

The capabilities of both vertex and pixel shaders have been increased. The number of instructions possible has gone up, more textures can be accessed, and shaders can be more complicated. Instead of just limiting the improvements to the previous shader types, Direct3D 11 introduces compute shaders and hull and domain shaders. These new shaders are accompanied by Direct3D 10's introduction to geometry shaders and vertex and pixel shaders, which have been around since DirectX 8.

History of Programmable Shaders

Graphics programming before shaders used a set of fixed algorithms that collectively was known as the fixed function pipeline. To enable various features and effects, the fixed function pipeline essentially served as a way to enable and disable built-in states. This was very limiting to developers because what could be done in graphics APIs such as Direct3D and OpenGL was fixed by those in control of the API and was not expandable.

In DirectX 8, the graphics pipeline in Direct3D first offered programmable shaders, along with the fixed function algorithms. The graphics pipeline was programmable via assembly instructions or HLSL, the High Level Shading Language. In Direct3D 10, HLSL became the only way to write programmable shaders, and not even assembly instructions are supported. Also in Direct3D 10, the graphics pipeline became 100% programmable, and the fixed function pipeline was completely removed.

Because Direct3D no longer supports the fixed function pipeline, it falls to you to designate the behavior of how vertices and pixels are handled. The fixed function pipeline previously had a set way of processing vertices as they passed through on their way to being drawn. This restricted the options you had to fully control the pipeline, limiting you to the functionality the pipeline supported. There was a single method for handling lighting and a set maximum value of textures you could work with. This severely limited the effects you could achieve using Direct3D.

Today, as each vertex is processed by the system, you get the opportunity to manipulate it or to allow it to pass through unchanged. The same can be said for pixels. Any pixel being rendered by the system also is provided to you to be changed before going to the screen. The functionality to change vertices and pixels is contained within Direct3D's shader mechanism.

Shaders are Direct3D's way of exposing pieces of the pipeline to be dynamically reprogrammed by you. Direct3D supports several types of shaders: vertex, pixel, geometry, compute, hull, and domain.

Vertex shaders operate on just what you'd expect: vertices. Every vertex going through the pipeline is made available to the current vertex shader before being output. Likewise, any pixel being rendered must also pass through the pixel shaders. Geometry shaders are a special type of shader introduced with Direct3D 10. Geometry shaders allow for multiple vertices to be manipulated simultaneously, giving the option of controlling entire primitives of geometry.

One of the new shader types in Direct3D 11 is compute shaders. A compute shader, which requires at least hardware that supports shader model 4.0, is used to perform general parallel computing on graphics units. Compute shaders can be used for anything from graphics to physics, video encoding and decoding, etc. Not all tasks are suitable to be executed by a GPU because of the GPU's design, but those tasks that do fit the architecture can see an increase in performance by taking advantage of the additional processing power.

The two other types of shaders new to Direct3D 11 are hull and domain shaders, as well as bringing an additional stage known as the tessellator. The tessellating stage is not programmable, but the shaders that accompany it (hull and domain) are. The hull shader basically is used to transform incoming surface data as it runs on the source control mesh's control points, whereas the domain shader executes for each generated vertex. The idea of tessellation is to take a control mesh defined by surface (not triangle lists as we have done throughout this book) and a subdivide it dynamically to generate a mesh of varying levels of detail. Ideally this means that we can generate very high polygonal models within the graphics hardware without actually having to send that detail to the graphics hardware. Think of it as dynamic level of detail for advanced graphics programming.

EFFECT FILES

In Direct3D there are what are known as effect files. Shaders created via these files are bundled together in what's called an effect. Most of the time, you'll be using a combination of vertex and pixel shaders together to create a certain behavior, called a technique. A technique defines a rendering effect, and an effect file can have multiple rendering techniques within.

While using shaders individually is still possible with Direct3D 11, you'll find them extremely useful when grouped together into an effect. An effect is a simple way of packaging the needed shaders together to render objects in a particular way. The effect is loaded as a single object, and the included shaders are executed when necessary. By changing the effect you're applying to your scene, you easily change the method Direct3D is using to do the rendering.

Effects are defined with an effect file, a text format that is loaded in from disk, compiled, and executed.

Although you can use effect files in Direct3D, they are not necessary. All demos throughout this book loaded the code for the individual shaders one at a time. The difference between effect files and what we have been doing so far is that effect files have additional information other than just the shaders themselves, such as rendering states, blend states, etc.

Effect File Layout

Effect files are a way of containing a particular set of rendering functionality. Each effect, applied when drawing objects in your scene, dictates what the objects look like and how they're drawn. For example, you may create an effect whose job it is to texture objects, or you may create an effect to generate lighting bloom or blur. You could also have different versions of these effects within an effect file, which could be useful if you had to target lower-end machines but also offer an alternative to an effect designed for high-end machines. Effects have an amazing versatility in how they can be used.

Previously, vertex and pixel shaders were loaded and applied separately. Effects combine the shaders into a self-contained unit that encompasses functionality of multiple shader types.

Effects are comprised of a couple of different sections:

- External variables—Variables that get their data from the calling program.
- Input structures—Structures that define the information being passed between shaders.
- Shaders—Shader's code (an effect file can have many shaders within).
- Technique block(s)—Defines the shaders and passes available within the effect.

The simplest form of effect contains a technique with a vertex shader that allows the incoming data from the vertex structure to just pass through. This means the vertex position and other properties will not be changed in any way and are passed on to the next stage in the pipeline.

A simple pixel shader will perform no calculations and return only a single color. Geometry shaders, and also domain and hull shaders, are optional and can be null. The contents of a basic effect file are shown next.

```
struct VS_OUTPUT
{
    float4 Pos : SV_POSITION;
    float4 Color : COLOR0;
};


VS_OUTPUT VS( float4 Pos : POSITION )
{
    VS_OUTPUT psInput;
    psInput.Pos = Pos;
    psInput.Color = float4( 1.0f, 1.0f, 0.0f, 1.0f );

    return psInput;
}


float4 PS( VS_OUTPUT psInput ) : SV_Target
{
    return psInput.Color;
}


technique11 Render
{
    pass P0
    {
        SetVertexShader( CompileShader( vs_4_0, VS( ) ) );
        SetGeometryShader( NULL );
        SetPixelShader( CompileShader( ps_4_0, PS( ) ) );
    }
}
```

Loading an Effect File

Effects are usually loaded in from a buffer using the D3DX11CreateEffectFrom-Memory function. Because this function loads the effect from essentially a buffer, you can read an effect off a file using `std::ifstream` and pass along the file's contents to this function. `D3DX11CreateEffectFromMemory` has the following function prototype:

```
HRESULT D3DX11CreateEffectFromMemory(
    void* pData,
    SIZE_T DataLength,
    UINT FXFlags,
    ID3D11Device* pDevice,
    ID3DX11Effect** ppEffect
);
```

The parameters for the `D3DX11CreateEffectFromMemory` starts with the data of the effect file (the HLSL effect source code). The parameters that follow the source include the size of the source code in bytes, compilation flags, the Direct3D 11 device, and a pointer to an `ID3DX11Effect` object that will hold the effect.

External Variables and Constant Buffers

Most effects will need additional input past just the list of vertices; this is where external variables are useful. External variables are those variables declared within your effects that are visible from within your application code. Variables that receive information like current frame time, world projection, or light positions can be declared within the effect, so they can be updated from the calling program.

With the introduction of Direct3D 10, all external variables now reside in constant buffers. Constant buffers are used to group variables visible to the calling program so that they can be optimized for access. Constant buffers are similar in definition to structures and are created using the `cbuffer` keyword. An example can be seen in the following HLSL code snippet:

```
cbuffer Variables
{
    matrix Projection;
};
```

Constant buffers are commonly declared at the top of an effect file and reside outside of any other section. For ease of use, it can be useful to group together variables based on the amount they are accessed. For instance, variables that get an initial value would be grouped separately from variables that are updated on a frame by frame basis. You have the ability to create multiple constant buffers.

When the effect file is loaded, you can bind the external variables to the effect variables within your application. The following code shows how the external variable "Projection" is bound to the ID3DX11EffectMatrixVariable in the application.

```
ID3DX11EffectMatrixVariable * projMatrixVar = 0;

projMatrixVar = pEffect->GetVariableByName( "Projection" )->AsMatrix( );
projMatrixVar->SetMatrix( ( float* )&finalMatrix );
```

Input and Output Structures

Effect files consistently need to pass multiple values between shaders; to keep things simple, the variables are passed within a structure. The structure allows for more than one variable to be bundled together into an easy-to-send package and helps to minimize the work needed when adding a new variable.

For instance, vertex shaders commonly need to pass values like vertex position, color, or normal value along to the pixel shader. Since the vertex shader has the limitation of a single return value, it simply packages the needed variables into the structure and sends it to the pixel shader. The pixel shader then accesses the variables within the structure. An example structure called VS_OUTPUT is shown next.

```
struct VS_OUTPUT
{
    float4 Pos : SV_POSITION;
    float4 Color : COLOR0;
};
```

Using the structures is simple. First, an instance of the structure is created within the vertex shader. Next, the individual structure variables are filled out, and then the structure is returned. The next shader in the pipeline will use the VS_OUTPUT structure as its input and have access to the variables you set. A simple vertex shader is shown here to demonstrate the definition and usage of a structure.

```
VS_OUTPUT VS( float4 Pos : POSITION, float4 Color : COLOR )
{
    VS_OUTPUT psInput;

    psInput.Pos = mul( Pos, Projection );
    psInput.Color = Color;

    return psInput;
}
```

Technique Blocks

Effect files combine the functionality of multiple shaders into a single block called a technique. Techniques are a way to define how something should be drawn. For instance, you can define a technique that supports translucency or opaqueness. By switching between techniques, the objects being drawn will go from solid to see-through.

Techniques are defined within a shader using the technique11 keyword followed by the name of the technique being created.

```
technique11 Render
{
    // technique definition
}
```

Each technique has a set of vertex and pixel shaders that it uses as vertices, and pixels are passed through the pipeline. Effects allow for multiple techniques to be defined, but you must have at least one technique defined in an effect file. Each technique can also contain multiple passes. Most techniques you come across will contain only one pass, but just be aware that multiple passes are possible for more complicated effects. Each pass uses the available shader hardware to perform different kinds of special effects.

After loading the effect file, you need to gain access to its technique in order to use it. The technique is then stored in an ID3DX11EffectTechnique object for use later when rendering or defining a vertex layout. A small code sample showing how to create the technique object from an effect is shown here:

```
ID3DX11EffectTechnique* shadowTech;

shadowTech = effect->GetTechniqueByName( "ShadowMap" );
```

Because you can create simple or complex rendering techniques, techniques apply their functionality in passes. Each pass updates or changes the render state and shaders being applied to the scene. Because not all the effects you come up with can be applied in a single pass, techniques give you the ability to define more than one. Some post-processing effects such as depth of field require more than one pass. Keep in mind that utilizing multiple passes will cause objects to be drawn multiple times, which can slow down rendering times.

You now have a technique object ready to use when drawing your objects. Techniques are used by looping through the available passes and calling your draw functions. Before drawing with the shader technique in a pass, the technique is applied preparing the hardware for drawing. The Apply function is used to set the current technique along with all of its rendering states and data. An example can be seen in the following:

```
D3DX11_TECHNIQUE_DESC techDesc;

ShadowTech->GetDesc( &techDesc );

for( UINT p = 0; p < techDesc.Passes; p++ )
{
    ShadowTech->GetPassByIndex( p )->Apply( 0, d3dContext_ );

    // Draw function
}
```

Each pass is created using the pass keyword in the HLSL effect file, followed by its pass level. The pass level is a combination of the letter P followed by the number of the pass.

In the following example, there are two passes, P0 and P1, being defined. At least one pass must be defined for the technique to be valid.

```
technique11 Render
{
    pass P0
    {
        // pass shader definitions
    }

    pass P1
```

```
    {
        // pass shader definitions
    }
}
```

The main job of each pass is the setting of the shaders. Because the shaders you use can differ for each pass, they must be specifically defined using the functions SetVertexShader, SetGeometryShader, SetPixelShader, etc.

```
technique11 Render
{
    pass P0
    {
        SetVertexShader( CompileShader( vs_4_0, VS( ) ) );
        SetGeometryShader( NULL );
        SetPixelShader( CompileShader( ps_4_0, PS( ) ) );
    }
}
```

As you can see, the shader setting functions include a call to the function CompileShader. The CompileShader HLSL function takes the shader type of version (e.g., vertex shader 5.0 is vs_5_0) and takes the name of the function you've written in the HLSL file that is the main entry point to that shader.

Rasterizer States

Effect files allow you to set the rasterizer states from within the shader rather than on the application level. You've probably seen 3D modeling software display objects in wireframe mode. This mode displays 3D objects using only their outline. This lets you see how objects are made up, sort of like seeing the frame of a house without the walls getting in the way.

By default, Direct3D operates in solid mode, which causes faces to be drawn opaquely. This can be changed though by altering the rasterizer state. The rasterizer state tells Direct3D how things in the rasterizer stage should behave, such as what type of culling should take place, whether features like multi-sampling and scissoring are enabled, and the type of fill mode that should be used.

Rasterizer state objects are inherited from the ID3D11RasterizerState interface and are created using the CreateRasterizerState function, which has the following function prototype:

```
HRESULT CreateRasterizerState(
    const D3D11_RASTERIZER_DESC* pRasterizerDesc,
    ID3D11RasterizerState** ppRasterizerState
);
```

The functions used to set states in HLSL mimic what they look like on the application side. The D3D11_RASTERIZER_DESC is used to define the various state options and has the following structure:

```
typedef struct D3D11_RASTERIZER_DESC {
    D3D11_FILL_MODE FillMode;
    D3D11_CULL_MODE CullMode;
    BOOL            FrontCounterClockwise;
    INT             DepthBias;
    FLOAT           DepthBiasClamp;
    FLOAT           SlopeScaledDepthBias;
    BOOL            DepthClipEnable;
    BOOL            ScissorEnable;
    BOOL            MultisampleEnable;
    BOOL            AntialiasedLineEnable;
} D3D11_RASTERIZER_DESC;
```

The D3D11_FILL_MODE parameter controls how the geometry will be drawn. If you use the value D3D11_FILL_WIREFRAME, the geometry will be drawn in wire frame mode; otherwise, pass the value D3D11_FILL_SOLID to have all geometry drawn solid.

The second parameter is the culling mode parameter named D3D11_CULL_MODE. The culling mode tells the rasterizer which faces to draw and which to ignore. Imagine that you had a sphere made up of triangles. No matter which way you faced the sphere, not all of the triangles that make it up will be visible at any one time; only those triangles directly in front of you could be seen. The triangles on the back of the sphere are said to be back facing. Because of how the vertices that make up the triangles are defined, they have a particular winding order to them. The winding order is the direction in which vertices for a triangle are defined, clockwise or counterclockwise. Because of the nature of 3D objects, even if you defined all your triangles using the same winding order, just the act of rotating the object causes some of the triangles to be reversed from the camera point of view. Going back to the sphere, from the camera's perspective, some of the triangles are clockwise, and some are counterclockwise. The culling mode tells Direct3D which triangles it can safely ignore and not draw. The D3D11_CULL_MODE has three options. D3D11_CULL_NONE uses no culling, D3D11_CULL_FRONT culls all polygons facing the camera, and D3D11_CULL_BACK culls all polygons facing away from the camera. By specifying a culling mode, this cuts down on the number of triangles that you're asking Direct3D to draw.

If you want the details on all the other parameters in the D3D10_RASTERIZER_DESC structure, please consult the DirectX SDK documentation. Once you have the structure filled out, it is safe to call the CreateRasterizerState function to create the new rasterizer state.

After the new rasterizer state is created, it must be set before its effects take place. You use the function RSSetState to change the currently active rasterizer state, which is provided by the ID3D11DeviceContext interface.

```
void RSSetState( ID3D11RasterizerState* pRasterizerState );
```

High Level Shading Language

As we know, the High Level Shading Language (HLSL) is the programming language used to write shaders. Very similar in syntax and structure to C, HLSL allows you to create small shader programs that are loaded onto the video hardware and executed. With shader model 5.0 we can also use object-oriented programming concepts. Shader model 5.0 is a superset of shader model 4.0.

In this section we will briefly look at HLSL syntax a little more closely.

Variable Types

HLSL contains many of the variable types that you'll find in C++ such as int, bool, and float; you'll also find a few new ones like half, int1x4, and float4, which we discussed in Chapter 6.

Some variable types can contain multiple components allowing you to pack more than a single value into them. For instance, the variable type float4 allows you to store four float values within it. By storing values using these specialized types, the video hardware can optimize access to the data, ensuring quicker access.

```
float4 tempFloat = float4(1.0f, 2.0f, 3.0f, 4.0f );
```

Any variable that contains multiple components can have each individual component accessed using swizzling. Swizzling enables you to split, for instance, a `float3` variable into its three components by specifying X, Y, or Z after the variable name. Take a look at the following example; the `singleFloat` variable is filled with the value found in the `newFloat` X component.

```
float3 newFloat = float3( 0.0f, 1.0f, 2.0f );
float singleFloat = newFloat.x;
```

Any variable containing multiple components can be accessed in this way.

Semantics

Semantics are a way of letting the shader know what certain variables will be used so their access can be optimized. Semantics follow a variable declaration and have types such as `COLOR0`, `TEXCOORD0`, and `POSITION`. As you can see in the following structure, the two variables `Pos` and `Color` are followed by semantics specifying their use.

```
struct VS_OUTPUT
{
    float4 Pos : SV_POSITION;
    float4 Color : COLOR0;
};
```

Some commonly used semantics include:

- `SV_POSITION`—A float4 value specifying a transformed position.
- `NORMAL0`—Semantic that is used when defining a normal vector.
- `COLOR0`—Semantic used when defining a color value.

There are many more semantics available; take a look at the HLSL documentation in the DirectX SDK for a complete list. A lot of semantics end in a numerical value because it is possible to define multiples of those types.

Function Declarations

Functions within HLSL are defined in pretty much the same way they are within other languages.

```
ReturnValue FunctionName( parameterName : semantic )
{
    // function code goes here
}
```

The function return value can be any of the defined HLSL types, including packed types and void.

When you're defining a parameter list for a shader function, it is perfectly valid to specify a semantic following the variable. There are a few things you need to be aware of though when defining function parameters. Since HLSL doesn't have a specific way for you to return a value by reference within your parameter list, it defines a few keywords that can be used to achieve the same results.

Using the `out` keyword before your parameter declaration lets the compiler know that the variable will be used as an output. Additionally, the keyword `inout` allows the variable to be used both as an input and output.

```
void GetColor( out float3 color )
{
    color = float3( 0.0f, 1.0f, 1.0f );
}
```

Vertex Shaders

Vertex shaders are the part of the pipeline where you are given control of every vertex that gets processed by the system. In previous versions of Direct3D, you had the option of using the fixed function pipeline, which has a built-in set of functionality that it uses when processing vertices. Now with the latest Direct3D, you must do all the processing yourself. To that end, you'll need to write at least a simple vertex shader.

A vertex shader is one of three shaders that can exist within an effect file. As objects are sent to be drawn, their vertices are sent to your vertex shader. If you don't want to do any additional processing to the vertices, you can pass them along to the pixel shader to be drawn. In most cases, though, you'll at least want to apply a world or projection transform so the vertices are placed in the proper space to be rendered.

Using vertex shaders, you have a lot of power to manipulate the vertices past just doing a simple transform. The vertex can be translated along any of the axes, its color changed, or any of its other properties manipulated.

PIXEL SHADERS

Pixel shaders give you access to every pixel being put through the pipeline. Before anything is drawn, you're given the chance to make changes to the color of each pixel. In some cases you'll simply return the pixel color passed in from the vertex or geometry shaders, but in most cases you'll apply lighting or textures that affect the color of the resulting pixel.

Texture Color Inversion

In this chapter we will create a simple pixel shader effect that inverts the color of a rendered surface, which is located on the companion website in the Chapter7/ColorInversion folder. This demo will use the exact same code from Chapter 6's Cube demo, with the exception of a change we'll be making in the pixel shader and that we are using an effect file with a technique.

The goal of this effect is to render the colors of a surface negated. This means white becomes black, black becomes white, and all other colors switch places with colors on the opposite side of the intensity chart. The effect to perform this is fairly easy and requires us to do 1 minus the color in the pixel shader to perform the inversion. This makes sense because 1 minus 1 (white) will equal 0 (changes white to black), whereas 1 minus 0 equals 1 (changes black to white).

The HLSL shader that performs the color inversion can be seen in Listing 7.1. This shader is exactly the same as the Cube demo from Chapter 6, with the exception that we are doing 1 − color in the pixel shader. Keep in mind that SV_TARGET is the output semantic that specifies that the pixel shader's output is being used for the rendering target. A screenshot of the running demo can be seen in Figure 7.1.

Listing 7.1 The Color Inversion demo's HLSL shader.

```
Texture2D colorMap : register( t0 );
SamplerState colorSampler : register( s0 );


cbuffer cbChangesEveryFrame : register( b0 )
{
    matrix worldMatrix;
};
```

Figure 7.1
Screenshot from the Color Inversion demo.

```
cbuffer cbNeverChanges : register( b1 )
{
    matrix viewMatrix;
};

cbuffer cbChangeOnResize : register( b2 )
{
    matrix projMatrix;
};


struct VS_Input
{
    float4 pos  : POSITION;
    float2 tex0 : TEXCOORD0;
};

struct PS_Input
{
    float4 pos  : SV_POSITION;
    float2 tex0 : TEXCOORD0;
};
```

```
PS_Input VS_Main( VS_Input vertex )
{
    PS_Input vsOut = ( PS_Input )0;
    vsOut.pos = mul( vertex.pos, worldMatrix );
    vsOut.pos = mul( vsOut.pos, viewMatrix );
    vsOut.pos = mul( vsOut.pos, projMatrix );
    vsOut.tex0 = vertex.tex0;

    return vsOut;
}



float4 PS_Main( PS_Input frag ) : SV_TARGET
{
    return 1.0f - colorMap.Sample( colorSampler, frag.tex0 );
}



technique11 ColorInversion
{
    pass P0
    {
        SetVertexShader( CompileShader( vs_5_0, VS_Main() ) );
        SetGeometryShader( NULL );
        SetPixelShader( CompileShader( ps_5_0, PS_Main() ) );
    }
}
```

The demo class uses an effect object of the type ID3DX11Effect (seen in Listing 7.2), and the code used to load the effect can be seen in the LoadContent function in Listing 7.3, which is limited only to the code used to load the effect and the code used to create the input layout, since the remainder of the function's contents is not new.

Listing 7.2 The Color Inversion demo's class definition.

```
#include"Dx11DemoBase.h"
#include<xnamath.h>
#include<d3dx11effect.h>
```

```
class ColorInversionDemo : public Dx11DemoBase
{
    public:
        ColorInversionDemo( );
        virtual ~ColorInversionDemo( );

        bool LoadContent( );
        void UnloadContent( );

        void Update( float dt );
        void Render( );

    private:
        ID3DX11Effect* effect_;
        ID3D11InputLayout* inputLayout_;

        ID3D11Buffer* vertexBuffer_;
        ID3D11Buffer* indexBuffer_;

        ID3D11ShaderResourceView* colorMap_;
        ID3D11SamplerState* colorMapSampler_;

        XMMATRIX viewMatrix_;
        XMMATRIX projMatrix_;
};
```

Listing 7.3 The Color Inversion LoadContent function.

```
bool ColorInversionDemo::LoadContent( )
{
    ID3DBlob* buffer = 0;

    bool compileResult = CompileD3DShader( "ColorInversion.fx", 0,
        "fx_5_0", &buffer );

    if( compileResult == false )
    {
        DXTRACE_MSG( "Error compiling the effect shader!" );
        return false;
    }
```

```
HRESULT d3dResult;

d3dResult = D3DX11CreateEffectFromMemory( buffer->GetBufferPointer( ),
    buffer->GetBufferSize( ), 0, d3dDevice_, &effect_ );

if( FAILED( d3dResult ) )
{
    DXTRACE_MSG( "Error creating the effect shader!" );

    if( buffer )
        buffer->Release( );

    return false;
}

D3D11_INPUT_ELEMENT_DESC solidColorLayout[] =
{
    { "POSITION", 0, DXGI_FORMAT_R32G32B32_FLOAT, 0, 0,
        D3D11_INPUT_PER_VERTEX_DATA, 0 },
    { "TEXCOORD", 0, DXGI_FORMAT_R32G32_FLOAT, 0, 12,
        D3D11_INPUT_PER_VERTEX_DATA, 0 }
};

unsigned int totalLayoutElements = ARRAYSIZE( solidColorLayout );

ID3DX11EffectTechnique* colorInvTechnique;
colorInvTechnique = effect_->GetTechniqueByName( "ColorInversion" );
ID3DX11EffectPass* effectPass = colorInvTechnique->GetPassByIndex( 0 );

D3DX11_PASS_SHADER_DESC passDesc;
D3DX11_EFFECT_SHADER_DESC shaderDesc;
effectPass->GetVertexShaderDesc( &passDesc );
passDesc.pShaderVariable->GetShaderDesc(passDesc.ShaderIndex,
&shaderDesc);

d3dResult = d3dDevice_->CreateInputLayout( solidColorLayout,
    totalLayoutElements, shaderDesc.pBytecode,
    shaderDesc.BytecodeLength, &inputLayout_ );

buffer->Release( );
```

```
        if( FAILED( d3dResult ) )
        {
            DXTRACE_MSG( "Error creating the input layout!" );
            return false;
        }


        ...

    }
```

In Listing 7.3 we are able to use the same CompileD3DShader code that we've used throughout this book to compile the effect file, with the exception that we are not specifying an entry function name and that we are using a profile of "fx_5_0", where fx represents effect files rather than "vs_5_0" for vertex shaders, "ps_5_0" for pixel shaders, etc.

When we create the input layout, we must use a vertex shader from within the effect file that will correspond to that specific input layout. To do this we first obtain a pointer to the technique that specifies the vertex shader we wish to base the input layout on, which allows us to access the technique's passes. Since each pass can use a different vertex shader, we must also obtain a pointer to the pass we are basing this input layout on. Using the pass, we can call GetVertexShaderDesc to get a description object of the vertex shader used by that pass, followed by calling that object's GetShaderDesc function, which will provide the vertex shader's bytecode and size. We use the bytecode and the size of that code to create the input layout.

The last function with modified code to allow this demo to use an effect file is the rendering code seen in Listing 7.4. In the Render function we can set constant variables in shaders by using various effect variable objects such as ID3DX11EffectShaderResourceVariable for shader resource variables, ID3DX11EffectSamplerVariable for samplers, ID3DX11EffectMatrixVariable for matrices, and so forth.

To obtain a pointer to the variable we can use a function such as GetVariableByName (or GetVariableByIndex). We then would call a form of "AsType" to convert it into the type we know the variable to be. For example, we would call AsShaderResource to obtain the variable as a shader resource, AsSampler to obtain it as a sampler, AsMatrix to obtain it as a matrix, and so forth.

Once we have a pointer to the variable we can call various functions to bind data to it (for example, call `SetMatrix` of a `ID3DX11EffectMatrixVariable` variable to pass along the data we wish to set to it). Once we're done setting the shader variables, we can obtain a pointer to the technique we wish to render with and loop over each pass; drawing the mesh's geometry. The `Render` function is shown in Listing 7.4.

Listing 7.4 The rendering code for the Color Inversion demo.

```
void ColorInversionDemo::Render( )
{
    if( d3dContext_ == 0 )
        return;

    float clearColor[4] = { 0.0f, 0.0f, 0.25f, 1.0f };
    d3dContext_->ClearRenderTargetView( backBufferTarget_, clearColor );
    d3dContext_->ClearDepthStencilView( depthStencilView_,
        D3D11_CLEAR_DEPTH, 1.0f, 0 );

    unsigned int stride = sizeof( VertexPos );
    unsigned int offset = 0;

    d3dContext_->IASetInputLayout( inputLayout_ );
    d3dContext_->IASetVertexBuffers( 0, 1, &vertexBuffer_, &stride, &offset );
    d3dContext_->IASetIndexBuffer( indexBuffer_, DXGI_FORMAT_R16_UINT, 0 );
    d3dContext_->IASetPrimitiveTopology(D3D11_PRIMITIVE_TOPOLOGY_
TRIANGLELIST);

    XMMATRIX rotationMat = XMMatrixRotationRollPitchYaw( 0.0f, 0.7f, 0.7f );
    XMMATRIX translationMat = XMMatrixTranslation( 0.0f, 0.0f, 6.0f );
    XMMATRIX worldMat = rotationMat * translationMat;

    ID3DX11EffectShaderResourceVariable* colorMap;
    colorMap = effect_->GetVariableByName( "colorMap" )->AsShaderResource( );
    colorMap->SetResource( colorMap_ );

    ID3DX11EffectSamplerVariable* colorMapSampler;
    colorMapSampler = effect_->GetVariableByName("colorSampler")->AsSampler( );
    colorMapSampler->SetSampler( 0, colorMapSampler_ );
    ID3DX11EffectMatrixVariable* worldMatrix;
```

```
worldMatrix = effect_->GetVariableByName( "worldMatrix" )->AsMatrix( );
worldMatrix->SetMatrix( ( float* )&worldMat );

ID3DX11EffectMatrixVariable* viewMatrix;
viewMatrix = effect_->GetVariableByName( "viewMatrix" )->AsMatrix( );
viewMatrix->SetMatrix( ( float* )&viewMatrix_ );

ID3DX11EffectMatrixVariable* projMatrix;
projMatrix = effect_->GetVariableByName( "projMatrix" )->AsMatrix( );
projMatrix->SetMatrix( ( float* )&projMatrix_ );

ID3DX11EffectTechnique* colorInvTechnique;
colorInvTechnique = effect_->GetTechniqueByName( "ColorInversion" );

D3DX11_TECHNIQUE_DESC techDesc;
colorInvTechnique->GetDesc( &techDesc );

for( unsigned int p = 0; p < techDesc.Passes; p++ )
{
    ID3DX11EffectPass* pass = colorInvTechnique->GetPassByIndex( p );

    if( pass != 0 )
    {
        pass->Apply( 0, d3dContext_ );
        d3dContext_->DrawIndexed( 36, 0, 0 );
    }
}

swapChain_->Present( 0, 0 );
}
```

One last thing to note: Direct3D 11 does not offer the effect support code in the same directories as the other includes and libraries. You can find d3dx11effect.h in the DirectX SDK folder under Samples\C++\Effects11\Inc, and you can find the solution that we must build in Samples\C++\Effects11 called Effects11_2010.sln (if you are using Visual Studio 2010). This solution is used to build a static library that we can link in order to use effect files in Direct3D. It is a little work to do these extra steps the first time, but it must be done for Direct3D 11. We only need to create this static library once, and then we can reuse it for all of our projects.

Color Shifting

Next we will create another simple pixel shader effect that shifts the color components of a rendered surface around, which is located on the companion website in the Chapter7/ColorShift folder. This demo will also use the exact same code from Chapter 6's Cube demo, with the exception of a change we'll be doing in the pixel shader.

For this effect we will simply transpose the color components of the texture's sampled color so that the output is Red = Blue, Blue = Green, and Green = Red. We do this in the pixel shader by first obtaining the texture's color, and then we create another float4 object to store the new shifted component values. The HLSL shader for this effect can be seen in Listing 7.5, and a screenshot can be seen in Figure 7.2.

Listing 7.5 The Color Shift demo's HLSL shader.

```
Texture2D colorMap : register( t0 );
SamplerState colorSampler : register( s0 );


cbuffer cbChangesEveryFrame : register( b0 )
{
```

Figure 7.2
Screenshot from the Color Shift demo.

```
    matrix worldMatrix;
};

cbuffer cbNeverChanges : register( b1 )
{
    matrix viewMatrix;
};

cbuffer cbChangeOnResize : register( b2 )
{
    matrix projMatrix;
};


struct VS_Input
{
    float4 pos   : POSITION;
    float2 tex0 : TEXCOORD0;
};

struct PS_Input
{
    float4 pos   : SV_POSITION;
    float2 tex0 : TEXCOORD0;
};


PS_Input VS_Main( VS_Input vertex )
{
    PS_Input vsOut = ( PS_Input )0;
    vsOut.pos = mul( vertex.pos, worldMatrix );
    vsOut.pos = mul( vsOut.pos, viewMatrix );
    vsOut.pos = mul( vsOut.pos, projMatrix );
    vsOut.tex0 = vertex.tex0;

    return vsOut;
}


float4 PS_Main( PS_Input frag ) : SV_TARGET
```

```
{
    float4 col = colorMap.Sample( colorSampler, frag.tex0 );
    float4 finalCol;

    finalCol.x = col.y;
    finalCol.y = col.z;
    finalCol.z = col.x;
    finalCol.w = 1.0f;

    return finalCol;
}


technique11 ColorShift
{
    pass P0
    {
        SetVertexShader( CompileShader( vs_5_0, VS_Main() ) );
        SetGeometryShader( NULL );
        SetPixelShader( CompileShader( ps_5_0, PS_Main() ) );
    }
}
```

Multitexturing

The last demo we will create will perform multitexturing, which is located on the companion website in the Chapter7/ColorShift folder. Multitexturing is an effect that displays two texture images on one surface. We can do this by sampling both texture images and using color1 × color2 as the final pixel's results.

Multitexturing can be a useful technique. Sometimes we need to perform tasks such as light mapping, shadow mapping, detail mapping, etc., and the ability to use multiple images at one time does come in handy.

For the Multitexture demo we load a second texture image and pass that along to our shader like we do the first texture. Listing 7.6 shows the `MultiTextureDemo` class with the added resource view for the second texture. Throughout the demo's code we can simply copy the same code we used for the first texture and use it for the second. Within the shader's code we simply sample both texture images and multiply their results to get the final render. Keep in mind that the

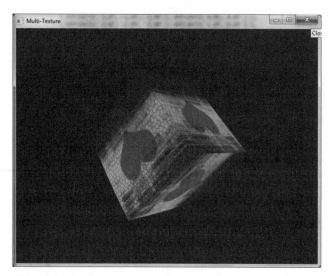

Figure 7.3
Multitexture demo.

second texture uses t1, while the first uses t0 in the HLSL file, which can be seen in Listing 7.7. A screenshot of the effect can be seen in Figure 7.3.

Listing 7.6 The Multitexture demo's class with added texture.

```
class MultiTextureDemo : public Dx11DemoBase
{
    public:
        MultiTextureDemo( );
        virtual ~MultiTextureDemo( );

        bool LoadContent( );
        void UnloadContent( );

        void Update( float dt );
        void Render( );

    private:
        ID3DX11Effect* effect_;
        ID3D11InputLayout* inputLayout_;

        ID3D11Buffer* vertexBuffer_;
```

```
        ID3D11Buffer* indexBuffer_;

        ID3D11ShaderResourceView* colorMap_;
        ID3D11ShaderResourceView* secondMap_;
        ID3D11SamplerState* colorMapSampler_;

        XMMATRIX viewMatrix_;
        XMMATRIX projMatrix_;
};
```

Listing 7.7 Multitexture demo's HLSL source code.

```
Texture2D colorMap : register( t0 );
Texture2D secondMap : register( t1 );
SamplerState colorSampler : register( s0 );


cbuffer cbChangesEveryFrame : register( b0 )
{
    matrix worldMatrix;
};

cbuffer cbNeverChanges : register( b1 )
{
    matrix viewMatrix;
};

cbuffer cbChangeOnResize : register( b2 )
{
    matrix projMatrix;
};


struct VS_Input
{
    float4 pos  : POSITION;
    float2 tex0 : TEXCOORD0;
};

struct PS_Input
{
```

```
    float4 pos   : SV_POSITION;
    float2 tex0 : TEXCOORD0;
};


PS_Input VS_Main( VS_Input vertex )
{
    PS_Input vsOut = ( PS_Input )0;
    vsOut.pos = mul( vertex.pos, worldMatrix );
    vsOut.pos = mul( vsOut.pos, viewMatrix );
    vsOut.pos = mul( vsOut.pos, projMatrix );
    vsOut.tex0 = vertex.tex0;

    return vsOut;
}


float4 PS_Main( PS_Input frag ) : SV_TARGET
{
    float4 col = colorMap.Sample( colorSampler, frag.tex0 );
    float4 col2 = secondMap.Sample( colorSampler, frag.tex0 );

    return col * col2;
}
```

GEOMETRY SHADERS

Geometry shaders are a bit more complicated than the shaders you've worked with so far. Unlike vertex and pixel shaders, geometry shaders are able to output more or less than they take in. Vertex shaders must accept a single vertex and output a single vertex; pixel shaders work the same way. Geometry shaders, on the other hand, can be used to remove or add vertices as they pass through this portion of the pipeline. This is useful if you want to clip geometry based on some set criteria, or maybe you want to increase the resolution of the object through tessellation.

Geometry shaders exist within an effect file between the vertex and pixel shader stages. Since geometry shaders are optional, you may commonly see them set to a null value in effect techniques. When a geometry shader is necessary, though, it is set in an identical way as vertex and pixel shaders.

To give you an example of what geometry shaders can do, take a look at the following code. It contains the full geometry shader function, along with the structures and constant buffer to support it. The job of this particular shader is to take as input a single point from a point list and generate a full triangle to send along to the pixel shader.

```
cbuffer TriangleVerts
{
    float3 triPositions[3] =
    {
        float3( -0.25, 0.25, 0 ),
        float3( 0.25, 0.25, 0 ),
        float3( -0.25, -0.25, 0 )
    };
};


struct VS_OUTPUT
{
    float4 Pos : SV_POSITION;
    float4 Color : COLOR0;
};


[maxvertexcount(3)]
void GS( point VS_OUTPUT input[1], inout TriangleStream<VS_OUTPUT>
triangleStream )
{
    VS_OUTPUT psInput;

    for( int i = 0; i < 3; i++ )
    {
        float3 position = triPositions[i];

        position = position + input[0].Pos;

        psInput.Pos = mul( float4( position, 1.0f ), Projection );
        psInput.Color = input[0].Color;

        triangleStream.Append( psInput );
```

```
        }
    }
```

Geometry Shader Function Declaration

Geometry shaders are declared slightly differently than vertex and pixel shaders. Instead of designating the return type for the function, the vertices this shader outputs are done so in the parameter list. The geometry shader itself has a return type of void.

Every geometry shader needs to designate the number of vertices that it will return and must be declared above the function using the maxvertexcount keyword. This particular function is meant to return a single triangle, so three vertices are required.

```
[maxvertexcount(3)]
void GS( point VS_OUTPUT input[1],
    inout TriangleStream<VS_OUTPUT> triangleStream )
```

Geometry shader functions take two parameters. The first parameter is an array of vertices for the incoming geometry. The type of geometry being passed into this function is based on the topology you used in your application code. Since this example uses a point list, the type of geometry coming into the function is a point, and there is only one item in the array. If the application used a triangle list, the type would be set as triangle, and three vertices would be in the array.

The second parameter is the stream object. The stream object is the list of vertices that are output from the geometry shader and passed to the next shader stage. This list of vertices must use the structure format that is used as the input to the pixel shader. Based on the type of geometry you're creating within this shader, there are three stream object types available: PointStream, Triangle-Stream, and LineStream.

When adding vertices to a stream object, it will be occasionally necessary to end the strip being created. In that instance, you should make a call to the restartstrip function. This is useful when generating a series of interconnected triangles.

The Geometry Shader Explained

The geometry shader in the previous example generates three vertices for every point from a point list passed to it. The vertices are created by taking the initial position vertex and merging it with the vertex positions found in the `triPositions` variable. This variable holds a list of three vertices that are used to create a triangle at any position.

Because each triangle the shader is trying to create requires three vertices, a for-loop within the shader loops three times, generating a new vertex for each point of the triangle.

The final triangle points are then multiplied by the projection matrix to create the final positions. Each point in the triangle is added to the triangle stream after its creation.

Introduction to Lighting

In this section we'll take a quick look at performing lighting in Direct3D. We will use code based on the Models demo from Chapter 8 to demonstrate the effect on a complex object, but we'll defer explaining the model loading part of the demo until you reach the "Models" section in the next chapter. In this chapter, we'll talk about lighting in general and the shaders used to achieve it. Once you finish Chapter 8 you will see how all of the demo's code ties together.

Real-time lighting in games is evaluated these days in shaders, where lighting equations performed in vertex shaders are known as per-vertex lighting, and lighting done in the pixel shader is known as per-pixel lighting. Since there are many more pixels than vertices, and those pixels are extremely close together in distance, the lighting quality of performing these equations in a pixel shader is often much higher.

There are also a number of different algorithms for performing lighting. In this chapter we'll examine a simple algorithm for performing the effect based on the standard lighting model used by Direct3D during the fixed-function pipeline days.

In general, the rendering equation in computer graphics is highly complex, math intensive, and definitely something you'll need to research once you start to move toward advanced lighting topics, global illumination, and shadows, but in this chapter we will examine the three most common parts of this equation. These parts are known as the ambient, diffuse, and specular terms. Since this is a beginner's book, we will briefly touch upon the easiest to understand concepts to at least introduce you to the topic for later use.

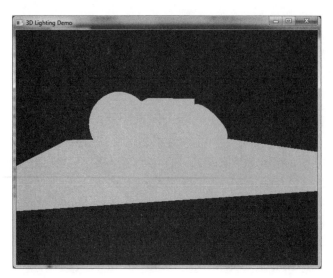

Figure 7.4
Ambient-only light.

The Ambient Term

The ambient term is a value used to simulate light that has bounced off of the environment and onto the surface being shaded. In its basic form this is just a color value that is added to the total lighting value such as `float4( 0.3f, 0.3f, 0.3f, 1.0f)`. In reality this term is nothing more than a solid color that slightly brightens the scene, which is highly unrealistic—an example of which can be seen in Figure 7.4.

In more complex lighting equations such as various global illumination algorithms and other techniques such as ambient occlusion, the value that represents bounced light is highly realistic and complex but often not possible to do in real time.

The Diffuse Term

The diffuse term is used to simulate light that has bounced off of a surface and into your eyes. This is not the same as light that has bounced off of other objects in the environment first and then off of the surface being shaded, which can be used to simulate many different phenomena, such as light bleeding in global illumination, soft shadows, etc.

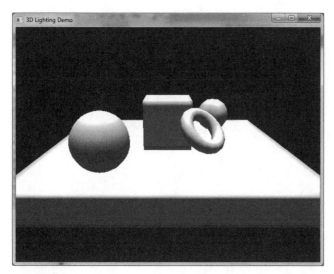

Figure 7.5
Light angles.

The diffuse term is a light intensity that is modulated with the surface color (and/or surface texture, light color if it is anything other than pure white, etc.) to shade the surface in a way that looks appropriate for real-time games. Distance aside, light that shines directly on an object should fully light the object, and lights that are behind a surface should not affect the surface at all. Lights at an angle to a surface should partially light the surface as that angle decreases and the light becomes more parallel to the surface, which is shown in Figure 7.5.

To perform diffuse lighting we can use a simple equation based on the dot product calculation of two vectors. If we take the surface normal and the light vector, we can use the dot product to give us the diffuse intensity. The surface normal is simply just that, the normal of the triangle, and the light vector is a vector that is calculated by the subtraction of the light's position and the vertex's position (or pixel's position when looking at per-pixel lighting).

Looking back again at Figure 7.5, if the light's position is directly above the point, then the dot product between the light vector and the surface normal is equal to 1.0. since they are moving toward each other. (You can calculate this by doing the dot product math from Chapter 6 on a piece of paper.) If the light is behind the surface, the direction of the vectors will point in an opposite direction, causing the dot product to equal a value less than 0. All other angles between being directly above (1.0) and parallel to the surface (0.0) we know are a shade of the light's intensity. We can literally multiply the diffuse term by the surface color to apply the diffuse contribution to the mix. The diffuse lighting equation is as follows:

```
float diffuse = clamp( dot( normal, lightVec ), 0.0, 1.0 );
```

If we are using a light color other than pure light, we would use the following equation:

```
float diffuse = clamp( dot( normal, lightVec ), 0.0, 1.0 );
float4 diffuseLight = lightColor * diffuse;
```

If we want to apply the diffuse light color to the surface color, assuming the surface color is just a color we fetched from a color map texture, we can use the following:

```
float diffuse = clamp( dot( normal, lightVec ), 0.0, 1.0 );
float4 diffuseLight = lightColor * diffuse;
float4 finalColor = textureColor * diffuseLight;
```

We clamp the diffuse term because we want anything less than 0.0 to equal 0.0 so that when we multiple that diffuse term with the light's color or directly to the surface color it will make the final diffuse color black, which would represent no diffuse color. We don't want negative numbers affecting other parts of the lighting equation in ways we don't desire. An example of the diffuse-only light can be seen in Figure 7.6.

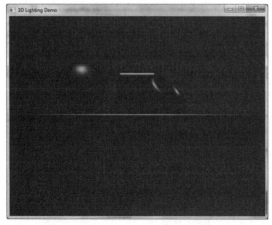

Figure 7.6
Diffuse-only light.

Specular Term

Specular lighting is similar to diffuse lighting, with the exception that specular lighting simulates sharp reflections of light as it bounces off of an object and hits the eyes. Diffuse light is used for rough surfaces, where the more microscopic bumpiness of a surface (the rougher it is) will cause light to scatter in a pattern that generally looks even in all directions. This is why if you rotate a highly diffuse lit object or view it from another angle, the intensity should remain the same.

With specular light, the smoothness of the surface is what will cause light to reflect back in its mirror direction. The smoother the surface is, the more sharp light reflections can be observed. Take for example a shiny piece of metal. The smoothness of this surface will cause light to reflect more sharply than chaotically (like diffuse). In computer graphics this creates the highlight you see on shiny objects. On non-shiny or smooth surfaces, the specular light will be low or non existent. When we model our surfaces, we must mix the right amount of diffuse and specular light to create a believable effect. For example, a slice of bread would not be as shiny as a metal ball. A mirror in real life is so smooth that light reflects in such a way that we can see a perfect mirror image on the surface. Another example can be seen with soft drink bottles, where if you rotate the object in your hand, the shiny highlight will seem to move and dance as the rotational relationship with the surface and the light source changes.

From the description of diffuse and specular light, we can say that diffuse light is *not* view dependent, but specular light is. That means the equation to perform specular light will use the camera vector instead of the light vector. The camera vector is the vector calculated from:

```
float4 cameraVec = cameraPosition - vertexPosition;
```

From the camera vector we can create what is also known as the half vector. We can then calculate the specular contribution using the following equation:

```
float3 halfVec = normalize( lightVec + cameraVec );
```

```
float specularTerm = pow( saturate( dot( normal, halfVec ) ), 25 );
```

An example of specular-only lighting can be seen in Figure 7.7.

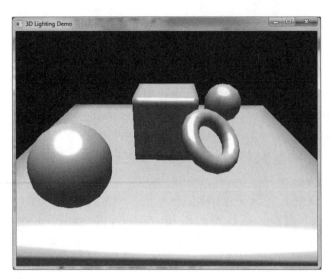

Figure 7.7
Specular-only light.

Putting It All Together

The lighting demo can be found with the accompanying book code in the Chapter7/Lighting folder. In this demo we perform lighting within the pixel shader that uses the ambient, diffuse, and specular contributions. This demo is essentially the Models demo from Chapter 8 with the lighting effect added to it. Keep in mind that we will only look at the shaders in this chapter. In the next chapter, Chapter 8, we will cover how to load and render 3D models from a file.

The HLSL shader code for performing the lighting effect can be seen in Listing 7.8. In the vertex shader we transform the incoming position to calculate the outgoing vertex position, and we transform the normal by the 3×3 world matrix. We transform the normal because the final and true normal's orientation is dependent on the object's rotation. This transformation of the normal must be done to get the correct results.

Listing 7.8 The lighting HLSL shader.

```
Texture2D colorMap : register( t0 );
SamplerState colorSampler : register( s0 );

cbuffer cbChangesEveryFrame : register( b0 )
```

```
{
    matrix worldMatrix;
};

cbuffer cbNeverChanges : register( b1 )
{
    matrix viewMatrix;
};

cbuffer cbChangeOnResize : register( b2 )
{
    matrix projMatrix;
};

cbuffer cbCameraData : register( b3 )
{
    float3 cameraPos;
};


struct VS_Input
{
    float4 pos  : POSITION;
    float2 tex0 : TEXCOORD0;
    float3 norm : NORMAL;
};

struct PS_Input
{
    float4 pos  : SV_POSITION;
    float2 tex0 : TEXCOORD0;
    float3 norm : NORMAL;
    float3 lightVec : TEXCOORD1;
    float3 viewVec : TEXCOORD2;
};


PS_Input VS_Main( VS_Input vertex )
{
    PS_Input vsOut = ( PS_Input )0;
```

```
    float4 worldPos = mul( vertex.pos, worldMatrix );
    vsOut.pos = mul( worldPos, viewMatrix );
    vsOut.pos = mul( vsOut.pos, projMatrix );

    vsOut.tex0 = vertex.tex0;
    vsOut.norm = mul( vertex.norm, (float3x3)worldMatrix );
    vsOut.norm = normalize( vsOut.norm );

    float3 lightPos = float3( 0.0f, 500.0f, 50.0f );
    vsOut.lightVec = normalize( lightPos - worldPos );

    vsOut.viewVec = normalize( cameraPos - worldPos );

    return vsOut;
}


float4 PS_Main( PS_Input frag ) : SV_TARGET
{
    float3 ambientColor = float3( 0.2f, 0.2f, 0.2f );
    float3 lightColor = float3( 0.7f, 0.7f, 0.7f );

    float3 lightVec = normalize( frag.lightVec );
    float3 normal = normalize( frag.norm );

    float diffuseTerm = clamp( dot( normal, lightVec ), 0.0f, 1.0f );
    float specularTerm = 0;

    if( diffuseTerm > 0.0f )
    {
        float3 viewVec = normalize( frag.viewVec );
        float3 halfVec = normalize( lightVec + viewVec );

        specularTerm = pow( saturate( dot( normal, halfVec ) ), 25 );
    }

    float3 finalColor = ambientColor + lightColor *
        diffuseTerm + lightColor * specularTerm;
```

```
        return float4( finalColor, 1.0f );
}
```

In the pixel shader we use a constant for the ambient term, perform N dot L (the dot product of the surface normal and the light vector) to find the diffuse contribution, and we perform N dot H (dot product of the normal and half vector) to find the specular contribution. We add all of these terms together to get the final light color. Take note that we are assuming a white diffuse and specular color, but if you want, you can adjust these colors to see how the results change the final output. As a bonus exercise, you can use constant buffer variables to specify the light color, camera position, and light position to allow you to manipulate these values with the keyboard to see how it affects the lit object in real time.

SUMMARY

You should now be familiar with at least the basics of shader programming and what benefits it provides. The best way to continue learning shader programming is to play around with the shader code you've already written and see what effects you can come up with. A small change can have profound effects.

This chapter served as a brief reference to the level of shaders we've been writing throughout this book. There is a lot that can be done with HLSL, and much of learning to master it is to practice and experiment.

WHAT YOU HAVE LEARNED

- How to write vertex, pixel, and geometry shaders
- How to use the High Level Shading Language
- How to provide lighting in your scene

CHAPTER QUESTIONS

You can find the answers to the chapter review questions in Appendix A on this book's companion website.

1. Effect files are loaded using which function?
2. What is HLSL?

3. What is the purpose of a geometry shader?

4. What is the purpose of domain and hull shaders?

5. What are the two modes the rasterizer can operate in?

6. Define *semantics*.

7. What are compute shaders, and what is the lowest version that can be used?

8. Define HLSL techniques and passes.

9. What is the fixed function pipeline? How does Direct3D 11 make use of it?

10. What is the tessellator unit used for?

On Your Own

1. Implement an effect file with a single technique and pass and render an object using it.

2. Build off of the previous "On Your Own" and take all of the shaders created in demos throughout this chapter and place them in a single effect file. Create a different technique for each effect. On the application side, allow the user to switch between the rendering techniques being applied by using the arrow keys.

3. Modify the lighting demo to allow you to move the light position using the arrow keys of the keyboard. To do this you will need to send the light's position to the shader via a constant buffer.

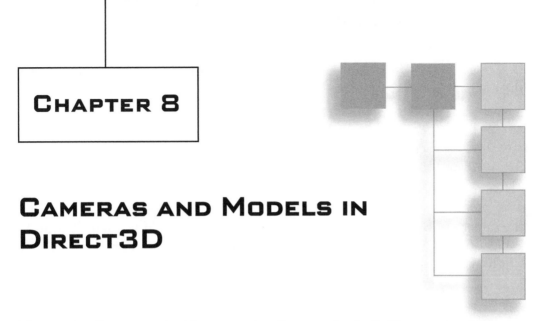

CHAPTER 8

CAMERAS AND MODELS IN DIRECT3D

The topic of cameras in 3D scenes is often overlooked. The camera is a very important actor in the game scene, and the cameras seen in today's games are often fairly complex. Cameras are critical because if the camera is frustrating or bad in any way, the gamer can have a negative opinion of the experience.

In this chapter we will look at two topics briefly. The first is the creation of two different types of cameras, and the second will show us how to load 3D models from a file.

In this chapter you will learn:

- How to create a look-at camera
- How to create an arc rotation camera
- How to load models in OBJ format

CAMERAS IN DIRECT3D

In game programming we create a view matrix that represents the virtual camera. This view matrix in XNA Math can be created with a function called

XMMatrixLookAtLH (the right-handed version is XMMatrixLookAtRH), which has the following prototype:

```
XMMATRIX XMMatrixLookAtLH(
    XMVECTOR EyePosition,
    XMVECTOR FocusPosition,
    XMVECTOR UpDirection
);
```

The XMMatrixLookAtLH function takes the position of the camera, the position the camera is looking at, and the direction that points up in the game world. In addition to XMMatrixLookAtLH, we could have alternatively used XMMatrixLookToLH, which has the following prototype:

```
XMMATRIX XMMatrixLookToLH(
    XMVECTOR EyePosition,
    XMVECTOR EyeDirection,
    XMVECTOR UpDirection
);
```

The difference between XMMatrixLookAtLH and XMMatrixLookToLH is that the second function specifies a direction to look toward, not a fixed point to look at. When building cameras, the idea is that we want to manipulate the properties of our camera during the game's update, and when it comes time to draw from the camera's perspective, we generate the three vectors that are passed to one of these matrix functions.

In this chapter we will create a stationary look-at camera and a camera that rotates around a point along an arc.

Look-At Camera Demo

Stationary cameras are fairly straightforward; their purpose is to sit at a location and look in a direction. There are two main types of stationary cameras: fixed-position and dynamic position. Fixed-position cameras are given a set position, and that position does not change. This was used heavily in the original *Resident Evil* games. Dynamic fixed-position cameras are those cameras whose position is dynamically placed in the game world—for example in *Halo Reach*, when the player drives off a cliff and the chase camera turns into a stationary camera at the moment it is determined that the player has passed a certain plane and is considered dead.

We will create a simply stationary camera that will create the most basic camera system possible. On the companion website you can find this demo in the Chapter8/LookAtCamera/ folder.

The look-at camera needs to have a position, a target position, and a direction that specifies which way is up. Since up can usually be defined as (0,1,0), we will create a class, called LookAtCamera, that takes just a position and a target. The LookAtCamera class can be seen in Listing 8.1.

Listing 8.1 The LookAtCamera.h header file.

```
#include<xnamath.h>


class LookAtCamera
{
    public:
        LookAtCamera( );
        LookAtCamera( XMFLOAT3 pos, XMFLOAT3 target );

        void SetPositions( XMFLOAT3 pos, XMFLOAT3 target );
        XMMATRIX GetViewMatrix( );

    private:
        XMFLOAT3 position_;
        XMFLOAT3 target_;
        XMFLOAT3 up_;
};
```

The LookAtCamera class is fairly small. The first constructor initializes the vectors to have components of all zeros, with the exception of the up direction, which is set to (0,1,0). If we use this class with this first constructor, we will have a view that looks like all of our demos so far. The second constructor will set our member objects to the position and target parameters, and the SetPositions function will do the same.

When it is time to render the scene using this camera, we can call GetViewMatrix to call XMMatrixLookAtLH with our position, target, and up member vectors to create the desired view matrix. Since XMMatrixLookAtLH requires the XMVECTOR type, we use XMLoadFloat3 to efficiently turn our XMFLOAT3 into an XMVECTOR. If we wanted to use XMVECTOR as our member variables, we'd have to align the memory of the class and take special care in order to get the code to correctly compile.

The functions for the LookAtCamera class can be seen in Listing 8.2.

Listing 8.2 The functions for the LookAtCamera class.

```
#include<d3d11.h>
#include"LookAtCamera.h"


LookAtCamera::LookAtCamera( ) : position_( XMFLOAT3( 0.0f, 0.0f, 0.0f ) ),
    target_( XMFLOAT3( 0.0f, 0.0f, 0.0f ) ), up_( XMFLOAT3( 0.0f, 1.0f, 0.0f ) )
{

}


LookAtCamera::LookAtCamera( XMFLOAT3 pos, XMFLOAT3 target ) :
    position_( pos ), target_( target ), up_( XMFLOAT3( 0.0f, 1.0f, 0.0f ) )
{

}


void LookAtCamera::SetPositions( XMFLOAT3 pos, XMFLOAT3 target )
{
    position_ = pos;
    target_ = target;
}


XMMATRIX LookAtCamera::GetViewMatrix( )
{
    XMMATRIX viewMat = XMMatrixLookAtLH( XMLoadFloat3( &position_ ),
        XMLoadFloat3( &target_ ), XMLoadFloat3( &up_ ) );

    return viewMat;
}
```

The demo's class, called `CameraDemo`, builds directly off of the 3DCube demo from Chapter 6. The difference here is that we are adding our stationary camera to the demo, and before we render we will obtain the view matrix from this camera. The `CameraDemo` class with our new camera can be seen in Listing 8.3.

Listing 8.3 The `CameraDemo` class.

```
#include"Dx11DemoBase.h"
#include"LookAtCamera.h"


class CameraDemo : public Dx11DemoBase
{
    public:
        CameraDemo( );
        virtual ~CameraDemo( );

        bool LoadContent( );
        void UnloadContent( );

        void Update( float dt );
        void Render( );

    private:
        ID3D11VertexShader* solidColorVS_;
        ID3D11PixelShader* solidColorPS_;

        ID3D11InputLayout* inputLayout_;
        ID3D11Buffer* vertexBuffer_;
        ID3D11Buffer* indexBuffer_;

        ID3D11ShaderResourceView* colorMap_;
        ID3D11SamplerState* colorMapSampler_;

        ID3D11Buffer* viewCB_;
        ID3D11Buffer* projCB_;
        ID3D11Buffer* worldCB_;
        XMMATRIX projMatrix_;
```

```
        LookAtCamera camera_;
};
```

We set up our camera in the LoadContent function. The camera for this demo is positioned at the 3 X axis, 3 Y axis, and -12 Z axis. This will allow the object to appear on the screen with a camera that is slightly above and to the side of it, giving us a bit of an angle on the object. The LoadContent function can be seen in Listing 8.4.

Listing 8.4 Setting up our camera in the LoadContent function.

```
bool CameraDemo::LoadContent( )
{
    // ... Previous demo's code ...


    XMMATRIX projection = XMMatrixPerspectiveFovLH( XM_PIDIV4,
        800.0f / 600.0f, 0.01f, 100.0f );

    projection = XMMatrixTranspose( projection );
    XMStoreFloat4x4( &projMatrix_, projection );

    camera_.SetPositions( XMFLOAT3( 3.0f, 3.0f, -12.0f ),
        XMFLOAT3( 0.0f, 0.0f, 0.0f ) );

    return true;
}
```

The last bit of code is the Render function, where we call the GetViewMatrix of our stationary camera to obtain the view matrix that is passed to the view matrix's constant buffer. This is the only changed code from the 3D Cube demo of Chapter 6. A screenshot of the Look-At Camera demo can be seen in Figure 8.1.

Listing 8.5 Using our camera in the Render function.

```
void CameraDemo::Render( )
{
    if( d3dContext_ == 0 )
        return;
```

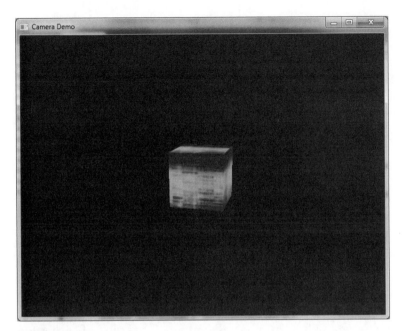

Figure 8.1
A screenshot of the Look-At Camera demo.

```
float clearColor[4] = { 0.0f, 0.0f, 0.25f, 1.0f };
d3dContext_->ClearRenderTargetView( backBufferTarget_, clearColor );
d3dContext_->ClearDepthStencilView( depthStencilView_,
    D3D11_CLEAR_DEPTH, 1.0f, 0 );

unsigned int stride = sizeof( VertexPos );
unsigned int offset = 0;

d3dContext_->IASetInputLayout( inputLayout_ );
d3dContext_->IASetVertexBuffers( 0, 1, &vertexBuffer_, &stride, &offset );
d3dContext_->IASetIndexBuffer( indexBuffer_, DXGI_FORMAT_R16_UINT, 0 );
d3dContext_->IASetPrimitiveTopology(D3D11_PRIMITIVE_TOPOLOGY_TRIANGLELIST);

d3dContext_->VSSetShader( solidColorVS_, 0, 0 );
d3dContext_->PSSetShader( solidColorPS_, 0, 0 );
d3dContext_->PSSetShaderResources( 0, 1, &colorMap_ );
d3dContext_->PSSetSamplers( 0, 1, &colorMapSampler_ );

XMMATRIX worldMat = XMMatrixIdentity( );
worldMat = XMMatrixTranspose( worldMat );
```

```
        XMMATRIX viewMat = camera_.GetViewMatrix( );
        viewMat = XMMatrixTranspose( viewMat );

        d3dContext_->UpdateSubresource( worldCB_, 0, 0, &worldMat, 0, 0 );
        d3dContext_->UpdateSubresource( viewCB_, 0, 0, &viewMat, 0, 0 );
        d3dContext_->UpdateSubresource( projCB_, 0, 0, & projMatrix_, 0, 0 );

        d3dContext_->VSSetConstantBuffers( 0, 1, &worldCB_ );
        d3dContext_->VSSetConstantBuffers( 1, 1, &viewCB_ );
        d3dContext_->VSSetConstantBuffers( 2, 1, &projCB_ );

        d3dContext_->DrawIndexed( 36, 0, 0 );

        swapChain_->Present( 0, 0 );
}
```

Arc-Ball Camera Demo

The next camera we will create will be an arc-ball camera. This type of camera is good for editors or moments in a game where an object is the target and the camera needs to rotate around that target in a spherical manner. The code for this demo can be found on the companion website in the Chapter8/ArcBall Camera/ folder.

For this demo we will need a few things. Since the target position is the one the camera is focusing on, it is the one position that is supplied. The camera's position itself will rotate around the target, meaning that the position will be calculated in the GetViewMatrix function.

Another set of properties we can use for this type of camera is the distance from the object and restraints along the X axis rotation. The distance will work as a zoom, allowing us to move closer or further from the target position. The restraints will allow us to rotate along an arc 180 degrees, which will keep our camera from reaching a rotation where it is then upside down.

Listing 8.6 shows the ArcCamera class. Its members includes the current distance the camera is from the target position, the min and max distance the camera can be if we want to limit how close or how far the camera can be, and the X and Y rotation values. We also have the min and max rotation values so that we can add restraints to the camera.

Listing 8.6 The ArcCamera class.

```
#include<xnamath.h>


class ArcCamera
{
    public:
        ArcCamera( );

        void SetDistance(float distance, float minDistance, float maxDistance);
        void SetRotation( float x, float y, float minY, float maxY );
        void SetTarget( XMFLOAT3& target );

        void ApplyZoom( float zoomDelta );
        void ApplyRotation( float yawDelta, float pitchDelta );

        XMMATRIX GetViewMatrix( );

    private:
        XMFLOAT3 position_;
        XMFLOAT3 target_;

        float distance_, minDistance_, maxDistance_;
        float xRotation_, yRotation_, yMin_, yMax_;
};
```

The arc camera has a constructor that defaults a target at the origin, a position at the origin, a distance of two units away from the target, and a set of rotation restraints that total 180 degrees (−90 to 90). The restraints allow us to go all the way up to the highest peak before the camera starts to turn upside down. Since GetViewMatrix will calculate the position, the constructor is simply giving it a default value that will eventually be replaced with a real position.

The other functions are SetDistance, which will set the current distance from the camera as well as setting the new min and max distance limits, SetRotation to set the current X and Y rotation as well as its limits, and SetTarget, which will set the current target position. Each of these functions is straightforward and can be seen in Listing 8.7.

Listing 8.7 Initializing functions of the `ArcCamera`.

```
ArcCamera::ArcCamera( ) : target_( XMFLOAT3( 0.0f, 0.0f, 0.0f ) ),
    position_( XMFLOAT3( 0.0f, 0.0f, 0.0f ) )
{
    SetDistance( 2.0f, 1.0f, 10.0f );
    SetRotation( 0.0f, 0.0f, -XM_PIDIV2, XM_PIDIV2 );
}


void ArcCamera::SetDistance( float distance, float minDistance,
    float maxDistance )
{
    distance_ = distance;
    minDistance_ = minDistance;
    maxDistance_ = maxDistance;

    if( distance_ < minDistance_ ) distance_ = minDistance_;
    if( distance_ > maxDistance_ ) distance_ = maxDistance_;
}


void ArcCamera::SetRotation( float x, float y, float minY, float maxY )
{
    xRotation_ = x;
    yRotation_ = y;
    yMin_ = minY;
    yMax_ = maxY;

    if( yRotation_ < yMin_ ) yRotation_ = yMin_;
    if( yRotation_ > yMax_ ) yRotation_ = yMax_;
}


void ArcCamera::SetTarget( XMFLOAT3& target )
{
    target_ = target;
}
```

Next we have our functions to apply movement. First is the `ApplyZoom` function, which will increase or decrease the distance amount while clamping the result to our desired `min` and `max` distances. `ApplyRotation` does the same thing, but since the rotation along the X axis will control the camera appearing to move up or down, it is the axis that has the limits applied to it. Both of these functions add deltas to the values, which means it adds the change in value and not the absolute distance or rotation. This allows us to build pseudo-forces upon our camera until the final view matrix is calculated with a call to `GetViewMatrix`.

The `GetViewMatrix` function, which can be seen in Listing 8.8 along with `ApplyZoom` and `ApplyRotation`, is also fairly straightforward, thanks to XNA Math. First we create the position in local space, and then we'll call its variable zoom in the code listing. With no rotation at all, this zoom position is our camera's final position. The beauty of XNA Math and of matrices in general is that for us to transform this local position into its real position, we must apply the rotation of the camera. As we rotate the camera, we are only technically rotating the camera's position around the target. If the target has a local position of (0,0,0), and our camera's position has a local position of (0,0,distance), then to transform our camera to the correct world locations we must translate our target to the target position (which means we must make our target vector the target position since anything added to 0 is itself), we rotate the local position by the camera's rotation matrix, and then we translate (i.e., offset) the rotated camera's position by the target position. The translation is a simple vector addition.

The last step we need to perform is to calculate the up vector. This is as simple as creating a local space up vector of (0,1,0) and rotating it by our camera's rotation matrix to get the true up vector. We use our calculated position, target position, and calculated up vector to pass along to `XMMatrixLookAtLH` to create our arc-ball controlled view matrix. The rotation matrix is created with a call to `XMMatrix-RotationRollPitchYaw`, which takes the yaw, pitch, and the roll rotation values and returns to us a rotation matrix. We supply our X and Y axis rotation values to this function, and XNA Math does the work for us.

Listing 8.8 The `ApplyZoom`, `ApplyRotation`, and `GetViewMatrix` functions.

```
void ArcCamera::ApplyZoom( float zoomDelta )
{
    distance_ += zoomDelta;
```

```
        if( distance_ < minDistance_ ) distance_ = minDistance_;
        if( distance_ > maxDistance_ ) distance_ = maxDistance_;
}


void ArcCamera::ApplyRotation( float yawDelta, float pitchDelta )
{
    xRotation_ += yawDelta;
    yRotation_ += pitchDelta;

    if( xRotation_ < yMin_ ) xRotation_ = yMin_;
    if( xRotation_ > yMax_ ) xRotation_ = yMax_;
}


XMMATRIX ArcCamera::GetViewMatrix( )
{
    XMVECTOR zoom = XMVectorSet( 0.0f, 0.0f, distance_, 1.0f );
    XMMATRIX rotation = XMMatrixRotationRollPitchYaw( xRotation_,
        -yRotation_, 0.0f );

    zoom = XMVector3Transform( zoom, rotation );

    XMVECTOR pos = XMLoadFloat3( &position_ );
    XMVECTOR lookAt = XMLoadFloat3( &target_ );

    pos = lookAt + zoom;
    XMStoreFloat3( &position_, pos );

    XMVECTOR up = XMVectorSet( 0.0f, 1.0f, 0.0f, 1.0f );
    up = XMVector3Transform( up, rotation );

    XMMATRIX viewMat = XMMatrixLookAtLH( pos, lookAt, up );

    return viewMat;
}
```

This demo is the same as the Look-At Camera demo, with the minor exceptions that we've replaced our camera with an ArcCamera (see Listing 8.9) and we replaced our camera setup code to just specify the camera's default distance, since the constructor already gives us all we really need (see Listing 8.10).

Listing 8.9 The Arc Camera demo's application class.

```
#include"Dx11DemoBase.h"
#include"ArcCamera.h"
#include<XInput.h>


class CameraDemo2 : public Dx11DemoBase
{
    public:
        CameraDemo2( );
        virtual ~CameraDemo2( );

        bool LoadContent( );
        void UnloadContent( );

        void Update( float dt );
        void Render( );

    private:
        ID3D11VertexShader* solidColorVS_;
        ID3D11PixelShader* solidColorPS_;

        ID3D11InputLayout* inputLayout_;
        ID3D11Buffer* vertexBuffer_;
        ID3D11Buffer* indexBuffer_;

        ID3D11ShaderResourceView* colorMap_;
        ID3D11SamplerState* colorMapSampler_;

        ID3D11Buffer* viewCB_;
        ID3D11Buffer* projCB_;
        ID3D11Buffer* worldCB_;
        XMMATRIX projMatrix_;

        ArcCamera camera_;

        XINPUT_STATE controller1State_;
        XINPUT_STATE prevController1State_;
};
```

Listing 8.10 Changing our camera setup code in LoadContent to a single line.

```
camera_.SetDistance( 6.0f, 4.0f, 20.0f );
```

The Arc Camera demo builds off of not only the Look-At Camera demo (which is a modified version of the 3D Cube demo from Chapter 6) but also the XInput demo from Chapter 5. In this demo we are using XInput and an Xbox 360 controller to rotate our view around the target position. This all occurs in the Update function, which can be seen in Listing 8.11.

The Update function starts by obtaining the state of the device. If no device is plugged in, we cannot obtain any information from the device. Next we add code that allows us to exit the application via the Back button on the controller. This is not necessary but is a nice touch.

Next the Update function checks to see if the B face button was pressed. If so, it moves the camera a little bit away from the target. If the A button is pressed, the camera is moved closer toward the target.

The remainder of the function will use the right thumb-stick to rotate the camera. We do this by taking a fairly simple approach. If the X and Y axes of the thumb-stick have been moved a meaningful amount, then we move the yaw (Y rotation) and pitch (X rotation) in a positive or negative direction. In the demo we look to see if the sticks have been moved at least a value 1000, because anything smaller might cause the stick to be too sensitive to the touch.

A screenshot of the Arc Camera demo can be seen in Figure 8.2.

Listing 8.11 The demo's Update function.

```
void CameraDemo2::Update( float dt )
{
    unsigned long result = XInputGetState( 0, &controller1State_ );

    if( result != ERROR_SUCCESS )
    {
        return;
    }

    // Button press event.
    if( controller1State_.Gamepad.wButtons & XINPUT_GAMEPAD_BACK )
```

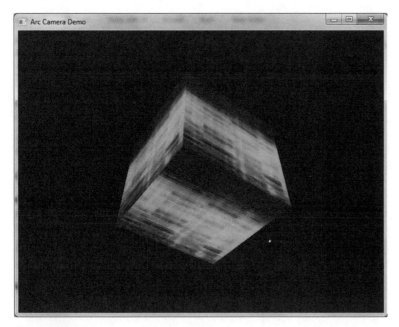

Figure 8.2
A screenshot of the Arc Camera demo.

```
    {
        PostQuitMessage( 0 );
    }

    // Button up event.
    if( ( prevController1State_.Gamepad.wButtons & XINPUT_GAMEPAD_B ) &&
        !( controller1State_.Gamepad.wButtons & XINPUT_GAMEPAD_B ) )

    {
        camera_.ApplyZoom( -1.0f );
    }

    // Button up event.
    if( ( prevController1State_.Gamepad.wButtons & XINPUT_GAMEPAD_A ) &&
        !( controller1State_.Gamepad.wButtons & XINPUT_GAMEPAD_A ) )

    {
        camera_.ApplyZoom( 1.0f );
    }
```

```
float yawDelta = 0.0f;
float pitchDelta = 0.0f;

if( controller1State_.Gamepad.sThumbRY < -1000 ) yawDelta = -0.001f;
else if( controller1State_.Gamepad.sThumbRY > 1000 ) yawDelta = 0.001f;

if( controller1State_.Gamepad.sThumbRX < -1000 ) pitchDelta = -0.001f;
else if( controller1State_.Gamepad.sThumbRX > 1000 ) pitchDelta = 0.001f;

camera_.ApplyRotation( yawDelta, pitchDelta );

memcpy( &prevController1State_, &controller1State_, sizeof( XINPUT_STATE ) );
}
```

MESHES AND MODELS

Throughout this book, the most complex model we've created was a cube for which we manually specified its geometry by hand (3D Cube demo from Chapter 6). This cube was essentially a mesh, and it marked the simplest closed-volume 3D object you can create. A mesh, as you will recall, is a geometry object that has one or more polygons, materials, textures, etc. A model, on the other hand, is a collection of meshes where the meshes collectively represent a larger entity. This can be a vehicle where the wheels, body, doors, windows, etc. are all meshes of the larger vehicle model.

The problem with manually specifying geometry is that eventually objects become too complex to create by hand, and we will have to use tools to get the job done. In this section we'll briefly look at how we can load models from files and tools to create these models.

The final demo of this chapter is the Models demo, which can be found on the companion website in the Chapter8/Models/ folder. This demo builds directly off of the Arc Camera demo from earlier in this chapter.

The OBJ File Format

Wavefront OBJ files are text files that can be opened and edited in any text editor. The format is fairly simple, and its layout is usually to list vertices first, followed by texture coordinates, vertex normal vectors, and triangle indices. On each line is a different piece of information, and the starting character dictates what the rest of the line represents. For example, lines that are comments start with a # symbol, which can be seen as follows:

```
# 1104 triangles in group
```

Vertex position is on lines that start with a v. Each value after the v is for the X, Y, and Z positions, each separated by a whitespace. An example can be seen in the following:

```
v 0.000000 2.933333 -0.000000
```

Texture coordinates start with a vt and have two floating-point values that follow the keyword, and normals start with a vn. An example of each is as following:

```
vt 1.000000 0.916667
vn 0.000000 -1.000000 0.000000
```

Triangle information is on lines that start with an f. After the f there are three groups of values. Each group has the vertex position index into the vertex list, texture coordinate index into the texture coordinate list, and normal index into the normal list. Since each vertex position, texture coordinate, and normal specified in the file are unique, the face information in an OBJ file is not the same as indices using indexed geometry. When using index geometry, we have one index that is used for all attributes of a vertex (i.e., position, texture coordinate, etc.), whereas in the OBJ file it has separate indices for each attribute. An example of a triangle in the OBJ file can be seen in the following, where each index is separated by a /, and each group (vertex) is separated by a whitespace:

```
f 2/1/1 3/2/2 4/3/3
```

There are other keywords in an OBJ file. The keyword mtllib is used to specify the material file used by the mesh:

```
mtllib Sphere.mtl
```

The usemtl keyword is used to specify that the following mesh is to use the material specified in the file loaded by mtllib:

```
usemtl Material01
```

And the g keyword specifies the start of a new mesh:

```
g Sphere02
```

Reading Tokens from a File

The OBJ file is simply a text file. Each piece of information we want to read is on its own line, which means we need to write code that can parse lines of text from a file and break down the lines into smaller pieces of text. These smaller pieces of text are called tokens.

To do this we'll create a simple class that can return to use tokens from within a text file. This class is called TokenStream, and it can be found in TokenStream.h and TokenStream.cpp in the Chapter8/Models/ folder on the companion website. Listing 8.12 shows the TokenStream.h header file.

Listing 8.12 The TokenStream.h header file.

```
class TokenStream
{
   public:
      TokenStream( );

      void ResetStream( );

      void SetTokenStream( char* data );

      bool GetNextToken( std::string* buffer, char* delimiters,
         int totalDelimiters );

      bool MoveToNextLine( std::string *buffer );

   private:
      int startIndex_, endIndex_;
      std::string data_;
};
```

The TokenStream object will just store the entire file's data and the current read indices (start and end) that mark the current positions it is reading from. We'll see how this is used soon. First we'll look at the constructor, ResetStream, and SetTokenStream functions in Listing 8.13. The constructor and ResetStream simply set the read indices to 0, and SetTokenStream will set the data member variable that will store the file's text.

Listing 8.13 The constructor, `ResetStream`, and `SetTokenStream` functions.

```
TokenStream::TokenStream( )
{
    ResetStream( );
}


void TokenStream::ResetStream( )
{
    startIndex_ = endIndex_ = 0;
}


void TokenStream::SetTokenStream( char *data )
{
    ResetStream( );
    data_ = data;
}
```

Next are two helper functions from the TokenStream.cpp source file. These functions simply test whether or not a character is a delimiter. A delimiter is a character that marks the separation of text. Taking the following text as an example, we can see that each word is separated by a whitespace. This whitespace is the delimiter.

"Hello world. How are you?"

The first `isValidIdentifier` function simply looks to see if the character is a number, letter, or symbol. This is usually used as a default check, whereas the overloaded `isValidIdentifier` function will check the character with an array of desired delimiters. If you open the spheres.obj model file for this demo, you will see that the only delimiters in this file are new lines, whitespaces, and /. The `isValidIdentifier` functions are listed in Listing 8.14.

Listing 8.14 The `isValidIdentifier` functions.

```
bool isValidIdentifier( char c )
{
    // Ascii from ! to ~.
    if( ( int )c > 32 && ( int )c < 127 )
        return true;
```

```
        return false;
}


bool isValidIdentifier( char c, char* delimiters, int totalDelimiters )
{
    if( delimiters == 0 || totalDelimiters == 0 )
        return isValidIdentifier( c );

    for( int i = 0; i < totalDelimiters; i++ )
    {
        if( c == delimiters[i] )
            return false;
    }

    return true;
}
```

The next function is GetNextToken. This function will loop through the text until it reaches a delimiter. Once it finds a delimiter, it uses the start index (the position at which it began reading) and the end index (the position before the delimiter) to identify a token. This token is returned to the caller as the first parameter, which is the address of the object that will return this token. The function also returns true or false, depending on whether it was able to find a new token (which can be used to determine when we have reached the end of the data buffer). The GetNextToken function can be seen in Listing 8.15.

Listing 8.15 The GetNextToken function.

```
bool TokenStream::GetNextToken( std::string* buffer, char* delimiters,
    int totalDelimiters )
{
    startIndex_ = endIndex_;

    bool inString = false;
    int length = ( int )data_.length( );

    if( startIndex_ >= length - 1 )
        return false;
```

```
while( startIndex_ < length && isValidIdentifier( data_[startIndex_],
    delimiters, totalDelimiters ) == false )
{
    startIndex_++;
}

endIndex_ = startIndex_ + 1;

if( data_[startIndex_] == '"' )
    inString = !inString;

if( startIndex_ < length )
{
    while( endIndex_ < length && ( isValidIdentifier(
    data_[endIndex_], delimiters, totalDelimiters ) || inString == true ) )
    {
        if( data_[endIndex_] == '"' )
            inString = !inString;

        endIndex_++;
    }

    if( buffer != NULL )
    {
        int size = ( endIndex_ - startIndex_ );
        int index = startIndex_;

        buffer->reserve( size + 1 );
        buffer->clear( );

        for( int i = 0; i < size; i++ )
        {
            buffer->push_back( data_[index++] );
        }
    }

    return true;
}

return false;
}
```

The next and last function that is part of the `TokenStream` class is the `Move-ToNextLine` function, which will move from the current read indices to the next line of the data. We also return this line via the pointer parameter, and we do this because our data is a continuous array of characters and we want our read indices to stay ready to read the next token, or to read the remainder of a line from its current position. The `MoveToNextLine` function can be seen in Listing 8.16.

Listing 8.16 The `MoveToNextLine` function.

```cpp
bool TokenStream::MoveToNextLine( std::string* buffer )
{
    int length = ( int )data_.length( );

    if( startIndex_ < length && endIndex_ < length )
    {
        endIndex_ = startIndex_;

        while( endIndex_ < length && ( isValidIdentifier( data_[endIndex_] ) ||
            data_[endIndex_] == ' ' ) )
        {
            endIndex_++;
        }

        if( ( endIndex_ - startIndex_ ) == 0 )
            return false;

        if( endIndex_ - startIndex_ >= length )
            return false;

        if( buffer != NULL )
        {
            int size = ( endIndex_ - startIndex_ );
            int index = startIndex_;

            buffer->reserve( size + 1 );
            buffer->clear( );

            for( int i = 0; i < size; i++ )
            {
```

```
                buffer->push_back( data_[index++] );
            }
        }
    }
    else
    {
        return false;
    }

    endIndex_++;
    startIndex_ = endIndex_ + 1;

    return true;
}
```

Loading Meshes from OBJ Files

The class that will actually load the OBJ file is called `ObjModel`. This class uses the `TokenStream` class to parse the data and to create the triangle list of information from it. The OBJ file has vertex positions, texture coordinates, and normal vectors, so our `ObjModel` class will store pointers for each, as you can see in Listing 8.17.

Listing 8.17 The ObjModel class.

```
class ObjModel
{
    public:
        ObjModel( );
        ~ObjModel( );

        void Release( );
        bool LoadOBJ( char *fileName );

        float *GetVertices()   { return vertices_; }
        float *GetNormals()    { return normals_; }
        float *GetTexCoords()  { return texCoords_; }
        int    GetTotalVerts() { return totalVerts_; }

    private:
        float *vertices_;
```

```
        float *normals_;
        float *texCoords_;
        int totalVerts_;
};
```

The LoadOBJ function (seen in Listing 8.18 and Listing 8.19) is more straightforward than it appears. The function first opens a file and determines the size of the file in bytes. It then reads this information into a temporary buffer that is then passed to a TokenStream object.

The first TokenStream object is used to read lines out of the data by calling MoveToNextLine. We'll use a second TokenStream object to further parse each individual line for the specific information we are looking for.

When we parse a line, we look at the first character of the line to determine what information it has. If it starts with a v it is a position, if it starts with a vt it is a texture coordinate, or if it starts with a vn it is a vertex normal. We can use the whitespace delimiter to break down these lines into their components.

If we are reading a face (triangle indices) from the file, which appears after the f keyword, then we need to use another TokenStream object to break down the indices using the whitespace and / characters as a delimiter.

Listing 8.18 The first half of the LoadOBJ function.

```
bool ObjModel::LoadOBJ( char *fileName )
{
    std::ifstream fileStream;
    int fileSize = 0;

    fileStream.open( fileName, std::ifstream::in );

    if( fileStream.is_open( ) == false )
        return false;

    fileStream.seekg( 0, std::ios::end );
    fileSize = ( int )fileStream.tellg( );
    fileStream.seekg( 0, std::ios::beg );

    if( fileSize <= 0 )
        return false;
```

```
char *buffer = new char[fileSize];

if( buffer == 0 )
    return false;

memset( buffer, '\0', fileSize );

TokenStream tokenStream, lineStream, faceStream;
std::string tempLine, token;

fileStream.read( buffer, fileSize );
tokenStream.SetTokenStream( buffer );

delete[] buffer;

tokenStream.ResetStream( );

std::vector<float> verts, norms, texC;
std::vector<int> faces;

char lineDelimiters[2] = { '\n', ' ' };

while( tokenStream.MoveToNextLine( &tempLine ) )
{
    lineStream.SetTokenStream( ( char* )tempLine.c_str( ) );
    tokenStream.GetNextToken( 0, 0, 0 );

    if( !lineStream.GetNextToken( &token, lineDelimiters, 2 ) )
        continue;

    if( strcmp( token.c_str( ), "v" ) == 0 )
    {
        lineStream.GetNextToken( &token, lineDelimiters, 2 );
        verts.push_back( ( float )atof( token.c_str( ) ) );

        lineStream.GetNextToken( &token, lineDelimiters, 2 );
        verts.push_back( ( float )atof( token.c_str( ) ) );

        lineStream.GetNextToken( &token, lineDelimiters, 2 );
        verts.push_back( ( float )atof( token.c_str( ) ) );
    }
```

```
else if( strcmp( token.c_str( ), "vn" ) == 0 )
{
    lineStream.GetNextToken( &token, lineDelimiters, 2 );
    norms.push_back( ( float )atof( token.c_str( ) ) );

    lineStream.GetNextToken( &token, lineDelimiters, 2 );
    norms.push_back( ( float )atof( token.c_str( ) ) );

    lineStream.GetNextToken( &token, lineDelimiters, 2 );
    norms.push_back( ( float )atof( token.c_str( ) ) );
}
else if( strcmp( token.c_str( ), "vt" ) == 0 )
{
    lineStream.GetNextToken( &token, lineDelimiters, 2 );
    texC.push_back( ( float )atof( token.c_str( ) ) );

    lineStream.GetNextToken( &token, lineDelimiters, 2 );
    texC.push_back( ( float )atof( token.c_str( ) ) );
}
else if( strcmp( token.c_str( ), "f" ) == 0 )
{
    char faceTokens[3] = { '\n', ' ', '/' };
    std::string faceIndex;

    faceStream.SetTokenStream( ( char* )tempLine.c_str( ) );
    faceStream.GetNextToken( 0, 0, 0 );

    for( int i = 0; i < 3; i++ )
    {
        faceStream.GetNextToken( &faceIndex, faceTokens, 3 );
        faces.push_back( ( int )atoi( faceIndex.c_str( ) ) );

        faceStream.GetNextToken( &faceIndex, faceTokens, 3 );
        faces.push_back( ( int )atoi( faceIndex.c_str( ) ) );

        faceStream.GetNextToken( &faceIndex, faceTokens, 3 );
        faces.push_back( ( int )atoi( faceIndex.c_str( ) ) );
    }
}
else if( strcmp( token.c_str( ), "#" ) == 0 )
{
```

```
            int a = 0;
            int b = a;
    }

    token[0] = '\0';
}
```

Once we have the data, we use the face information to generate a triangle list array of geometry. We cannot use the information in an OBJ file directly because the indices are defined per attribute, not per vertex. Once we generate the information in a manner Direct3D will be happy with, we return true after releasing all of our temporary data. The second half of the LoadOBJ function can be seen in Listing 8.19.

Listing 8.19 The second half of the LoadOBJ function.

```
{
    // "Unroll" the loaded obj information into a list of triangles.

    int vIndex = 0, nIndex = 0, tIndex = 0;
    int numFaces = ( int )faces.size( ) / 9;

    totalVerts_ = numFaces * 3;

    vertices_ = new float[totalVerts_ * 3];

    if( ( int )norms.size( ) != 0 )
    {
        normals_ = new float[totalVerts_ * 3];
    }

    if( ( int )texC.size( ) != 0 )
    {
        texCoords_ = new float[totalVerts_ * 2];
    }

    for( int f = 0; f < ( int )faces.size( ); f+=3 )
    {
        vertices_[vIndex + 0] = verts[( faces[f + 0] - 1 ) * 3 + 0];
        vertices_[vIndex + 1] = verts[( faces[f + 0] - 1 ) * 3 + 1];
        vertices_[vIndex + 2] = verts[( faces[f + 0] - 1 ) * 3 + 2];
```

```
            vIndex += 3;

            if(texCoords_)
            {
                texCoords_[tIndex + 0] = texC[( faces[f + 1] - 1 ) * 2 + 0];
                texCoords_[tIndex + 1] = texC[( faces[f + 1] - 1 ) * 2 + 1];
                tIndex += 2;
            }

            if(normals_)
            {
                normals_[nIndex + 0] = norms[( faces[f + 2] - 1 ) * 3 + 0];
                normals_[nIndex + 1] = norms[( faces[f + 2] - 1 ) * 3 + 1];
                normals_[nIndex + 2] = norms[( faces[f + 2] - 1 ) * 3 + 2];
                nIndex += 3;
            }
        }

    verts.clear( );
    norms.clear( );
    texC.clear( );
    faces.clear( );

    return true;
}
```

The last code to look at lies within LoadContent. When we load our OBJ model, we create a new ObjModel object, called LoadOBJ, and use the pointers to the attributes to fill out our vertex structure array that will be passed to the vertex buffer. Once this information is in our vertex buffer, it is rendered as a normal triangle list, and our model should appear on the screen. You can try many different models of different complexities with this code besides the sphere model that comes with the demo. The code specific to loading the vertex buffer can be seen in Listing 8.20. A screenshot of the demo can be seen in Figure 8.3.

Listing 8.20 The code in LoadContent specific to loading the vertex buffer.

```
// Load the models from the file.
ObjModel objModel;
```

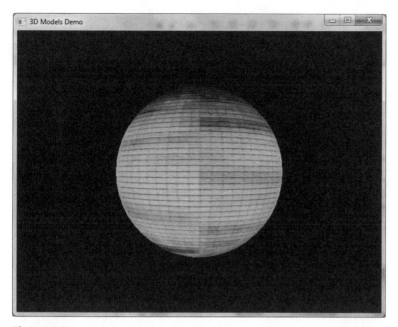

Figure 8.3
A screenshot of the Models demo.

```
if( objModel.LoadOBJ( "sphere.obj" ) == false )
{
    DXTRACE_MSG( "Error loading 3D model!" );
    return false;
}

totalVerts_ = objModel.GetTotalVerts( );

VertexPos* vertices = new VertexPos[totalVerts_];
float* vertsPtr = objModel.GetVertices( );
float* texCPtr = objModel.GetTexCoords( );

for( int i = 0; i < totalVerts_; i++ )
{
    vertices[i].pos = XMFLOAT3( *(vertsPtr + 0), *(vertsPtr + 1), *(vertsPtr + 2) );
    vertsPtr += 3;
```

```
    vertices[i].tex0 = XMFLOAT2( *(texCPtr + 0), *(texCPtr + 1) );
    texCPtr += 2;
}


D3D11_BUFFER_DESC vertexDesc;
ZeroMemory( &vertexDesc, sizeof( vertexDesc ) );
vertexDesc.Usage = D3D11_USAGE_DEFAULT;
vertexDesc.BindFlags = D3D11_BIND_VERTEX_BUFFER;
vertexDesc.ByteWidth = sizeof( VertexPos ) * totalVerts_;

D3D11_SUBRESOURCE_DATA resourceData;
ZeroMemory( &resourceData, sizeof( resourceData ) );
resourceData.pSysMem = vertices;

d3dResult = d3dDevice_->CreateBuffer( &vertexDesc, &resourceData,
    &vertexBuffer_ );

if( FAILED( d3dResult ) )
{
    DXTRACE_MSG( "Failed to create vertex buffer!" );
    return false;
}

delete[] vertices;
objModel.Release( );
```

ADVANCED TOPICS

This chapter has just begun to scratch the surface of what is possible in 3D video game scenes. Although some of these topics can quickly become quite advanced, some of them you can begin to experiment with sooner rather than later. Just looking at the camera code we wrote earlier in this chapter should give you an indication that, with a little more work, you can create a camera system that allows you to create a wide range of various viewports for many different types of games.

In this section we will take a moment to discuss some topics that, even as a beginner, you can begin to explore once you are done with this book. With the right art assets, you can even create some impressive-looking demos or games using these general ideas as a foundation.

Complex Cameras

We touched upon two types of cameras in this chapter. The first camera was a simple stationary camera that had properties that directly fed the creation of the look-at view matrix. This type of camera has its purposes, but it alone would not have been enough to adequately discuss cameras in Direct3D.

The second type of camera was a little more useful when examining our 3D objects. The arc camera allowed us to freely rotate along the X axis, as well as impose limited rotations along the Y axis. Many 3D editors use cameras similar to this, where the target position becomes the driving force of the view, and the position is determined dynamically based upon rotation around that target.

There are many more cameras we could create in our 3D games. Following is a limited list of some of the more common 3D camera systems:

- First-person
- Free (ghost)
- Chase (third-person)
- Flight
- Scripted
- AI
- Framing

First-person cameras are used greatly in first-person shooting games. With a first-person camera, the player is given the perspective of seeing through the avatar's eyes. In first-person shooters (FPS), the player's weapon(s) and parts of the avatar's body can be visible, along with any interface elements such as crosshairs to help with aiming. Epic Game's UDK (Figure 8.4) is a prime example of the first-person camera.

A free camera, also known as a ghost camera, is a cam that is able to freely move around the environment in all axes. This type of camera is often done in spectator modes of popular FPS games such as the sample demo from the UDK (Figure 8.5), in replay modes such as Bungie's Halo Reach Theater, and many more. Although a free camera might or might not physically interact with the game world via collisions, it often has free flight throughout the scene with very few restrictions in movement.

Figure 8.4
First-person view in the UDK sample demo.

Figure 8.5
Free camera in Epic's UDK sample.

Figure 8.6
Chase camera in UDK's sample demo.

A chase camera is the type of camera that chases an object inside of the scene. This is commonly used for third-person games (see Figure 8.6), flight games, etc., where the player's camera is usually stationed behind the avatar. These cameras also have damping effects so that the camera gradually catches up to the rotation instead of moving as if it was attach to a rigid pole.

In flight games we often have many different types of cameras working together. There is the cockpit view that acts as a first-person camera, there are stationary cameras during replays, there can be free cameras for guided missiles and rockets, and there are chase cameras for a flight view behind the avatar (airplane, jet, etc.). In a modified version of the Chase Camera (Figure 8.7) sample demo for XNA Game Studio Express (available from http://create.msdn.com), the chase camera also has the ability to turn into an arc camera when the player uses the right joystick to arc around the aircraft while the left stick controls the aircraft, causing the chase camera to "chase" after it.

Scripted and artificial intelligence guided cameras are controlled by sources other than the player. For scripted cameras we can script the camera's movements and play it back in real time. Scripting a camera, along with scripting the movements and animations of game objects and models, makes it possible to create real-time, in-game cinematic scenes, also known as cut-scenes.

Figure 8.7
Going from chase to arc.

Many games also use multiple types of cameras during gameplay. For example, some games might switch between first- and third-person perspectives based on the current context the player is in, games with split-screen views can have multiple cameras for each player rendering to different areas of the screen, and some games give you the option to decide which perspective you wish to use (e.g., XNA's Ship Game Starter Kit in Figure 8.8).

XNA is a Microsoft development framework similar to the DirectX SDK so the permissions should be available to use SDK screenshots just like we can with the DirectX SDK.

3D Level Files

Loading 3D geometry from a file is the first step to loading entire environments. There are many aspects of an environment, many of which include the following:

- Skies
- Water
- Terrain (land)
- Buildings
- Vehicles
- Characters

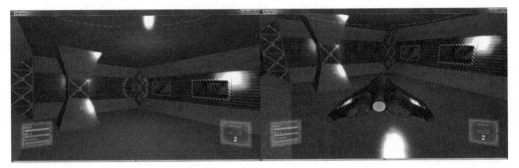

Figure 8.8
Switching camera perspective based on personal preference in XNA's Ship Game Starter Kit.

- Weapons
- Power-ups
- Trigger volumes (i.e., areas that trigger an event, like a cut-scene)
- Environment props (e.g., rocks, trees, grass, brush, etc.)
- Objective game props (e.g., flags for Capture the Flag, hill locations, etc.)
- And much more

There is a wide range of different objects you can have in a virtual world, some of which are not visible. In today's games, game levels are too large to manually specify by hand, and often an editor of some form is used. We generally refer to these as map or level editors.

Creating a level editor is no easy task and can often be very game specific. The file format that represents the game level is also highly game specific. As a quick example, let's look at a simple sample file that stores nothing but positions, rotations, and scaling information for 3D models. Take a look at the following:

```
Level Level1
{
    PlayerStart 0,0,-100 0,0,0 1,1,1
    WeaponStart Pistol


    Weapons
    {
```

```
        Pistol -421,66,932 0,90,0 1,1,1
        Sniper 25,532,235 0,0,0 1,1,1
        RocketLauncher 512,54,336 0,0,0, 1,1,1
        ...
    }


    Enemies
    {
        ...
    }


    Scripts
    {
        ...
    }


    Triggers
    {
        ...
    }
}
```

In the example above, imagine that PlayerStart specified the player's starting position, rotation, and scale in the game world when the level starts, and WeaponStart specifies which weapon the player has in his possession at the start. Let's imagine that all of the weapons and their starting positions in the game world are defined within the Weapons block, the enemies within the Enemies block, and the scripts and triggers in their own blocks. If scripts load upon the level's start, then triggers could potentially be invisible areas within the game world that trigger an action whenever the player enters it (such as opening a door when a player is near it, playing a cut-scene, etc.).

Even with this extremely basic and imaginary level file, you can already see that we barely have the details of many common games, and we've barely specified enough detail for the objects listed as is. Although this is not a real format of any kind, the amount of properties and information you can have for a single object or group of objects can become quite involved. Being able to create objects and edit them in an application can help make creating levels much easier and much more time efficient. Today many game companies utilize art tools such as 3D Studio Max or Maya and write custom exporters that create not just individual objects but the level/world data files that are loaded by the game.

SUMMARY

The goal of this chapter was to introduce two simple 3D cameras that you can use to help you learn how to create additional types of cameras later on. This chapter also showed how to load models from the OBJ file format, which many 3D modeling applications support. The OBJ file format is a simple format to start off with because it is a simple-to-read text file with straightforward syntax.

WHAT YOU HAVE LEARNED

- How to create a look-at (stationary) camera
- How to create an arc-ball camera
- How to load meshes from an OBJ file

CHAPTER QUESTIONS

You can find the answers to chapter review questions in Appendix A on this book's companion website.

1. What is a stationary camera?
2. What two types of stationary cameras did we discuss?
3. What is an arc-ball camera?
4. True or False: The OBJ file is a binary file for 3D models.
5. Describe what a token stream is.

INDEX